Aftermath of Climate Change

Editors

Dr. Mamta Sharma   Dr. Hukam Singh

Dr. Upendra Singh

Pustak Bharati
Toronto Canada

Editors : Dr. Mamta Sharma
Dr. Hukam Singh
Dr. Upendra Singh

Book Title : Emerging Trends In Sustainable Development

Cover Picture : By Dr. Anil Kumar Chhangani, D.Sc

Published by :
Pustak Bharati (Books India)
180 Torresdale Ave, Toronto Canada M2R 3E4
email : pustak.bharati.canada@gmail.com
Web : www.pustak-bharati-canada.com

Published for
Raj Rishi Government Autonomous College,
Alwar, Rajasthan, India

Financial Assistance
Rashtriya Uchchatar Shiksha Abhiyan
(RUSA-2.0)

Copyright ©2023

ISBN : 978-1-989416-13-6

© All rights reserved. No part of this book may be copied, reproduced or utilised in any manner or by any means, computerised, e-mail, scanning, photocopying or by recording in any information storage and retrieval system, without the permission in writing from the editors.

PREFACE

"Our planet is slowly dying, and if we don't do anything about it soon enough, it would eventually begin to deteriorate and everything would be used. The world would become a barren place without any resources. We need to cater to the needs of our planet, and we need to change our life styles so that it becomes beneficial to the planet. We need to become much more eco-friendly, so that no harm is dealt to the planet by our existence. Many people don't realize that they waste large amounts of energy and other resources in various unnecessary things that could otherwise be saved."

This series of books is an extension of the 3 days international conference on **Multidisciplinary Approach Towards Sustainable Development and Climate Change for A Viable Future (ICMSDC-2022)** held from 12th -14th August 2022 at Raj Rishi Government Autonomous College, Alwar, Rajasthan.

We are very happy and delighted to publish our series of books which are accumulation of research papers of knowledgeable experts in the field of sustainable development and climate change.

Climate change is the most significant challenge to achieving sustainable development, and it threatens to drag millions of people into grinding poverty. At the same time, we have never had better know-how and solutions available to avert the crisis and create opportunities for a better life for people all over the world. Climate change is not just a long-term issue. It is happening today, and it entails uncertainties for policy makers trying to shape the future.

There is a dual relationship between sustainable development and climate change. On the one hand, climate change influences key natural and human living conditions and thereby also the basis for social and economic development, while on the other hand, society's priorities on sustainable development influence both the greenhouse gas emissions that are causing climate change and the vulnerability.

Climate policies can be more effective when consistently embedded within broader strategies designed to make national and regional development paths more sustainable. This occurs because the impact of climate variability and change, climate policy responses, and associated socio-economic development will affect the ability of countries to achieve sustainable development goals. Conversely, the pursuit of those goals will in turn affect the opportunities for, and success of, climate policies.

With these books, we aim to reach to as many people as we can, and spread awareness about sustainable development and climate change and its in-depth analysis through our didactic research papers. We hope that the thought with which ICMSDC-2022 was executed is taken forward through this series of books and the inception of an idea of saving the environment is rooted in the minds of our readers.

The articles in these books have been contributed by eminent research scholars, scientists, academicians and industry experts whose contributions have enriched this book series. We thank our publisher, Pustak Bharati, Toronto, Canada for joining us in this initiative and helped in publishing this series of books.

Finally, we will always remain indebted to all our well-wishers for their blessings, without which ICMSDC-2022 and series of these book would have not come into existence.

Financial Assistance provided by Rashtriya Uchchatar Shiksha Abhiyan (RUSA-2.0) is gratefully acknowledged.

Dr. Mamta Sharma
Dr. Hukam Singh
Dr. Upendra Singh

Contents

Preface

1.	Greener Living and 3R Dr. Mamta Sharma Dr. Hukam Singh Dr. Upendra Singh	1
2.	सतत् विकास के आयाम उमेश कुमार	8
3.	जलवायु परिवर्तन का जैव विविधता पर प्रभाव लोकेश कुमार मीना	12
4.	Exploring Nutritional and Biochemical Traits of *Pseudomonas Virdiflava* for its Identification from *Capsicum Annum* Seeds Neetu Soni, Ashwani Kumar Verma and Laxmi Meena	20
5.	Socio-Economic Transformations to achieve Sustainable Development Goals Dr. Madhu Kumari	28
6.	Extent of Knowledge and Adoption Behaviour of Organic Farming Practices Among the Vegetables Farmers in Kadavoor Block in Karur District Manivannan. N and Gokula Krishnan M	42
7.	Contribution of Teacher-Education in Environment Preservation Neeraj Mohan Puri and Dr. Rashmi Tyagi	48
8.	Environmental Impacts of Tourism Industry Girdhari Lal Meeena	56
9.	Environmental Concern : A Facilitator for Practicing Sustainable Production Techniques in Textile and Garment Industries Dr.Ritu Gupta and Dr.Rachana Asopa	67
10.	Environment Protection : A New Dimension in Sustainable Tourism Development in India Dr. Beena Sharma	75

11.	Economic Growth and Sustainable Development Dr. Meghna Meena	79
12.	Ecological Restoration : Planning, Evaluation, Outcomes and Hurdles Pragya Dadhich, Anita Malav and Poonam Jaiswal	86
13.	Sustainable Development and Industrialization Dr. Dev Karan	103
14.	Sustainable Development Goals from a Gender Equality Perspective Dr. Aruna Kumari Paliya	110
15.	Green and Smart Technology for Environmental Sustainability in India : An Overview Dr. Sama Jain, Dr. Varsha Saxena, Dr. Neeraj Jain	121
16.	भारत में जल संकट एवं सतत विकास के लिए संरक्षण के उपाय डॉ. नीरज कारगवाल	130
17.	Effects of Fluoride Water (5.8 ppm) on Essential Biochemical Parameters, Histology of Testis and Reproductive Function of Male Albino Rats (*Rattus norvegicus*) Mamta Solanki	137
18.	Green Chemistry and their Twelve Principles for Sustainable Development of Environment D.T. Sakhare	152
19.	Green Chemistry Principles and Environmental Sustainability Dr. Varsha Saxena and Dr. Sama Jain	174
20	Doctrines of Environmental Law in India Dr. Pawan Kumar Srivastava	180

1. Greener Living and 3R

Dr. Mamta Sharma*
Dr. Hukam Singh**
Dr. Upendra Singh***

Introduction

The levels of pollution have begun to rise rapidly. The use of plastics and other forms of non-degradable substances has only added to it. One way to combat this is to reduce the use of such objects, recycle and reuse them. Hence the concept of reduce-reuse-recycle has become popular world over. Reuse is using an item more than once. This includes conventional reuse where the item is used again for the same function and new-life reuse where it is used for a new function. In contrast, recycling is the breaking down of the used item into raw materials which are used to make new items. Reuse can have financial and environmental benefits, either of which can be the main motivation for it. The financial motivation historically did, and in the developing world still does, lead to very high levels of reuse, but rising wages and consequent consumer demand for the convenience of disposable products made the reuse of low value items such as packaging uneconomic m richer countries, leading to the demise of many reuse schemes.

Detour

Reduce, Reuse, Recycle : these three 'R' words are an important part of sustainable living, as they help to cut down on the amount of waste we have to throw away.

The principle of reducing waste, reusing and recycling resources and products is often called the "3Rs." Reducing means choosing to use things with care to reduce the amount of waste generated. Reusing involves the repeated use of items or parts of items which still have usable aspects. Recycling means the use of waste itself as resources. Waste minimization can be achieved in an efficient way by focusing primarily on the first of the 3Rs, "reduce," followed by "reuse" and then "recycle."

1. Reduce the amount of waste you produce.
2. Reuse items as much as you can before replacing them.
3. Recycle items wherever possible.

Using the 3 'R's also helps to minimise the amount of space needed for landfill sites, where waste materials are disposed of.

Reduce

The most important way to reduce waste is to reduce spending. The secret is only to buy the things we need in the proper quantity. We wouldn't need to extract raw materials, create items from scratch, develop packaging, use more resources for shipping, and then figure out how to get rid of them if we never produced them in the first place.

How to Practice the Principle of Reduce

1. Shopping for Premium Good : High-quality goods may cost more but also perform better and cause fewer issues than inferior goods. Invest in long-lasting products like silverware, reusable cups, and reusable water bottles rather than disposables.

2. Using Minimal Packaging : Plastic bags, boxes, packing peanuts, and plastic wrappers are among the packaging materials that frequently end up in landfills. Bring your bags so you won't have to rely on plastic ones. Use paper bags rather than plastic ones if you don't have any shopping bags because they degrade more quickly. Reusable bags are frequently available at the register; some shops even provide customers with discarded plastic bags.

3. Purchasing Regional Good : By supporting local businesses, we can limit the negative impacts of transportation on the environment.

2. Reuse

The idea behind recycling is that the used materials in our lives can be repurposed as resources rather than waste. If we take a close look at the things we discard, we can learn to recognise them as resources that can be used to meet daily needs and solve issues. You can start brainstorming and coming up with ideas once you've decided to use waste for good. Reusing reduces costs, saves resources, and satisfies the creative drive-in people.

How To Practice the Principle of Reuse
- You can use old towels and sheets torn into little pieces as dust rags.
- When you go shopping, bring a reusable tote bag or bags with you to the store.
- Old tyres can be used in the play area and garden.
- Reuse cardboard boxes, plastic bags, wrapping paper, and lumber.
- Purchase drinks in reusable containers.
- Donate broken appliances to a local vocational school or charity so students can practice repairing them or utilize them in art workshops.

3. Recycle

Recycling is gathering and processing materials (such as bottles and cans) that would otherwise be thrown away to transform them into something fresh and beneficial. Recycling is essential for maintaining a clean environment and local communities. We lessen our influence on nature by employing recycled materials to create new products. Recycling generally prevents the waste of potentially useful materials, reduces the consumption of raw materials and reduces energy usage, and hence greenhouse gas emissions, compared to virgin production. Recycling is a key concept of modern waste management and is the third component of the waste hierarchy. Recyclable materials, also called "recyclables", may originate from a wide range of sources including the home and industry. They include glass, paper, aluminum, asphalt, iron, textiles and plastics. Biodegradable waste, such as food waste or garden waste, is also recyclable with the assistance of micro-organisms through composting or anaerobic digestion. Recyclates are sorted and separated into material types. Contamination of the recylates with other materials must be prevented to increase the recylates' value and facilitate easier reprocessing for the ultimate recycling facility. This sorting can be performed either by the producer of the waste or within semi- or fully-automated materials recovery facilities. There are two common household methods of recycling. In curbside collection, consumers leave presorted recyclable materials in front of their property to be collected by a recycling vehicle. With a "bring" or carry-in system the householder takes the materials to collection points, such as transfer stations or civic amenity sites.

The term recycling does not generally include reuse, in which existing items are used for a new purpose. The communication and identification are laid out in International Universal Recycling Codes. These codes outline what material an item is made from, to facilitate easier reprocessing. Recycling and reuse are ways to help combat the increasing pollution. But primarily one concept that can help negate the pollution rise is reducing the usage of non-degradable wastes. Biodegradable waste, such as food waste or garden waste, is also recyclable with the assistance of micro-organisms through composting or anaerobic digestion. Recyclates are sorted and separated into material types. Contamination of the recylates with other materials must be prevented to increase the recylates' value and facilitate easier reprocessing for the ultimate recycling facility.

Recycling is the process of converting waste materials into new materials and objects. The recovery of energy from waste materials is often included in this concept. The recyclability of a material depends on its ability to reacquire the properties it had in its original state. It is an alternative to "conventional" waste disposal that can save material and help lower greenhouse gas emissions. It can also prevent the waste of potentially useful materials and reduce the consumption of fresh raw materials, reducing energy use, air pollution (from incineration) and water pollution (from landfilling).

Recycling is a key component of modern waste reduction and is the third component of the "Reduce, Reuse, and Recycle" waste hierarchy. It promotes environmental sustainability by removing raw material input and redirecting waste output in the economic system.

Aftermath of Climate Change

Recyclable materials include many kinds of glass, paper, cardboard, metal, plastic, tires, textiles, batteries, and electronics. The composting and other reuse of biodegradable waste-such as food and garden waste-is also a form of recycling. Materials for recycling are either delivered to a household recycling center or picked up from curbside bins, then sorted, cleaned, and reprocessed into new materials for manufacturing new products.

In ideal implementations, recycling a material produces a fresh supply of the same material-for example, used office paper would be converted into new office paper, and used polystyrene foam into new polystyrene. Some types of materials, such as metal cans, can be remanufactured repeatedly without losing their purity.[6] With other materials, this is often difficult or too expensive (compared with producing the same product from raw materials or other sources), so "recycling" of many products and materials involves their reuse in producing different materials (for example, paperboard). Another form of recycling is the salvage of constituent materials from complex products, due to either their intrinsic value (such as lead from car batteries and gold from printed circuit boards), or their hazardous nature (e.g. removal and reuse of mercury from thermometers and thermostats).

Pollution levels have started to rise swiftly. The usage of plastics and other non-biodegradable materials has only made matters worse. Reducing the use of such items and recycling and reusing them are ways to combat this. Thus, the idea of "reduce, reuse, recycle" has gained popularity on a global scale.

How To Practice the Principle of Recycle

- **Glass :** Glass is broken down into fragments called "Cullet" not wider than 5 cm. Glass fragments are separated by color. Silica, which is melted down and shaped into new goods, is used to make glass.
- **Plastics :** Polyethylene terephthalate, high-density polyethene, polyvinyl chloride, low-density polyethene, polypropylene, and polystyrene are the six chemicals that makeup plastic. The physical characteristics of each plastic are determined by its molecular structure, which makes some plastics easier to recycle than others.

Large carbon chains make up plastic; therefore, some types can be melted down and reformed, others can be combined with new plastic, and yet others can only be molded into different shapes for various applications.

Conclusion

Recycling is an environmentally friendly method of converting trash and waste into usable products. It is a preventative approach to stop the demolition of things that might be valuable. Additionally, it aids in lowering the consumption of fresh raw materials, energy, and natural resources. Recycling includes composting or reusing biodegradable trash, such as food scraps, kitchen garbage, and garden waste. As a result, less rubbish is produced, significant environmental resources are preserved, environmental contamination is reduced, and greenhouse gas emissions are reduced. Hence, despite rising demands, our ecosystem is carefully cared for and conserved. Plastic, paper, glass, metal, tyres, electronics, and textiles are a few examples of recyclable materials used daily. Another eco-friendly method of conserving resources and energy and innovatively reusing products in the future is through reuse. Additionally, it eases the strain on industrial production, resulting in less industrial pollution—both the prices and requirements for disposal decrease simultaneously. In addition to its positive effects on the environment, recycling is a cost-effective strategy for both businesses and consumers because it is more affordable than buying new goods. Reusing is the best approach to conserving energy and cutting the cost of producing all goods and materials.

Since, there will be a significant reduction in the amount of waste thrown into the environment, the chances of spreading toxins also decrease. It automatically reduces the levels of greenhouse gas emissions and pollution. It eliminates the practice of improper waste disposal, i.e., burning waste and trash haphazardly in an uncontrolled manner. Rather it enables us to manage waste in an eco-friendly manner lessening the risk of damage to the environment. The primary objective of 3R principle is to lessen the use of newer resources and energy, making more efficient use of resources. It promotes resource efficiency by using the already available resources that are used multiple times, reprocessed, or entirely reduced. It contributes to more sustainable energy consumption as the resources available on hand are used, and excessive consumption is cut down. It promotes the sustainability of not only energy and resources but also the environment. It encourages the development of green technology that is ways to create cleaner, safer means of waste disposal while reducing the impact on the environment and all habitats. It helps increase the use of renewable energy sources like solar, wind, geothermal, etc. as well. The 3Rs conserve energy and resources and generate jobs in resource management and boost the economy.

References
Source of knowledge is the internet and it is highly acknowledged

*Associate Professor (Zoology)
*Professor
*** Associate Professor (Chemistry)
Raj Rishi Government (Autonomous) College
Alwar, Rajasthan 301001, India.
email : mamta810@gmail.com;
drhukamsingh63@gmail.com
dr.usingh09@gmail.com

2. सतत् विकास के आयाम

उमेश कुमार

संयुक्त राष्ट्र संघ ने वर्ष 1982 की जनरल असेम्बली में 'वर्ल्ड चेप्टर फॉर नेचर' का प्रस्ताव पारित किया, इसके बाद ब्रंटलैंड ने अपनी रिपोर्ट 'ऑवर कॉमन फ्यूचर' में सतत् विकास की अवधारणा प्रस्तुत की थी।

सतत् विकास (Sustainable Development) आर्थिक विकास की एक ऐसी अवधारणा है जिसमें संसाधनों का उपयोग विकास के लिए वर्तमान में मानवीय आवश्यकताओं को पूरा करने के लिए इस प्रकार से किया जाये कि पर्यावरण का पूर्ण संरक्षण हो सके ताकि भविष्य में आने वाली पीढ़ियों में अपनी आवश्यकताओं को पूरा करने की जो क्षमता है उससे समझौता किए बगैर वर्तमान मानव जाति की आवश्यकताओं को पूरा करना इस अवधारणा का मूल भाव है। सतत् विकास के तीन प्रमुख आधार स्तम्भ हैं—1. सामाजिक विकास, 2. आर्थिक विकास, 3. पर्यावरण संरक्षण।

भूमण्डलीय तापन तथा जलवायु परिवर्तन की समस्या के समाधान के लिए सतत् विकास आवश्यक है। सतत् विकास का तात्पर्य वर्तमान की आवश्यकताओं की आपूर्ति हो सके तथा आने वाली पीढ़ियां भी अपनी आवश्यकताओं की आपूर्ति कर सके तथा परितंत्र भी स्वस्थ व सतत् अवस्था में बना रहे।

सतत् विकास के सन्दर्भ में वैश्विक सीमाओं को पारिस्थितिकीय प्रभाव के संदर्भ से समझा जा सकता है, जो उस दबाव का परिचायक है जो मानवीय कार्यकलाप पारिस्थितिकी तंत्र पर डालते हैं। उनकी तुलना जब जैव क्षमता (उपयोगी जैव सामग्री सृजित करने और मानव द्वारा सृजित अपशिष्ट पदार्थों को खपाने की पारिस्थितिकी तंत्र की क्षमता का पैमाना) से की जाती है तो हमें पता चलता है कि हम लाभ कमा रहे हैं या घाटा उठा रहे हैं। आंकड़े बताते हैं कि विश्व पारिस्थितिकीय अतिक्रमण की स्थिति में रह रहा है। लिविंग प्लेनेट रिपोर्ट, 2014 के अनुसार वर्ष 2010 में वैश्विक पारिस्थितिकीय फुटप्रिंट 18.1 बिलियन वैश्विक हैक्टेयर (जी.एच.ए.) अथवा प्रति व्यक्ति 2.6 जी.एच.ए. था और पृथ्वी की कुल जैव क्षमता 12 बिलियन जी.एच.ए. अथवा प्रति व्यक्ति 1.7 जी.एच.ए. थी।

जैव क्षमता विश्वभर में समान रूप से व्याप्त नहीं है। दुर्भाग्यवश कम आय वाले देशों का सबसे छोटा फुटप्रिंट होता है, लेकिन वे सबसे बड़ी पारिस्थितिकीय हानियों को झेलते हैं। संयुक्त राष्ट्र के सामान्य परिदृश्य यह इंगित करते हैं कि यदि वर्तमान आबादी और खपत की प्रवृत्ति जारी रहती है तो वर्ष 2030 तक हमें अपने भरण-पोषण के लिए दो पृथ्वियों की जरूरत पड़ेगी।

किसी भी समाज के सतत् एवं सम्पोषणीय होने के लिए कुछ विशेषताओं

Aftermath of Climate Change

का होना जरूरी है, जो निम्न हैं—

1. पुनर्वीकरणीय—संसाधनों को पुनर्जनन की दर के बराबर या उससे कम उपयोग करने से संसाधनों का सतत् विकास संभव ळें
2. अनुकूलन—एक सम्पोषणीय रूप से विकासशील समाज में परिवर्तनशील पर्यावरण के प्रति अनुकूलन की क्षमता होती है।
3. प्रतिस्थापना—गैर नवीकरणीय प्राकृतिक संसाधनों को नवीकरणीय प्राकृतिक संसाधनों से प्रतिस्थापन करके तंत्र की सततता को बढ़ाया जा सकता है।
4. आत्मनिर्भरता—सम्पोषणीय समाजों में आत्मनिर्भरता की स्थिति सदैव सन्तुलित होती है। एक सम्पोषणीय समाज किसी अन्य समाज को क्षति पहुंचाकर संसाधनों का आयात अथवा निर्यात नहीं करता है।
5. संस्थागत प्रतिबद्धता—राजनैतिक समर्थन, संवैधानिक प्रावधान, विधिक ढांचा आदि सतत् विकास की प्राप्ति के लिए संस्थागत ढांचे का निर्माण करते हैं।
6. सतत् विकास के लिए भूमण्डलीय प्रयास—वर्ष 1972 में क्लब ऑफ रोम की रिपोर्ट वृद्धि की सीमाओं में असतत् विकास पर चिंता व्यक्त की गई। वर्ष 1972 में स्वीडन के स्टॉकहोम सम्मेलन के नाम से संयुक्त राष्ट्र द्वारा मानव एवं पर्यावरण पर आयोजित सम्मेलन भूमण्डलीय स्तर पर पर्यावरण सम्बन्धी समस्याओं को शामिल करने की दिशा में पहला प्रयास था। भारत का प्रतिनिधित्व श्रीमती इन्दिरा गांधी ने किया था तथा इसमें उन्होंने निर्धनता को सबसे बड़ा प्रदूषक बताया, स्पष्ट है कि विकसित राष्ट्रों में पर्यावरण की गम्भीर समस्याएं हैं वहीं विकासशील देषों में पर्यावरण की निर्धनता से जुड़ी समस्याएं है, जो अति दोहन एवं अधिक जनसंख्या का परिणाम है।

इस सम्मेलन के बाद संयुक्त राष्ट्र पर्यावरण कार्यक्रम (UNEP) नाम से संयुक्त राष्ट्र के द्वारा एक नये तंत्र का गठन किया गया। यह अन्य संगठनों के कार्यक्रमों में पर्यावरण सम्बन्धी महत्व के विकास एवं समन्वयक हेतु उत्प्रेरक का काम करता था। स्टॉकहोम सम्मेलन के 20 वर्ष बाद रियो भू-शिखर सम्मेलन वर्ष 1992 में ब्राजील के रियो-डी-जेनेरो में आयोजित किया गया। रियो भू शिखर सम्मेलन के पांच वर्ष बाद संयुक्त राष्ट्र महासभा का एक विशेष अधिवेषन हुआ, जिसे रियो + 5 कहा जाता है। इसमें रियो के बाद की प्रगति का मूल्यांकन किया गया। रियो के 10 वर्ष के बाद जोहान्सबर्ग में सतत् विकास शिखर सम्मेलन (रियो + 10) आयोजित किया गया, इसका लक्ष्य कार्यसूची 21 में निर्धारित लक्ष्यों में हुई प्रगति तथा उसमें पड़ने वाली अड़चनों का पुनरीक्षण करना था।

सतत् विकास पर संयुक्त राष्ट्र सम्मेलन (UNCSD) जून, 2012 में रियो-डी-जेनेरियो में आयोजित किया गया, जिसका प्रमुख उद्देश्य सतत् विकास हेतु संषोधित राजनीतिक प्रतिबद्धताओं को पूरा करना तथा 20 वर्ष पूर्व 1992 में हुए UNCSD से अब तक की प्रगति की समीक्षा तथा चुनौतियों का आकलन करना था। रियो +20 सम्मेलन विकासशील SDG (Sustainable Development

Aftermath of Climate Change

Goals) की प्रक्रिया के प्रारंभ करने के लिए यादगार रहेगा। यह सतत् विकास के तीनों आयामों एवं उनकी अन्तर्सम्बन्धता का समाधान सन्तुलित रूप में करेगी।

सतत् विकास के लिए आवश्यक दशाएं—मानव जनसंख्या को पर्यावरण की धारण क्षमता के स्तर तक सीमित करना होगा। नवीकरणीय संसाधनों का उत्खनन/निष्कर्षण धारणीय आधार पर हो, ताकि पुनर्सृजन की दर, निष्कर्षण की दर से अधिक हो। गैर-नवीकरणीय संसाधनों की अपक्षय दर नवीनीकृत प्रतिस्थापकों से अधिक नहीं होनी चाहिए। प्रदूषण के कारण उत्पन्न अक्षमताओं का सुधार करके। सतत् विकासशील समाज प्राप्ति के लिए स्थानीय तथा वैश्विक दोनों स्तरों पर नीतिगत एवं संस्थागत दोनों प्रकार के परिवर्तन करने आवश्यक हैं। साथ ही दृष्टिकोण के वैश्विक सोच एवं स्थानीय कार्यान्वयन बनाने की आवश्यकता है। इसके लिए निम्न क्षेत्रों में नीतिगत परिवर्तन की आवश्यकता है :–

प्रौद्योगिकी : उन्नत प्रौद्योगिकी ने समस्त विश्व में पर्यावरण में ह्रास एवं नष्ट किए जाने में महत्वपूर्ण भूमिका निर्वाह किया है। अधिक ऊर्जा कुशल, अधिक स्वच्छ एवं लोकहितकारी तकनीकी के विकास को प्राप्त किया जा सकता है।

जनसंख्या : जनसंख्या वृद्धि की गतिकी का सतत् विकास से निकट सम्बन्ध है। विकसित देश यद्यपि 2 प्रतिशत से कम जनसंख्या वृद्धि रखते हैं, लेकिन यहां के उपभोग स्तर एवं प्रति व्यक्ति ऊर्जा खपत का स्तर ऊँचा पाया जाता है। विकासशील देशों में यद्यपि प्रति व्यक्ति उपभोग कम है, लेकिन जनसंख्या आधार अधिक होने एवं प्रौद्योगिकी का स्तर निम्न होने के कारण पर्यावरण पर दबाव अधिक है।

संरक्षण : सतत् विकासशील के आधार पर हमारी आवश्यकताओं की पूर्ति के लिए पृथ्वी के संसाधन सुरक्षित किए तथा बढ़ाए जाने चाहिए। पर्यावरण सुचारू प्रौद्योगिकी की ओर बदलाव लाकर तथा नवीकरणीय संसाधनों जैसे—सौर ऊर्जा, पवन ऊर्जा आदि का कार्यशील एवं अधिकारिक इस्तेमाल हमारे प्राकृतिक संसाधनों के संरक्षण में सहायता कर सकता है। विकास लक्ष्यों की प्राप्ति के अतिरिक्त अन्य जीवों तथा स्वयं हमारी भावी पीढ़ियों के लिए प्रकृति का संरक्षण भी हमारा नैतिक उत्तरदायित्व है।

भारत एवं सतत् विकास—मैकेन्जी रिपोर्ट के अनुसार भारत शहरी दावानल की दहलीज पर खड़ा है। भारतीय शहरों की आबादी 2008 में 340 मिलियन से बढ़कर वर्ष 2030 तक 590 मिलियन हो जाएगी। 2030 के दशक में भारत के सबसे बड़े शहर बहुत से बड़े-बड़े देशों से भी अधिक बड़े होंगे। जैसे-जैसे आबादी बढ़ेगी, प्रत्येक मुख्य सेवा की मांग से पांच से सात गुना बढ़ोतरी हो जायेगी। गरीबी उन्मूलन, खाद्य और ऊर्जा सुरक्षा, शहरी अपशिष्ट प्रबन्धन और पानी की कमी मौजूदा चुनौतियों के साथ मिलकर हमारे निर्मित संसाधनों पर और अधिक दबाव डालेगी। यदि दोनों घटकों को और अधिक अलग नहीं किया तो इसके परिणामस्वरूप ऊर्जा की जरूरतों में बढ़ोतरी होगी और उत्सर्जनों में वृद्धि होगी। लेकिन साथ ही इस चुनौती में बड़े अवसर छुपे बैठे हैं। बहुत से देशों के

Aftermath of Climate Change

विपरीत, भारत की आबादी युवा है और इसलिए मानव आबादी से लाभ उठाए जा सकते हैं। वर्ष 2030 तक भारत का आधे से अधिक हिस्सा अभी निर्मित किया जाना शेष है। हमारे पास मौका है कि हम जीवाश्म ईंधन पर आधारित ऊर्जा प्रणालियों और कार्बन लॉक इन पर अत्यधिक निर्भर होने से बचे जिसका सामना आज बहुत से ओद्योगीकृत देश कर रहे हैं। एक सजग नीतिगत फ्रेमवर्क, जिसमें विकास सम्बन्धी जरूरतों और पर्यावरणीय मुद्दों दोनों का ध्यान रखा जाए, इन चुनौतियों को अवसरों में बदल सकता है।

सतत् विकास की प्राप्ति के लिए पर्यावरणनुकूल प्रौद्योगिकी पर निवेश करने की आवश्यकता है। पर्यावरणनुकूल प्रौद्योगिकी पर निवेश करने की आवश्यकता है। पर्यावरणनुकूल प्रौद्योगिकियों ने कृषि उद्योग तथा ऊर्जा क्षेत्र में क्रांतिकारी परिवर्तन लाए हैं। प्रकृति अनुकूल नियमों पर आधारित होने से यह बिना किसी पारिस्थितिक हानि के उत्पादकता में वृद्धि संभव बना सकता है। इसके लिए ऊर्जा के गैर परम्परागत स्रोतों को प्रोत्साहित किया जा रहा है।

सतत् कृषि—सतत् कृषि पादप उत्पादन एवं पशुपालन की समन्वित कृषि प्रणाली है, जो पर्यावरणीय सिद्धान्तों को ध्यान में रखकर की जाती है। सतत् कृषि दीर्घावधि में मानव के भोजन एवं रेशों की आवश्यकताओं की पूर्ति करेगी। जहां संभव हो वहां ऊर्जा के स्रोतों का अधिकतम दक्षता के साथ कम से कम उपयोग करेगी तथा कृषि कार्यों को आर्थिक रूप से स्वपोषित बनाएगी।

पर्यावरण जैविक—अजैविक संघटकों की एक व्यवस्था है। मानव ने इस व्यवस्था में व्यवधान उत्पन्न कर दिया है। अतः सतत् विकास के लिए मानव की अनियमित क्रियाओं को नियंत्रित करना आवश्यक है।

सतत् कृषि के लाभ—मृदा की उर्वरक शक्ति को न केवल बनाए रखता है, बल्कि उसमें वृद्धि भी करता है। पोषक तत्वों को सन्तुलित एवं दीर्घकालीन उपयोगी बनाता है। भूमिगत जल स्तर को बनाये रखता है। रसायनों के अत्यधिक उपयोग से होने वाले प्रदूषण को कम करता है। मृदा में लाभकारी सूक्ष्म जीवों की पर्याप्त जनसंख्या को बनाए रखता है।

सहायक आचार्य, हिन्दी
राजकीय वाणिज्य महाविद्यालय, अलवर
email : drukumar7@gmail.com

3. जलवायु परिवर्तन का जैव विविधता पर प्रभाव

लोकेश कुमार मीना

जलवायु एक क्षेत्र में दीर्घकालिक मौसम पैटर्न है, जो आमतौर पर 30 वर्षों में औसत होता है। (1) (2) सरल शब्दों में यह महीनों से लेकर लाखों वर्षों तक के समय में मौसम संबंधी चरों का माध्य और परिवर्तनशीलता है । (1) कुछ मौसम संबंधी चर जिन्हे आमतौर पर मापा जाता है, वे है-तापमान, आर्द्रता, वायुमंडलीय दबाव, हवा और वर्षा। व्यापक अर्थ में, जलवायु, जलवायु प्रणाली के घटकों की स्थिति है, जिसमें वायुमंडल, जलमंडल, क्रायोस्फीयर, स्थलमंडल और जीवमंडल शामिल है । (1) किसी स्थान की जलवायु उसके अक्षांश / देशांतर भू-भाग ऊंचाई और आसपास के जल निकायों और उनकी धाराओं से प्रभावित होती है ।

पेलियोक्लाइमेटोलॉजी प्राचीन जलवायु का अध्ययन है । चूंकि (2) 19वीं शताब्दी से पहले जलवायु के बहुत कम प्रत्यक्ष अवलोकन उपलब्ध थे । इसलिए पेलियोक्लाइमेंट का अनुमान प्रॉक्सी चर से लगाया जाता है। इनमें गैर-जैविक साक्ष्य शामिल है- जैसे की झील के तल और बर्फ के कोर में पाए जाने वाले तलछट और जैविक साक्ष्य- जैसे कि पेड़ के छल्ले और मूंगा ।

विश्व मौसम विज्ञान संगठन (WHO) "जलवायु मानदंड" (सी एन) का वर्णन क्लाइमेटोलॉजिस्ट द्वारा उपयोग किए जाने वाले संदर्भ बिंदुओं के रूप में करता है, जो वर्तमान जलवायु संबंधी रुझानों की तुलना अतीत के या विशिष्ट माना जाता है । एक सी एन को एक जलवायु तत्व के अंकगणितीय औसत के रूप में परिभाषित किया गया है । (उदाहरण के लिए तापमान) 30 साल की अवधि में । 30 साल की अवधि का उपयोग किया जाता है, क्योंकि यह किसी भी अंतर वार्षिकी भिन्नता या विसंगतियों को फिल्टर करने के लिए पर्याप्त है, लेकिन लंबी जलवायु प्रवृत्तियों को दिखाने में सक्षम होने के लिए भी पर्याप्त है ।(3)

(3) जलवायु वर्गीकरण :

जलवायु वर्गीकरण वे प्रणालियां है, जो विश्व की जलवायु को वर्गीकृत करती है । एक जलवायु वर्गीकरण बायोम वर्गीकरण के साथ निकटता से संबंधित हो सकता है, क्योंकि जलवायु एक क्षेत्र में जीवन पर एक प्रमुख प्रभाव है । सबसे अधिक इस्तेमाल में से एक कोपेन जलवायु वर्गीकरण योजना है जिसे पहली बार 1899 में विकसित किया गया था । (4)

Aftermath of Climate Change

जलवायु को समान व्यवस्थाओं में वर्गीकृत करने के कई तरीके हैं । मूल रूप से, किसी स्थान के अक्षांश के आधार पर मौसम का वर्णन करने के लिए प्राचीन ग्रीस में जलवायु को परिभाषित किया गया था । आधुनिक जलवायु वर्गीकरण विधियों को मोटे तौर पर आनुवांशिक तरीकों में विभाजित किया जा सकता है, जो जलवायु के कारणों पर ध्यान केंद्रित करते हैं । आनुवांशिक वर्गीकरण में विभिन्न वायु द्रव्यमान प्रकारों की सापेक्ष आवर्ती के आधार पर या समकालिक मौसम की गड़बड़ी के भीतर के स्थान शामिल हैं । अनुभवजन्य वर्गीकरण के उदाहरणों के द्वारा परिभाषित जलवायु क्षेत्र शामिल हैं - पौधों की कठोरता (5) वाष्पीकरण या अधिक सामान्यत: कोपेन जलवायु वर्गीकरण जिसे मूल रूप से कुछ बायोम से जुड़े जलवायु की पहचान करने के लिए डिजाइन किया गया था । इन वर्गीकरण योजनाओं की एक सामान्य कमी यह है कि वे प्रकृति में अधिक सामान्य जलवायु गुणों के कृत्रिम संक्रमण के बजाय उन क्षेत्रों के बीच अलग-अलग सीमाएं उत्पन्न करती है जिन्हें वे परिभाषित करते हैं ।

जलवायु परिवर्तन :

जलवायु परिवर्तन समय के साथ वैश्विक या क्षेत्रीय जलवायु में बदलाव है । (6) यह दशकों से लेकर लाखों वर्षों तक के समय के पैमाने के साथ वातावरण की परिवर्तनशीलता या औसत स्थिति में परिवर्तन को दर्शाता है । ये परिवर्तन पृथ्वी की आंतरिक प्रक्रियाओं, बाहरी शक्तियों (जैसे सूर्य के प्रकाश की तीव्रता में भिन्नता) या हाल ही में मानवीय गतिविधियों के कारण हो सकते है । (7) हाल के उपयोग में, विशेष रूप से पर्यावरण नीति के संदर्भ में शब्द "जलवायु परिवर्तन" अक्सर केवल आधुनिक जलवायु में परिवर्तन को संदर्भित करता है, जिसमें औसत सतह के तापमान में वृद्धि शामिल है, जिसे ग्लोबल वार्मिंग के रूप में जाना जाता है । कुछ मामलों में, इस शब्द का प्रयोग मानवीय कार्य-करण के अनुमान के साथ भी किया जाता है, जैसा कि जलवायु परिवर्तन पर संयुक्त राष्ट्र फ्रेमवर्क कन्वेंशन (UNFCCC). UNFCCC गैर मानव जनित विविधताओं के लिए "जलवायु परिवर्तनशीलता" का उपयोग करता है ।(8)

पृथ्वी ने अतीत में समय समय पर जलवायु परिवर्तन किया है - जिसमें प्रमुख हिमयुग शामिल है इसमें हिमनद काल शामिल होते हैं । जहां स्थितियां सामान्य से अधिक ठंडी होती है, जो अंत: विषम काल से अलग होती है । हिमनदो की अवधि के दौरान बर्फ और बर्फ का संचय सतह एल्बिडो को बढ़ाता है, जो सूर्य की ऊर्जा को अंतरिक्ष में अधिक दर्शाता है और कम वायुमंडलीय तापमान बनाए रखता है। ग्रीन हाउस गैसों में वृद्धि जैसे ज्वालामुखी गतिविधियों से, वैश्विक तापमान में वृद्धि हो सकती है और एक अंतराल अवधि उत्पन्न हो सकती है । हिम युग काल के सुझाए गए

Aftermath of Climate Change

कारणों में महाद्वीपों की स्थिति, पृथ्वी की कक्षा में भिन्नता, सौर उत्पादन में परिवर्तन और ज्वालामुखी शामिल है । (12)

जलवायु परिवर्तन के कारक :

पृथ्वी की जलवायु गतिशील है जो प्राकृतिक-चक्र के अनुसार सदैव बदलती रहती है अर्थात जलवायु परिवर्तन एक प्राकृतिक प्रक्रिया है, किंतु मानवीय गतिविधियों द्वारा जलवायु परिवर्तन की दर में आई वृद्धि चिंता का विषय है । जलवायु में आये परिवर्तन के कारणों को दो भागों में बांटा जा सकता है । (8) पहला-प्राकृतिक और दूसरा-मानवीय गतिविधियां । प्राकृतिक कारणों से होने वाले जलवायु परिवर्तन से पर्यावरण प्रभावित होता है तथा मानव गतिविधियों द्वारा पर्यावरण प्रदूषित होने से जलवायु प्रदूषित होती है । इस प्रकार जलवायु और पर्यावरण एक दूसरे को प्रभावित करते हैं -

(अ) प्राकृतिक गतिविधियां :

(I) **महाद्वीपीय संवहन :** सृष्टि के प्रारंभ में सभी महाद्वीप एक ही बड़े धरातल के रूप में पृथ्वी पर विद्यमान थे किंतु सागरों के कारण धीरे-धीरे वे एक दूसरे से दूर होते गए और आज उनके अलग-अलग खंड बन गए हैं महाद्वीपों का खिसकना आज भी जारी है, जिसकी वजह से समुद्री धाराएं तथा हवाएं प्रभावित होती है और इनका सीधा प्रभाव पृथ्वी की जलवायु पर पड़ता है । हिमालय पर्वत की श्रंखला प्रति वर्ष 1 मिलीमीटर की दर से ऊंची हो रही है, जिसका मुख्य कारण भारतीय उपखंड का धीरे-धीरे एशियाई महाद्वीप की ओर खिसकना माना जाता है ।

(II) **ज्वालामुखी विस्फोट :** ज्वालामुखी विस्फोट होने पर बड़ी मात्रा में विभिन्न गैसे जैसे CO_2, SO_2 जलवाष्प आदि तथा धूलकण वायुमंडल में उत्सर्जित होते हैं, जो कि वायुमंडल की ऊपरी परत समताप मंडल में जाकर फैल जाते हैं तथा पृथ्वी पर आने वाले सूर्य प्रकाश की मात्रा घटा देते हैं । जिससे पृथ्वी का तापमान कम हो जाता है । एक अनुमान के अनुसार, प्रतिवर्ष लगभग 100लाख टन CO_2 गैस ज्वालामुखी विस्फोट द्वारा वायुमंडल में फैल जाती है । सन् 1816 में इंग्लैंड, अमेरिका तथा पश्चिमी यूरोपीय देशों में ग्रीष्म ऋतु में जो अचानक ठंड आई थी जिसे "किलिंग समर फ्रास्ट" कहा गया, उसका कारण सन 1815 में इंडोनेशिया में हुए अनेक ज्वालामुखी विस्फोटों को माना जाता है ।

Aftermath of Climate Change

(III) **पृथ्वी का झुकाव :** पृथ्वी के झुकाव में बदलाव के कारण ऋतुओं में परिवर्तन होता है। अधिक झुकाव अर्थात अधिक गर्मी तथा अधिक सर्दी और कम झुकाव अर्थात कम गर्मी तथा कम सर्दी का मौसम। इस प्रकार पृथ्वी के झुकाव के कारण जलवायु प्रभावित होती है।

(IV) **समुद्री धाराएं :** जलवायु को संतुलित रखने में सागरों का बड़ा योगदान रहता है। पृथ्वी के 71 प्रतिशत भाग में समुद्र व्याप्त है, जो कि वातावरण तथा जमीन की तुलना में दोगुना सूर्य का प्रकाश का अवशोषण करते हैं। सागरों को CO_2 का सबसे बड़ा सिंक कहा जाता है। वायुमंडल की अपेक्षा 50 गुना अधिक CO_2 गैस समुद्र में होती है। समुद्री बहाव में बदलाव आने से जलवायु प्रभावित होती है।

(ब) मानव गतिविधियां :

(I) **शहरीकरण :** 19वीं सदी में हुई औद्योगिक क्रांति की ओर सभी का ध्यान आकर्षित हुआ है। रोजगार पाने के लिए गांवों में स्थित आबादी शहरों की तरफ प्रस्थान करने लगी और शहरों का आकार दिन-प्रतिदिन बढ़ने लगा। मुंबई, कोलकाता, लंदन, पेरिस, जैसे महानगरों में उनकी क्षमता से कई गुना अधिक आबादी निवास कर रही है, जिससे शहरों के संसाधनों का असीमित दोहन हो रहा है। जैसे-जैसे शहर बढ़ रहे हैं, वहां पर उपलब्ध भू-भाग दिन-प्रतिदिन ऊंची-ऊंची इमारतों से ढकता जा रहा है, जिससे उस स्थान की जल संवर्धन क्षमता कम हो रही है तथा बारिश के पानी से प्राप्त होने वाली शीतलता में भी कमी हो रही है, जिससे वहां की जलवायु और पर्यावरण पर निरंतर प्रभाव पड़ रहा है।

(II) **औद्योगिकीकरण :** जलवायु परिवर्तन में औद्योगिकीकरण की बड़ी भूमिका है उद्योगों से विभिन्न प्रकार की गैस CO_2, NO_2, SO_2 तथा अन्य जहरीले गैसें और धूलकण हवा में छोड़ती है, जो वायुमंडल में काफी वर्षों तक विद्यमान रहती है। यह ग्रीन हाउस प्रभाव, ओजोन परत का क्षरण तथा भूमंडलीय तापमान में वृद्धि जैसी समस्याओं का कारण बनते हैं। वायु, जल एवं भूमि प्रदूषण भी औद्योगिकीकरण की देन है।

(III) **वनोन्मूलन :** निरंतर बढ़ती हुई आबादी की निरंतर बढ़ती हुई जरूरतों को पूरा करने के लिए वृक्ष काटे जा रहे हैं। रहने की जगह, खेती तथा लकड़ी और वन संसाधनों की चाहत में वनों की अंधाधुंध कटाई हो रही है, जिससे पृथ्वी का हरित क्षेत्र

तेजी से घट रहा है और साथ ही जलवायु के परिवर्तन में तेजी आ रही है ।

(IV) रासायनिक कीटनाशकों एवं उर्वरकों का प्रयोग : पिछले कुछ दशकों में रासायनिक उर्वरकों की मांग इतनी तेजी से बढ़ रही है कि आज विश्व भर में 1000 से भी अधिक कीटनाशी उपलब्ध है । जैसे-जैसे इनका उपयोग बढ़ता जा रहा है, वैसे-वैसे वायु, जल तथा भूमि में इनकी मात्रा भी बढ़ती जा रही है, जो कि पर्यावरण को निरंतर प्रदूषित कर घातक स्थिति में पहुंचा रहे हैं ।

(V) अन्य मानवीय गतिविधियां : आजकल परिवहन संसाधनों विशेषकर वाहनों का योगदान वायु प्रदूषण बढ़ाने तथा जलवायु को प्रभावित करने में अधिक माना जा रहा है ।(8)

जैव विविधता : जैव विविधता जीवन और विविधता के सहयोग से निर्मित शब्द है, जो आमतौर पर पृथ्वी पर मौजूद जीवन की विविधता और परिवर्तनशीलता को संदर्भित करता है । संयुक्त राष्ट्र पर्यावरण कार्यक्रम UNEP के अनुसार जैव विविधता विशिष्टतया अनुवांशिक, प्रजाति तथा पारिस्थितिकी तंत्र के विविधता का स्तर मापता है । जैव विविधता किसी जैविक तंत्र के स्वास्थ्य का घोतक है । पृथ्वी पर जीवन आज लाखों विशिष्ट जैविक प्रजातियों के रूप में उपस्थित है । सन् 2010 को जैव विविधता का अंतरराष्ट्रीय वर्ष घोषित किया गया है । जैव विविधता एक प्राकृतिक संसाधन है जिससे हमारे जीवन की संपूर्ण आवश्यकताओं की पूर्ति होती है ।(9)

जैव विविधता शब्द पृथ्वी पर उसके सभी स्तरों पर जीवन की विविधता को संदर्भित करता है जीन से पारिस्थितिक तंत्र तक और जीवन को बनाए रखने वाली विकासवादी, परिस्थितिक और सांस्कृतिक प्रक्रियाओं को शामिल करता है । जैव विविधता में न केवल वे प्रजातियां शामिल है- मनुष्यों से लेकर जीवो तक जिनके बारे में हम बहुत कम जानते हैं जैसे कि रोगाणुओं, कवक, और अकशेरुकी(12)

जैव विविधता पृथ्वी पर समान रूप से वितरित नहीं है । यह आमतौर पर भूमध्य रेखा के पास के क्षेत्र में गर्म जलवायु और उच्च प्राथमिक उत्पादकता के परिणाम स्वरूप उष्णकटिबंधीय में अधिक है । यह उष्णकटिबंधीय वन पारिस्थितिक तंत्र पृथ्वी की सतह के 10% से कम को कवर करते हैं और इसमें दुनिया की लगभग 90% प्रजातियां शामिल है । समुद्री जैव विविधता आमतौर पर पश्चिमी प्रशांत में तटो के साथ अधिक होती है, जहां समुंद्र की सतह का तापमान उच्चतम होता है और सभी महासागरों के मध्य अक्षांशीय बैड गेप भी होता है । प्रजातियों की विविधता में अक्षांशीय प्रवणताएं है । जैव विविधता आमतौर पर हॉटस्पोंटस में कलस्टर होती है जो समय के साथ बढ़ रहा है, लेकिन भविष्य में वनों की कटाई के प्राथमिक परिणाम

के रूप में धीमा होने की संभावना है । 99.9% से अधिक प्रजातियां जो कभी पृथ्वी पर रहती थी, जिनमें से 5 मिलियन से अधिक प्रजातियों के विलुप्त होने का अनुमान है। पृथ्वी की वर्तमान प्रजातियों की संख्या का अनुमान 10 मिलियन से 14 मिलियन तक है, जिनमें से लगभग 1.2 मिलियन का दस्तावेजीकरण किया गया है और 86% से अधिक का अभी तक वर्णन नहीं किया गया है ।(9)

जलवायु परिवर्तन का जैव विविधता पर प्रभाव : जलवायु परिवर्तन और जैव विविधता के बीच की कड़ी लंबे समय से स्थापित है । यद्यपि पूरे पृथ्वी के इतिहास में पारिस्थितिक तंत्रों, प्रजातियों के आने और जाने के साथ जलवायु हमेशा बदलती है, तेजी से जलवायु परिवर्तन पारिस्थितिक तंत्र और प्रजातियों की अनुकूलन क्षमता को प्रभावित करता है और इसलिए जैव विविधता हॉनी बढ़ जाती है । मई 2010 में संयुक्त राष्ट्र के वैश्विक जैव विविधता आउटलुक-3 ने कुछ चिंताओं को संक्षेप में प्रस्तुत किया है की-जलवायु परिवर्तन पहले से ही जैव विविधता पर प्रभाव डाल रहा है और आने वाले दशकों में उत्तरोत्तर अधिक महत्वपूर्ण खतरा बनने का अनुमान है । आर्कटिक समुंद्री बर्फ के नुकसान से पूरे बायोम और उसके बाहर जैव विविधता को खतरा है। वातावरण में CO_2 की उच्च सांद्रता के परिणाम स्वरूप समुद्र के अम्लीकरण का संबंधित दबाव भी पहले से ही देखा जा रहा है । पारिस्थितिक तंत्र पहले से ही जलवायु परिवर्तन के मौजूद स्तरों के तहत नकारात्मक प्रभाव दिखा रहे हैं, जो कि भविष्य के अनुमानित परिवर्तनों की तुलना में मामूली है । गर्म तापमान के अलावा, अधिक लगातार चरम मौसम की घटनाएं और वर्षा और सूखे के बदलते पैटर्न से जैव विविधता पर महत्वपूर्ण प्रभाव पड़ने की उम्मीद की जा सकती है । (12)

भूमि जैव विविधता पर प्रभाव : बढ़ता तापमान पहले से ही दुनिया के ध्रुवीय क्षेत्रों को प्रभावित कर रहे हैं । घटते आइस पैक ध्रुवीय भालू, पेंगुइन, पफिन और अन्य आर्कटिक जीवो के आवास को कम करते हैं । जैसे ही बर्फ पिघलती है, यह समुद्र के स्तर को बढ़ाती है, जो समुद्र तट पर पारिस्थितिक तंत्र को प्रभावित और नष्ट कर सकती है । तापमान में परिवर्तन भी संभोग चक्रों में बदलाव का कारण बनेगा । विशेष रुप से प्रवासी जानवरों के लिए जो अपने परिवार और प्रजनन समय को इंगित करने के लिए बदलते मौसम पर भरोसा करते हैं। (11)

महासागर जैव विविधता पर प्रभाव : समुद्र के बढ़ते स्तर से समुद्र के तापमान और शायद धाराओं में भी बदलाव आएगा । इस तरह के बदलाव को समुद्र में खाद्य श्रृंखला का एक अनिवार्य हिस्सा जोप्लांकटन पर एक मजबूत प्रभाव पड़ेगा । प्लवक कहां रहते हैं और उनकी आबादी का आकार कितना बड़ा है, यह पृथ्वी के जल में जैव विविधता को हॉनि पहुंचा सकता है । व्हेल, विशेष रूप से, इसका खामियाजा भुगत

सकती है क्योंकि कहीं व्हेल प्रजातियों को जीवित रहने के लिए बड़े पैमाने पर प्लवक की आवश्यकता होती है । इसके अलावा बढी हुई CO_2 समुद्र के अम्लीकरण का कारण बनती है, जो जीवों और पौधों को प्रभावित करती है, जो PH संतुलन के प्रति संवेदनशील होते हैं । (11)

आर्कटिक में जैव विविधता पर प्रभाव : आर्कटिक, अंटार्कटिक और उच्च अक्षांशो में वार्मिंग की उच्चतम दर रहती है और यह जारी रहने का अनुमान है । आर्कटिक में यह न केवल समुद्री बर्फ की मात्रा में कमी है बल्कि इसकी मोटाई और उम्र भी है । कम परावर्तक सतह का अर्थ है - अधिक तेजी से पिघलना है । इसके अलावा पूरी प्रजातियों के संयोजन बर्फ के ऊपर या नीचे जीवन के लिए अनुकूलित होते हैं शैवाल से जो बह-वर्षीय बर्फ के नीचे उगते हैं, आर्कटिक महासागर के प्राथमिक उत्पादन का 25% तक अकशेरुकी, पक्षियों, मछली के लिए बनाते हैं । इसलिए उस खाद्य श्रृंखला के शीर्ष पर प्रतिष्ठित ध्रुवीय भालू जोखिम में एकमात्र प्रजाति नहीं है, भले ही इसे अधिक मीडिया का ध्यान मिल सका है । (10)

उपसंहार : जैसे-जैसे **जैव** विविधता घटती जाएगी इसके दूरगामी प्रभाव होंगे । खाद्य श्रृंखला में व्यवधान न केवल पारिस्थितिक तंत्र को प्रभावित कर सकता है बल्कि मानवता की बढती आबादी को खिलाने की क्षमता को प्रभावित कर सकता है । उदाहरण के लिए, विविध कीट प्रजातियों को खोने से पौधों के परागण में कमी आएगी। इसके अतिरिक्त यह मानवता की दवा बनाने की क्षमता को कम कर सकता है, क्योंकि विलुप्त होने का दावा अधिक से अधिक प्रमुख पौधों की प्रजातियों में होता है **जैव** विविधता प्राकृतिक आपदाओं से भी बचाती है, जैसे कि घास जो विशेष रूप से जंगल की आग के प्रसार का विरोध करने के लिए विकसित हुई है । जलवायु परिवर्तन की गति को धीमा करने के लिए दुनिया भर में लागू प्रकृति संरक्षण संबंधी नीतियों के माध्यम से कार्बन शोषण के स्रोतों जैसे जंगलों और दलदलों को बचाए जाने की आवश्यकता है । जलवायु परिवर्तन की मार सबसे ज्यादा उन आरक्षित प्रजातियों पर पड़ेगी जिनकी आबादी बहुत कम है, जो प्रतिबंधित क्षेत्रों में निवास करते हैं या वे जिनका बसेरा कुछ विशिष्ट स्थानों यथा कोरल रीफ, मेग्रोव वनो तथा हिम क्षेत्रों में होता है । पारिस्थितिक संतुलन बनाए रखने के लिए **जैव** विविधता अत्यंत महत्वपूर्ण है ।

Aftermath of Climate Change

संदर्भ सूची :

(1) ए बी सी मैथ्यूज, जेबी रोबिन, मोलर, विसेंट, वेन डायमेन, रेनी-जलवायु परिवर्तन पर अंतर सरकारी पैनल । IPCC 6वीं मूल्यांकन रिपोर्ट ।

(2) शेफर्ड, डॉ.जे. मार्शल, सिंथिया एम. : मौसम और जलवायु में क्या अंतर है ?

(3) "जलवायु डाटा और डाटा संबंधित उत्पाद" विश्व मौसम विज्ञान संगठन ।

(4) बेक, हिल्के ई. जीमर्मन. टिम आर., वुड., एरिक एफ., वर्तमान और भविष्य के कोपेन गीजर जलवायु वर्गिकरण ।

(5) "थार्नथवेट नमी सूचकांक", मौसम विज्ञान की शब्दावली ।

(6) "जलवायु परिवर्तन", नेशनल ज्योग्राफिक सोसायटी ।

(7) आर्कटिक जलवायु विज्ञान और मौसम विज्ञान, जलवायु परिवर्तन ।

(8) दिनेश मणि, आईसेक्ट विश्वविद्यालय द्वारा अनुसृजन परियोजना के अंतर्गत निर्मित पुस्तक जलवायु परिवर्तन-2015

(9) अमेरिकन म्यूजियम ऑफ नेशनल हिस्ट्री, **जैव** विविधता।

(10) WWW.GLOBALISSUES.ORG वेबसाइट का हिंदी अनुवाद, आर्कटिक में जैव विविधता ।

(11) WWW.SCIENCING.COM वेबसाइट का हिंदी अनुवाद-जलवायु परिवर्तन जैव विविधता को कैसे प्रभावित करता है, मैग मिशेल द्वारा

(12) इलेक्ट्रॉनिक मीडिया तथा इंटरनेट पर प्रकाशित खबर ।

सहायक आचार्य (गणित)
राजेश पायलट राजकीय महाविद्यालय, लालसोट ,दौसा
email : lokeshkumarmeena3093@gmail.com

4. Exploring Nutritional and Biochemical Traits of *Pseudomonas Virdiflava* for its Identification from *Capsicum Annum* Seeds

Neetu Soni*, Ashwani Kumar Verma and Laxmi Meena

Abstract

The present study has investigated presence of *Pseudomonas virdiflava* in seeds of *Capsicum annum* L. by use of its biochemical traits. Total twenty five bacterial colonies were obtained from the diseased seeds of capsicum and identified as pseudomonas spp. through numerous biochemical tests. Further these were confirmed as *Pseudomonas virdiflava* on the basis of LPOAT test, carbohydrate utilization, HR (hypersensitive reaction) and pathogenicity test. The discoloured and symptom showing seeds were plated on nutrient agar medium and total 42 bacterial colonies were selected on the basis of colony morphology and response on King's B medium. From these isolates, totally 25 colonies were sorted for further identification test. They were Gram negative, rod shaped, and utilized glucose, mannitol, inositol but unable to consume sucrose and starch in medium. Their host and pathogenicity test confirmed the pathovar as *Pseudomonas virdiflava*.

Keywords : Bacterial leaf spot, *Capsicum annum*, *Pseudomonas virdiflava*, biochemical test.

1. Introduction

The role of fresh fruits and vegetables in nutrition and healthy diet is well recognized and in recent years, many countries have undertaken various initiatives to encourage consumers to eat more of these products. The health aspect together with increasing consumer demands for variety and availability, and the changing structure of global trade has led to an increase in trade of fruits and vegetables (Abd-Alla et al. 2011).

Chilli (Capsicum annum L.) is most important spice. Chilli is grown for its fruit because its dried fruit have a good pungency. Chilli belong to the genus capsicum, family Solanaceae. Capsicum mainly cultivated in tropical region because it necessary a long and hot summer climate for its growth. It is originated in Mexico, Southern Peru and Bolivia (Villalon, 1981). The world's hottest chilli species is "Naga jolokia". India is largest producer, consumer and exporter of chilli in the world.

Agriculture products can be exposed to microbial contamination through a variety of sources. Since fruits and vegetables are produced in a natural environment, they are vulnerable to contamination by human pathogens. The majority of diseases associated with fresh fruits and vegetables are primarily those transmitted by the faecal-oral route, and therefore, are a results of contamination at some point in the process. (De Roeverv 1998).

Besides being used as Spice, medically, fungicide, it is attacked by many pathogenic bacteria which annually results in heavy yield losses (Aktar and Shamsi, 2014; Politi et al., 2012; Zhang et al., 2013; Salehi et al., 2018; Mir et al. 2019). Bacterial disease is leading cause of postharvest losses of potatoes (Ceponis et al. 1984), tomatoes (Ceponis et al. 1986), peppers (Ceponis et al. 1987), lettuce (Ceponis et al. 1985). It is causes by a group of plant pathogens that includes pectolytic, Pseudomonas fluorescence and P. virdiflava (Lund 1983).

The displaying characteristic symptoms of this disease start with water- soaked, dark brown- to- black, necrotic on pepper (Capsicum annum L.) leaves, irregular circles of chlorotic soft tissue. In some severe infected stage of disease plants show apical growth resulting in death of the infected plant is also observed. It shows variability in symptom development pattern also as sometimes little; moist, dark-green spots are emerged on lower side of leaves which is later covers upper layer also with brownish drawn-out de-coloration (Hellmers, 1955).

As mentioned above, the Capsicum has immense importance as a source of Spices compounds, details on its microbial pathogens and their early identification process is a necessity to decide approaches of crop protection so that monetary losses can be prevented, particularly for small-scale producers.

Materials and Methods
• Field Survey and Sample Collection
For collecting samples of *Capsicum annum* were performed in the year 2019-2020 and total 110 samples of seeds were collected from fields of different villages of Alwar districts, Rajasthan state. In initial investigation, the symptomatic seeds were distinguish on the basis of paleness of cotyledons, wrinkles or any other spot.

Screening of the Pathogen :
Out of the 110 samples, 65 samples showed discoloration and spots on seeds which later yielded in isolation of 42 bacterial colonies. On application of specific identification methods, 25 colonies were identified as *Pseudomonas* virdiflava capsici. Which were further confirmed by host and pathogenicity assays. Before doing biochemical tests, symptomatic seeds were washed with sterilized distilled water, and surface disinfested by washing in sodium hypochlorite (10%) for 1 min, a Second washing in ethyl alcohol (70%) for 1 min, followed by triple washing in sterile distilled water. (Cotter et al. 1985).Now the symptomatic tissue was investigated under a light microscope (40X) to check for bacterial streaming. The second test was electron microscopy screening for the presence of virus particles (Golding et al.2016). third an all seed tissue was plated on potato dextrose agar (PDA: Sogma Aldrich Ltd.) to check for the presence of fungi and lastly, the seeds sample was plated on agar medium to grow potentially present plant pathogenic bacteria. The different bacterial colony grown under the seeds were picked and transferred on semi selective King's B (KB) medium for further identification process. The isolates which showed *Pvc* type colony appearances were exposed to many biochemical tests.

Nutritional and Biochemical Analysis:
- In isolates 25 bacterial colony were selected for their reaction towards Gram's- stain, KOH solubility, and catalase activity, LOPAT test (Levan production, Oxidase activity, Potato soft rot, Arginine dihydrolase activity, and hypersensitive response) for early identification of pseudomonas spp. (Klement et al., 1990; Peix et al., 2018; Patyka et al., 2019).

- In addition to these initial tests, strains were eveluted for their ability to hydrolyase gelatin and esculin and to utilize betaine, L-lactate and homoserine as the sole carbon source according to Schaad et al. (2001).

Pathogenicity Test (Host test) :

The isolates showing characteristic test of *Pvc* were assessed for pathogenicity test on capsicum annum and other hosts such as Potato (*Solanum tuberosum*), Tomato (*Solanum lycopersicum* L.), eggplant (*Solanum melongena)*) (Robinson et al. 2004). The leaves of host plants were punctured and the bacterial suspension maintained at 1×10^7 CFU/mL was injected in the middle vein while the control was inoculated with sterile tap water only (Rhodehamel and Durbin 1985; Peix et al., 2018). The inoculated leaves were then placed in at $27 \pm 2°C$ and looked every day for development of any necrotic or pathogenic symptoms (Schaad and Kendrick, 1975; Saettler et al., 1989).

Results and Discussion :

The *P. virdiflava capsici* hosts members of family Solanaceae and incites apical chlorosis and bacterial leaf spots (Gulya et al., 1982; Hellmers, 1955; Rhodehamel and Durbin, 1985; Rhodehamel and Durbin, 1989; Shane and Baumer, 1984). Formerly also, it has been isolated from various plants and from weeds showing apical chlorosis. On the contrary, it is assessed for antagonistic activity for controlling Canada thistle in soybean and woolly leaf bursage in cotton (Budde and Ullrich et al. 2000; Sheikh et al.., 2001; Gronwald et al., 2002). In this study, overall 65 seed samples displayed atypical colour and spots on seed coat which further brought out 42 types of bacterial colonies. From these isolates, 25 colonies were developed on NA medium and characterized as *Pvc* on the basis of their response for nutritional and biochemical analytic tests as shown in table no. 1. The colonies developed on NA were whitish, mucoid, raised, smooth and glistering.

These fluorescent pseudomonads were looked for their group on the basis of LOPAT test and they were -+--+ (Fig. 1) and confirmed their position in LOPAT group IB (Young and Fletcher 1997). Suzuki et al. (2003) also used LOPAT and other test to differentiate

P. virdifalva pv. *Pisi* in infected pea plants. The most studied *P. virdifalva* bacterial models had same pattern in some other study viz. *Pseudomonas* pathovar from tomato (Whalen et al. 1991) and cauliflower (Weibe et al. 1993) showed same response for KB medium and LOPAT test.

The results of morphology of colony and LOPAT directed that all the purified colonies are strains of *Pseudomonas virdifalva capsici*. The results of different phenotypic (biochemical) tests lead to the confirmation of pathovar. Further positive results for D-Galctose, Gluconate, Glucose, inositol, mannitol, sorbitol utilization and negative results for starch hydrolysis and Glycerol and sucrose specified that all isolates are *pvc* which was further confirmed by host and HR test. In previous studies too, similar responses of biochemical and hypersensitivity reactions of *Pvc* have been observed in capsicum and other plants (Lydon et al. 2011; Song et al. 2015).

In some key studies, the selective characteristics of pathogen of Capsicum were established on the basis of specific biochemical features (Jeevan et al. 2021). For *B. altitudinis, P. aeruginosa, B. aryabhattai, B. wiedmannii* and many more, biochemical characterization method was applied successfully (Margarita et al. 2017; Shah et al. 2022). In experiments exploring antimicrobial properties of *Pvc* it was identified and distinguished on the basis of nutritional requirements Grădilă et al. 2022).

Conclusion :

We have performed an inclusive phenotypic and biochemical analysis of 25 strains of *Pseudomonas virdiflava capsici* isolated from the seeds of *Capsicum annum L*. The strains showed ability to utilize D-Galctose, Gluconate, Glucose, inositol, mannitol and sorbitol as sole carbon source in medium. We established an early detection of this seed borne pathogen of capsicum as yet there is no effective control measure known for this pathogen other than use of infection free seed lots in the field.

The significance of LOPAT and other biochemical tests has been established in many molecular detection experiments also and in our study we successfully demonstrated that these methods are vital to decide pathovar of *Pseudomonas* virdiflava. We have provided an extensive detail of these test methods and results which may be proven as a great source of reference in further

Table no. 1: Biochemical and physiological characterization of isolates strains of *Pseudomonas virdiflava capsici* isolated from seeds of Capsicum annum L

S. No.	Test	Response	S.no.	Test	Response
1.	Gram reaction	Negative	5.	Mannitol	Positive
2.	5% NaCl tolerance	Negative	6.	Utilization from Glucose	Positive
3.	7%NaCl tolerance	Negative	7.	Sucrose	Negative
4.	Catalase	Positive	8.	Sorbitol	Positive

Results of colony morphology, Gram's staining and KOH solubility test

A : White, glistening and mucoid colonies of *Pseudomonas viridiflava* on NA
B : Rod shaped colonies in Gram's staining
C : Whitish glistening colony on NA
D : Bubbles indicating KOH solubility test.

References
1. Klement, Z. 1963. Rapid detection and the pathogenicity of pathogenicity of phytopathogenic Pseudomonas. Nature. 199:299-300.
2. Ceponis MJ, Cappellini RA, Lightner GW (1985) Disorders in crisphead lettuce shipments to the New York market, 1972–1984. Plant Dis 69:1016–1020
3. Ceponis MJ, Cappellini PA, Lightner GW (1986) Disorders in tomato shipments to the New York market, 1972–1984. Plant Dis 70:261–265

4. Ceponis MJ, Cappellini RA, Lightner GW (1987) Disorders in fresh pepper shipments to the New York market, 1972–1984. Plant Dis 71:380–382
5. Cotter JL, Fader RC, Lilley C, Herndon DN (1985) Chemical parameters, antimicrobial activities, and tissue toxicity of 0.1 and 0.5% sodium hypochlorite solutions. Am Soc Microbiol 28:118–122
6. Abd-Alla MH (1994) Phosphatases and the utilization of organic phosphorus by Rhizobium leguminosarum biovar viceae phosphatases. Lett Appl Microbiol 18:294–296
7. Roever De (1998) Microbiological safety evaluations and recommendations on fresh produce. Food Control 6:321–347
8. Agrios GN. Plant Pathology. 5th Ed. The Netherlands: Elsevier Academic Press; 2005
9. Lund BM. Bacterial spoilage. In: Demis C (Ed.). Postharvest pathology of fruits and vegetables. London: Academic press; 1983: 219– 5
10. Abd-Alla MH, Bashandy SR, Schnell S, Ratering S (2011) Isolation and characterization of Serratia rubidaea from dark brown spots of tomato fruits. Phytoparasitica 39(2):175–183
11. Bruhn CM (1995) Consumer attitudes and market response to irradiated food. J Food Prot 58:175–181
12. Gronwald JW, Plaisance KL, Ide DA, Wyse DL. 2002. Assessment of *Pseudomonas* virdiflava as a biocontrol agent for Canada thistle. Weed Sci. 50:397-404.
13. Suzuki A, Togawa M, Ohta K, Takikawa Y. 2003. Occurrence of white top of pea caused by a new strain of *Pseudomonas viridiflava* Plant Dis. 87:1404-1410.
14. Krieg NR., Ludwig W., Whitman WB., Hedlund BP., Paster BJ., Staley JT., Ward N., Brown D. Bergey's manual of systematic bacteriology, 2nd edn, vol. 4, New York: Springer– Verlag; 2010
15. Lamichhane JR, Varvaro LA. 2013. New medium for the detection of fluorescent pigment production by pseudomonads. Plant Pathol. 62: 624–632.
16. Chaturvedi S, Kulshrestha S, & Agrawal KP. 2015. Characterization of *Pseudomonas savastoni* pv. *phaseolicola* in seed lots of mung bean (*Vigna radiata* L. Wilczek) collected from Rajasthan, India. Int. Res. J. Biological Sci. 4(10):57-61.

17. Marques E, Borges, RCF, Uesugi, CH. 2016. Identification and pathogenicity of *Pseudomonas cichorii* associated with a bacterial blight of gerbera in the Federal District. Horticultura Brasileira. 34:244-248. DOI http://dx.doi.org/10.1590/S0102-053620160000200015
18. Chaturvedi S, Agrawal K, Kulshrestha S, Narayan A. 2018. Molecular Identification of *Pseudomonas (savastoni)* pv. *phaseolicola* in Mung Bean (*Vigna radiata* L. Wilczek) Seeds Grown in Rajasthan State, India. Int. J. Curr. Microbiol. App. Sci. 7(11):1859-1866.
19. Peix A, Ramírez-Bahena MH, Velazquez E. 2018. The current status on the taxonomy of Pseudomonas revisited: An update. Infect. Genet. Evol. 57: 106–116.
20. Patyka V, Pasichnyk L, Butsenko L, Petrychenko V, Zubachev S, Dankevych L, Gnatiuk Y, Huliaiva H, Tokovenko I, Kalinichenko A. 2019. Express Diagnostics of Phytopathogenic Bacteria and Phytoplasmas in Agrophytocenosis. (Eds) Suszanowich D, Patyka V and Wyd-wo I. Drukarnia Swietego Krzyza, Opole, Poland. ISBN 978-83-7342-684-9.
21. Shah D, Khan MS, Aziz S, Ali H, Pecoraro L. 2022. Molecular and Biochemical Characterization, Antimicrobial Activity, Stress Tolerance, and Plant Growth- Promoting Effect of Endophytic Bacteria Isolated from Wheat Varieties. Microorganisms.10:21.https://doi.org/10.3390/microorganisms10010021
22. Höfte M., DeVos P. Plant pathogenic Pseudomonas species. In: plant-associated bacteria. Dordrecht. The Netherlands: Springer; 2007:507–33.

Dept. of Botany,
Raj Rishi Govt. College, Alwar (Raj.)
email : *sonineetu378@gmail.com

5. Socio-Economic Transformations to achieve Sustainable Development Goals

Dr. Madhu Kumari

Abstract

This paper is an analysis of projected economical changes in achieving SGDs and give a perspective of how we can achieve SGDs and sustain our economies. For this, we introduce six SDG Transformations as modular building-blocks of SDG achievement: (1) education, gender and inequality (2) health (3) Decarbonization and Energy (4) sustainable food, land, water (biosphere) (5) sustainable cities and communities; and (6) digital revolution. Each Transformation identifies priority investments and regulatory challenges. We also outline an action agenda to provide the knowledge required for designing, implementing and monitoring the SDG Transformations.These six Transformations require deep, deliberate, long-term structural changes in resource use, infrastructure, institutions, technologies and social relations that must be undertaken in a short period of time.

Transformation 1

Education builds human capital, which in turn promotes economic growth, the elimination of extreme poverty, decent work, and overcoming gender and other inequalities.

The knowledge and skills of workers available in the labour supply are a key determinant for both business and economic growth. A country's economy becomes more productive as the proportion of educated workers increases since educated workers can more efficiently carry out tasks that require literacy and critical thinking. However, obtaining a higher level of education also carries a cost. A country doesn't have to provide an extensive network of colleges or universities to benefit from education; it can provide basic literacy programs and still see economic improvements. An economy is more valuable when equal education and labour opportunities are available across gender, race, age, and ethnicities.

Countries with a greater portion of their population attending and graduating from schools see faster <u>economic growth</u> than countries with less-educated workers. As a result, many countries provide funding for primary and secondary education to improve economic performance. In this sense, education is an investment in <u>human capital</u>, similar to an investment in better equipment.

Gender Inequality : operational framework of gender equality with three dimensions :

The capabilities domain, which refers to basic human abilities as measured by education, health, and nutrition. These capabilities are fundamental to individual well-being and are the means through which individuals access other forms of well-being.

The access to resources and opportunities domain, which refers primarily to equality in the opportunity to use or apply basic capabilities through access to economic assets (such as land or housing) and resources (such as income and employment), as well as political opportunity (such as representation in parliaments and other political bodies). Without access to resources and opportunities, both political and economic, women will be unable to employ their capabilities for their well-being and that of their families, communities, and societies.

The security domain, which is defined to mean reduced vulnerability to violence and conflict. Violence and conflict result in physical and psychological harm and lessen the ability of individuals, households, and communities to fulfil their potential. Violence directed specifically at women and girls often aims at keeping them in "their place" through fear.

These seven interdependent priorities are the minimum necessary to empower women and alter the historical legacy of female disadvantage that remains in most societies of the world :

1. Strengthen opportunities for post primary education for girls while simultaneously meeting commitments to universal primary education.
2. Guarantee sexual and reproductive health and rights.
3. Invest in infrastructure to reduce women's and girls' time burdens.
4. Guarantee women's and girls' property and inheritance rights.

5. Eliminate gender inequality in employment by decreasing women's reliance on informal employment, closing gender gaps in earnings, and reducing occupational segregation.
6. Increase women's share of seats in national parliaments and local governmental bodies.
7. Combat violence against girls and women.

Transformation 2

As countries converge on the goal of universal health coverage, a number of common challenges are emerging. This paper explores three of them.

First is the challenge of making universal health coverage truly universal: while formal sector workers are easily covered by payroll deductions, and the poorest are often covered through government subsidies, the big challenge is to expand coverage to non-poor informal sector workers. made up mostly of informal workers and their families. Covering this group is proving challenging. There are two basic approaches to extend coverage to this group :

(i) Encourage contributions from the informal sector through financial and/or non-financial incentives and information campaigns, or (ii) use general tax revenues to cover not only the poor, but also the informal sector.

Second is the challenge of defining a common benefit package that is appropriate to the disease burden, represents good value for money and is socially acceptable. Third is the challenge of closing the gap between legal entitlements and citizens' actual ability to benefit from health services through ensuring supply-side readiness, i.e., the availability of quality health services within sufficiently close geographic proximity, especially in the larger countries.

Transformation 3

Since 1992, the United Nations Framework Convention on Climate Change Conference of the Parties (COP) has been seeking global solutions to this issue. In 2015, at COP21, there was a universal agreement to reduce global emissions to limit global warming to below 2 °C. In this so-called Paris Agreement, nations agreed to rapidly reduce their carbon emissions through a process of submitting intended nationally determined contributions (INDCs) to mitigate climate change.

India's Intended Nationally Determined Contribution (INDC) to Control Climate Change : On 28 September 2016, the President of India signed the Paris Agreement, and the Government of India formally ratified it on 2 October 2016. India communicated its INDC in response to COP decisions 1/CP.19 and 1/CP.20 for the period 2011 to 2030

It is difficult to estimate the cost of achieving India's INDCs at this time. But the preliminary assessment indicates implementing climate mitigation and adaptation measures in India through INDCs from 2015 to 2030 will cost approximately US$2.5 trillion at 2014–2015 prices. India has developed INDCs on the basis of its development agenda with existing resources and capacity base.

The major share of domestic funding of climate finance comes from different budgetary sources, as most of the resources for adaptation and mitigation are built into the ongoing sectoral programmes. A careful mix of market mechanisms, together with fiscal instruments and regulatory interventions, are made to augment the availability of funds.

India imposed a carbon tax called the Clean Energy Tax on 1 July 2010, but only on coal. It was initially set at 50 rupees (US$0.80) per ton of domestic and imported coal. In 2015, the tax quadrupled to 200 rupees (US$3.20) per ton of coal. The tax on coal production was renamed as the Clean Environment Tax, using the emission factor for coal of around US$2.00 per ton. So far, it has been a massive success for financing the National Clean Environment Fund used to invest in clean energy, technologies and related projects. The total collection of 170.84 billion Indian rupees (US$2.7 billion) up until 2014–2015 has been used for 46 clean energy projects worth 165.11 billion rupees (US$2.6 billion). In 2016, the coal tax was doubled from 200 rupees (US$3.20) to 400 rupees (US$6.40) per ton, to help finance more clean energy projects (Mondal, Irfan, & Ramaswamy, 2016).

India has also set up a National Adaptation Fund to address climate change adaptation needs with an initial allocation of 3500 million rupees (US$55.6million). This fund, in addition to sectoral spending by the respective ministries, will be used to fund sectors like agriculture, water, forestry, etc.

Subsidies Cut and Increased Taxes on Fossil Fuels (Petrol and Diesel) An important fiscal measure taken is a cut in subsidies and increased taxes on fossil fuels (petrol and diesel). This action leads to an implicit carbon tax (US$140 for petrol and US$64 for diesel) in absolute terms. This tax is considered to exceed the reasonable value in terms of an initial carbon tax and has led to a decrease in the petrol subsidy by approximately 25%. World Bank estimates suggest that these measures will help India to achieve a net reduction of 11 million tons of CO_2 emission in less than a year (Government of India, 2015b). In addition, India has implemented tax-free infrastructure bonds of 50 billion rupees (US$794 million) for funding of renewable energy projects during the year 2015–2016 (Government of India, 2015c).

Finance Commission Incentive for Creation of Carbon Sink This is the 14th Finance Commission recommendation on incentives for the forestry sector. This initiative has effectively given afforestation a massive boost, as US$6.9 billion will be transferred to the states. This will increase to US$12 billion by 2019–2020.

Renewable Energy Certificates Renewable energy certificates is a market instrument that endorses renewable energy and its participation in the energy market. This was established in 2010 by the Ministry of New and Renewable Energy (MNRE) and has been allowed to trade since March 2011. **Perform Achieve and Trade** Perform Achieve and Trade aims to improve energy efficiency by 1–2% per year for energy-intensive industries. In eight energy demanding sectors, 478 plants participated resulting in a 4–5% decline in energy consumption at the end of 2015 compared to 2012.

India's Mitigation Effort - According to the World Resource Institute report, the energy sector is the dominant source of greenhouse gas emissions, contributing 75% of global emissions. the primary emitting sectors in the country are electricity generation, transport, agriculture, industry, buildings, fugitive emissions and waste. Greenhouse gas emissions in 2007 from the energy sector constituted 58% of the net CO_2e emissions. The transport sector emissions are reported from road transport, aviation, railways and navigation. In 2007, 142.04 million tonnes of CO2e were emitted from the transport sector which is 12.9% of the total emissions. It is noted that electricity and transport sectors together account for more than 70% of CO_2 emissions. Therefore, we have focused our discussion on the energy sector from a sustainable development and mitigation angle.

Energy Sector Non-commercial energy sources like firewood, dung cake and agricultural waste were the main sources of energy (more than 70%) of the total energy consumed in India at the time of independence. The situation rapidly changed with urbanisation and the changing demographic situation. In 1965, primary commercial energy consumption was 53 Million Tonnes of Oil Equivalent (MTOE) and per capita energy consumption was about 110 kg of oil equivalent. Among the commercial energy sources, coal, due to its abundance, was a predominant source of energy, accounting for 55% (about 315 MTOE) of Indian energy consumption in 2002. This was followed by oil (31%), natural gas (8%), hydro (5%) and nuclear (1%) energy. Table 9.4 provides a breakdown over time.

As the GDP growth rate of India increases, the overall growth of the country shows the changing pattern of energy consumption. People are using electricity and gas as their primary source. The consumption of electricity is increasing with urbanisation.

Thermal Power In 2013, electricity coverage in India was only 81%; by 2050 it is estimated that there will be full coverage of electricity throughout India and per head consumption will also increase due to urbanisation. Coal is the most abundant source of commercial energy in India. The total coal reserves (as on 1 January 2014) have been assessed at about 301.56 billion tonnes.

The emission intensity of India's GDP declined by more than 30% during the period 1994–2007, due to the efforts and policies that India was following. India wants to further reduce the emission intensity of GDP by 20–25% between 2005 and 2020 following the path of inclusive growth. Experts say that GDP growth rate will fall by 2% and the inflation rate will also be high. In this situation, it will be difficult for the country to fulfil its commitments. The global scenario is also changing and will have great impact on the funding of the INDC. If the funding of projects becomes uncertain, their implementation will be difficult

Transformation 4

While agricultural activities are a major drain on water resources, high population growth continually escalates energy–water–food–land nexus pressures. Access to clean drinking water, energy, and food to meet the demographic needs are fundamental, but this is unlikely to be the case by 2050 due to the anticipated land scarcity. Land stress is endangering energy, water, and food security, and this works against ecological sustainable development. This research analysed the ecological balance of human activities and how policymakers have increasingly emphasized on energy–water–food nexus sectors separately without integrating land usage and population growth which poses an even more critical situation if left unattended to. The Multi-Scale Integrated Analysis of Societal and Ecosystem Metabolism (MuSIASEM) method as being appropriate to support the transition toward a sustainable economy because it is used to optimize resources, generate focused decisions, actions, investments, and policies that would combat nexus pressures and promote ecological sustainable development.

Since ecologically sustainable development is the environmental component of sustainable development, it is achieved by taking precautionary measures that curb any threats which could lead to environmental damage. This approach does not depend on scientific measures alone but also an integrated environmental and socioeconomic approach that depends on the valuation of assets and services to provide more incentive for the conservation of biological diversity and ecological integrity (Ecological sustainable development, 2019).

In many countries, food production affects water by causing changes in the way land is used as well as monitoring any changes in the river runoffs and groundwater discharge levels. Modern agriculture practices (SMART or Precision) that depend on fertilization for crop nutrition may cause groundwater pollution with nitrates, be energy-intensive and infrastructure intensive and yet less-labour intensive if adopted as a mitigation or adaptation technique. Further, the food and agriculture supply chain networks may use up more than the average 30% global consumption because its economy is 60% agricultural dependent. All these factors need careful analysis in the context of the food–water–energy–land–population growth nexus.

Transformation 5

At the global level, it is possible to see smart cities as indicators of neoclassical globalization and the next step in the evolution of 'new public management' philosophy where urban problems are converted into opportunities for corporate investment and profiteering. Thus, the spaces previously occupied mainly by local government institutions are opened up for involvement of new corporate actors. Estimates such as those by Grand View Research (2018) that the global market size of smart cities is about US dollars 550 billion in 2016 and projected to increase to US dollars 2.57 trillion by 2025 are indicative of this trend to see smart cities mainly as investment opportunities for digital technologies.

The second aspect of economics of smart cities is about what kind of data and approaches should cities use in selecting between different smart city projects and interventions. In ideal circumstances, smart city projects are no different to other public infrastructure projects and thus should be subject to cost benefit analysis. Presently there is limited guidance or literature on this (though there is some literature on economic appraisal of smart grid systems). However, valuing benefits from smart city interventions such as cloud platforms or building knowledge hubs can be a little bit challenging due to the lack of clarity on how to value something which is presently hidden from ultimate users. There is scope for developing and adapting valuation methods including those such as the survey-based contingent valuation method in some cases and perhaps qualitative and deliberative methods in other cases.

A third aspect is how cities can use an understanding of markets and competition to achieve good value for money in smart city project. This is the aspect that is most problematic due to the dominance of few large players in the smart city market and conceiving and presenting smart city project as a composite basket of various products. Such an approach favours monopolistic competition and cities especially in the Global South may find it difficult to unpack the different elements and negotiate a good deal for the city that delivers overall value for money for the city. Regulatory institutions needed to manage such a market also have not yet fully evolved. At present telecommunications regulators whose jurisdiction includes digital, mobile and broadband services are acting as de facto regulators for smart cities if at all.

A fourth aspect is in terms of how a smart city project can enhance or boost the strengths of the local economy and help the city to overcome the challenges such as youth unemployment or lack of skills among a section of the adult population or hurdles to innovation and business enterprise growth and sustainability. Many of these are deep social and economic issues and a smart city project can hardly be a quick fix but the real smart cities are those that are able to leverage technological and informational advantages to kickstart inclusive economic growth. This requires an innovation ecosystem approach with the involvement of a wide number of institutions and agents.

Besides the promising forecasts for Smart City market, many projects haven't taken off due to financial restrictions or unsustainable business models. There is an urgent need to build a holistic framework to analyze all business models included in the Smart City. As a matter of fact, the studies that analyze the business models in the context of Smart City refer mainly to e-government services, while there is a large number of dispersed studies that just focus on business models for specific applications within Smart City: e.g., smart mobility or smart energy.

There is a need to expand this framework beyond traditional expensive and unsustainable public infrastructures to provide eservices, towards an open and wide paradigm that includes multiple applications, agents, and technological and social innovations that can set the ground for sustainable financial models.

Transformation 6

The digital revolution is reinventing business models, reshaping economic sectors, and changing entire societal institutions. Big Data and Artificial Intelligence, profiling and targeting, and several other technological developments are now fundamentally changing the ways economies work.

Perhaps the greatest single enabler of sustainable development in the coming years would be the digital revolution, constituted by ongoing advances in AI, connectivity, digitization of information, additive manufacturing (3D printing), virtual reality, Internet of things (IoT), machine learning, block chain, robotics, quantum computing and synthetic biology.

The digital revolution has pervasive effects on all parts of the economy and society. It has been made possible by an interconnected set of discoveries and inventions, including semiconductors, logic gates, computer architecture, integrated circuits, microprocessors, packet switching, the Internet, mobile broadband, public-key cryptography, and global positioning system (GPS), among others. The pace of advance continues exponentially with imminent breakthrough prospects for AI, quantum computing, virtual reality, 5G broadband, and other technologies.

Digital technologies can raise productivity, lower production costs, reduce emissions, expand access, reduce resource intensity of production processes, improve matching in markets, enable the use of big data and make public services more readily available. They can also improve resource efficiencies, support the circular economy, enable zero-carbon energy systems, help monitor and protect ecosystems, and assume other critical roles.

As in the industrial revolution that initiated explosive development through the convergence of steel, steam and railways, coal and textile and other new manufacturing process, it was the convergence of these technologies, institutions, settlement patterns and lifestyles that generated the deep transformations. Likewise, the convergence of new digital technologies could be even more explosive with great winners and losers.

Yet there are risks and downsides that countries must identify and tackle through integrated strategies and a focus on the leave no-one-behind principle. This was fundamental in improving the lives of many including those previously excluded.

The digital revolution is already reshaping work, leisure, behaviour, education, and governance. Digital technologies are disrupting production processes in nearly every sector of the economy, from agriculture (precision agriculture), transport (self-driving cars), mining (autonomous vehicles), manufacturing (robotics. 3D printing), retail (e-commerce), finance (e-payments, AI trading strategies), media (social networks), health (AI diagnostics, telemedicine), education (online learning), public administration (e-governance, e-voting) and the IoT. In general, these contributions of digital technology can raise labour, energy, resource, and carbon productivity, lower production costs, expand access, dematerialize production (from physical books to e-books, for example), improve matching in markets (such as on electronic market places), enable the use of big data (disease epidemiology and drug design), and make public services more readily available (online voter registration, licenses and permits).

Yet there are risks and downsides that countries must identify and tackle through integrated strategies and a focus on the leave no- one-behind principle. Perhaps the most feared risk is the loss of jobs, particularly for lower-skilled workers, and the shift of income distribution from labour to capital. While new jobs might replace existing ones, these new jobs may come with lower real earnings and worse working conditions. Base erosion, profit shifting and the concentration of industries threaten to undermine countries tax bases. Other threats from the digital revolution include the theft of digital identities, invasion of privacy by governments or businesses, discrimination based on personal data, monopoly positions due to control of big data, challenges to deliberative decision-making processes, cyber warfare, hacking of election data and the manipulation of social media.

The digital transformation calls for a comprehensive set of regulatory standards and normative frameworks, physical infrastructure, and digital systems, to capture the benefits of the

digital revolution while avoiding the many potential downsides. An essential priority should be to develop science, technology and innovation roadmaps to better understand the potential benefits and dangers of digitalization

Conclusion

The six Transformations can be designed and directed in several ways. First, they must meet the standards of technical feasibility. Second, the Transformations need to address and resolve trade-offs. Third, they will be financed through a combination of public and private financing. Fourth, they need to accelerate development and deployment of new technologies. Fifth, policy coherence is needed across branches of government (horizontal), between levels of government (vertical) and through time (temporal) to manage trade-offs and ensure timely implementation. Sixth, business can provide co-financing and drive many of the organizational and technological changes required, so each Transformation must engage the business community through a coherent set of policies, market incentives and regulations. Finally, the transformations require civil-society engagement and public debates about sustainable development pathways.

References

1. TWI2050 *Transformations to Achieve the Sustainable Development Goals* (International Institute for Applied Systems Analysis, 2018).
2. *Transforming Our World: The 2030 Agenda for Sustainable Development* (United Nations, 2015)
3. *Review of the Sustainable Development Goals: The Science Perspective* (International Council for Science, International Social Science Council, 2015).
4. UN Millennium Project *Investing in Development: A Practical Plan to Achieve the MDGs* (Earthscan, 2005).
5. Sachs, J. D., Schmidt-Traub, G. & Williams, J. Pathways to zero emissions. *Nat. Geosci.* **9**, 799–801 (2016).
6. *Global Education Monitoring Report 2017/18: Accountability in Education : Meeting Our Commitments* (UNESCO, 2017).
7. *Tackling Inequality* (International Monetary Fund, 2017).
8. *Rules of the Game: A Brief Introduction to International Labour Standards* (International Labor Organization, 2014).

9. *Towards a Global Action Plan for Healthy Lives and Well-Being for All* (WHO, 2018).
10. *Sustainable Development Goal 6: Synthesis Report on Water and Sanitation 2018* (United Nations, 2018)
11. OECD. Policy coherence. In *27th Session on the Public Management Committee* GOV/PUMA(2003)4 (OECD, 2003); https://go.nature.com/2ys8c3E
12. Dharmapala, D. What do we know about base erosion and profit shifting? A review of the empirical literature. Fisc. Stud. 35, 421–448 (2014).
13. Perez, C. Capitalism, technology and a green global age: the role of history inhelping to shape the future. Polit. Q. 86, 191–217 (2015).
14. World Energy Outlook Special Report 2017: Energy Access Outlook (International Energy Agency, 2017).
15. World Energy Outlook Special Report 2016: Energy and Air Pollution (International Energy Agency, 2016).
16. Davis, S. J. et al. Net-zero emissions energy systems. Science 360, eaas9793 (2018).
17. Farmer, J. D. et al. Sensitive intervention points in the post-carbon transition. Science 364, 132–134 (2019).
18. Ramankutty, N. et al. Trends in global agricultural land use: implications for environmental health and food security. Annu. Rev. Plant Biol. 69, 789–815 (2018).
19. Williams, J. H. et al. The technology path to deep greenhouse gas emissions cuts by 2050: the pivotal role of electricity. Science 335, 53–59 (2012).
20. Brondizio, E. S. et al. (eds) Global Assessment Report on Biodiversity and Ecosystem Services of the Intergovernmental Science-Policy Platform on Biodiversity and Ecosystem Services (IPBES, 2019).
21. WHO 2014. WHO guidelines for indoor air quality: household fuel combustion. Geneva: World Health Organization.
22. WHO 2015. World report on ageing and health 2015. Geneva: World Health Organization.
23. World Bank 2016. World Development Report 2016: Digital Dividends. Washington, D.C.: The World Bank.

24. Kallis, G., Kerschner, C. & Martinez-Alier, J. 2012. The economics of degrowth. Ecological Economics, 84, 172-180.
25. Tilman, D., Balzer, C., Hill, J. & Befort, B. L. 2011. Global food demand and the sustainable intensification of agriculture. Proceedings of the National Academy of Sciences, 108, 20260-20264.
26. Arora, V. K. & Montenegro, A. 2011. Small temperature benefits provided by realistic afforestation efforts. Nature Geoscience,4, 5.
27. Arnell N, Kram T, Carter T, Ebi K, Edmonds J, Hallegatte S, Kriegler E, Mathur R, O'Neill B, Riahi K, Winkler H, van Vuuren D, Zwickel T (2011) A framework for a new generation of socioeconomic scenarios for climate change impact, adaptation, vulnerability, and mitigation research. http://www.isp.ucar.edu/socio-economic-pathways. Accessed 1 June 2012
28. Jakob M, Luderer G, Steckel JC, Tavoni M, Monjon S (2011) Time to act now? Assessing the costs of delaying climate measures and benefits of early action. Clim Chang. doi:10.1007/s10584-011-0128-3
29. Agudo-Peregrina, Ángel F., & Navío-Marco, Julio (2016). Extended framework for the analysis of innovative Smart City business models. 27th European Regional Conference of the international telecommunications society (ITS), Cambridge, United Kingdom.
30. Hollands, R. (2008). Will the real smart city please stand up? Intelligent, progressive or entrepreneurial? City, 12(3), 303–320
31. Picon, A. (2018). Urban infrastructure, imagination and politics: From the networked metropolis to the smart city. International Journal of Urban and Regional Research.
32. Walravens, N. (2015). Qualitative indicators for smart city business models: The case of mobile services and applications. Telecommunications Policy, 39(3–4), 218–240.

**Assistant Professor (Economics),
SRKP Government PG College, Kishangarh, Ajmer
madhu.saini4474@gmail.com**

6. Extent of Knowledge and Adoption Behaviour of Organic Farming Practices Among the Vegetables Farmers in Kadavoor Block in Karur District

Manivannan. N and Gokula Krishnan M

Abstract

Agriculture in developing countries must undergo a significant transformation in order to meet the related challenges of achieving food security and responding to climate. Organic farming is a production system which avoids or largely excludes the use synthetically compounded fertilizers, pesticides, growth regulators and livestock feed additives. The study entitled extent of knowledge and adoption behaviour of organic farming practices among the vegetables farmers in kadavoor block in karur district was aimed to study the extent of adoption of organic farming practices. Karurdistrict is predominantly an agricultural district with more than 75 per cent of population directly or indirectly associated with agriculture. They are so many organic farming practices followed for the cultivation, paddy, banana, vegetables, pulses were identified. Most of the farmers ready to adopt the organic farming practices due to well awareness about the eco-friendly farming practices. Majority of the practices were adopted by more than 70.00 per cent of the respondents. The important constraints reported by the respondents were labour scarcity, lack of training on organic farming, inability to attend training programmes, lack of knowledge to identify bio-agents, lack of credit facilities. Organic farming practices are associated with several advantages. It is right time for academicians, administrators, scientists, policy makers to promote organic farming in reality leading a new scenario in agriculture. Based on the findings of the study implication were drawn for promoting organic farming practices and suggestion were made for future research.

Keywords : Adoption, farming practices, vegetable growers, constraints

Introduction

Agriculture in developing countries must undergo a significant transformation in order to meet the related challenges of achieving food security and responding to climate. An organic farm, properly speaking, is not one that uses certain methods and substances and avoids others it is a farm whose structure is formed in limitation of the structure of a natural system that has the integrity the independence and the benign dependence of an organism. "Organic agriculture is a holistic production management system which promotes and enhances agro eco-system health, including bio-diversity, biological cycles and soil biological activity. It emphasizes the use of management practices in preference to the use of off-farm inputs, taking into account that regional conditions require locally adapted systems. This is accomplished by using wherever possible, agronomic, biological, and mechanical methods, as opposed to using synthetic materials, to fulfill a specific function within the system".Globally, 1.5% of the world's agricultural land is found to be organic with Australia, Argentina and China being the leading countries. India ranks 9th position in area with 78 million hectares of land. Also, India contributes to 30% of total organic producers of the world which is 1st position in terms of producers. Madhya Pradesh, Rajasthan and Maharashtra are some of the leading organic producing states in India and Sikkim is now the world's first 100 percent organic state. Tamil Nadu has 10,000 certified organic farmers with a total area of 2,765 ha of land under organic farming.An average Indian consumes much fewer vegetables (252 g) per day than is advised (300 g). Our vegetable consumption will surpass 250 million tonnes by 2020. Due to the restricted amount of accessible land and water resources, the only method to feed the people is to grow vertically or improve productivity per unit area per unit time. Food that is organic is highly sought after both domestically and abroad. Each year, the market for organic products is expanding at a rate that is faster (20–25%) than that of conventional products (5%). The fastest-growing economies are those in Japan, the US, Australia, and the EU. For a nation like India, which has been practicing organic farming since the beginning of time, export preferences for organic vegetables open up a lot of options.

Methodology

The farmer's responses were divided into two categories namely, adopted and non-adopted. A cumulative score of each item for each respondent was computed for arriving at the extent of adoption of organic farming practices. The scoring was done as given below.

S. No.	Response	Score
1	Adopted	2
2	Non-adopted	1

A score of two was given for adoption and non-adoption was given one score. The score for all these items were summed up for each respondent and his adoption score was arrived. Percentage analysis was also worked out to study the practice wise adoption of recommended organic farming practices.

Findings and Discussion

Extent of adoption of respondents on organic farming practices in vegetable cultivation

The findings on the extent of adoption of various organic farming practices in vegetable cultivation are presented in table 1.

Table 1. Distribution of respondents according to their adoption level on organic farming practices in vegetablecultivation (n=60)

S. No.	Organic farming practices in vegetable cultivation	Number of respondents	Per cent
1.	Summer ploughing	32	53.33
2.	In situ incorporation of crop residues	38	63.33
3.	Raising green manure and incorporation	40	66.67
4.	Resistant / tolerant variety	34	56.67
5.	Seed treatment with bio-fertilizers	28	46.67

Aftermath of Climate Change

6.	Application of FYM	38	63.33
7.	Application of	34	56.67
8.	Application of Poultry manure	52	86.67
9.	Application of oil cakes	44	73.33
10.	Timely irrigation	60	100.00
11.	Crop rotation	36	60.00
12.	Intercropping system	42	70.00
13.	Mulching	54	90.00
14.	Hand / mechanical weeding	52	86.67
15.	Collection and destruction of pests (egg, larvae and pupae) and diseased affected plants	06	10.00
16.	Use of light traps	16	26.67
17.	Ash / cowdung slurry spray	26	43.33
18.	Use of botanical pesticides	04	06.67
19.	Conservation of natural enemies	10	16.67

From the above table, regarding the adoption of organic farming 53.33per cent had full adoption towards summer ploughing followed by 63.33per cent who had full adoption towards in situ incorporation of crop residues. The analysis clearly revealed that more than half of the respondents 66.67 per cent and 63.33per cent had full adoption towards raising green manure and incorporation and applicationof FYM respectively. Regarding adoption of resistant/tolerant variety 56.67per cent had full adoption, 46.67per cent had full adoption towards treating seeds with bio-fertilizers. Regarding application of poultry manure and oil cakes 86.67per cent and a majority of the population of 73.33per cent had full adoption respectively. It was interesting to note that almost all the respondents (100%) had full adoption towards timely irrigation. Majority (90.00 per cent) of the farmers adopted the mulching practices. They also acknowledged that mulching was found to be highly beneficial for crop management as well as for crop nourishment and nitrogen fixation. Among the farmers 60.00per cent and 70.00per cent of farmers fully adopted crop rotation and intercropping systems which are one of the major components of organic farming. An overwhelming population i.e., 86.67 per cent had full adoption towards hand/mechanical weeding practices and more than one fourth of the respondents (26.67 per cent) had fully adopted light traps in field. 43.33 per centof the farmers adopted the of Ash / cowdung slurry spray in field. Only a minimum number of respondent's viz., 16.67per cent, 10.00per cent and 06.67per cent had full adoption towards conservation of natural enemies, collection and destruction of pests (egg, larvae and pupae) and diseased affected plants and use of botanical pesticidesrespectively. According to Singh et al., (2019)55.00 per cent had medium level adoption, followed by high (25.00 per cent), and low level adoption (20.00 per cent).

Conclusion

Farmers have gained timely and relevant information regarding the production of organic vegetables as a result of their participation in trainings and visits. Therefore, by creating awareness to conventional farmers regarding organic farming, we can encourage them to switch to organic farming methods. Farmers perceived organic practices as being in line with their current ideals, past knowledge, and current demands. Therefore, switching from inorganic to organic vegetable cultivation was not difficult for them. Creating awareness and introducing various capacity-building programs could also be a driving force in helping the conventional farmers adopts organic farming. Since both farmers and consumers are becoming more aware of the consequences of agrochemicals and the residues they leave in food, organic farming especially the cultivation of organic vegetables, could usher in a new revolution in terms of environmental, dietary, and health considerations. The assumption is that organic farming may produce veggies with greater quality, better nutritional content and no pesticide residues, hence creating a better satisfaction for farmers in terms of production as well as consumers in terms of consumption.

References
Adesope O, Matthews-Njoku E, Oguzor N, Ugwuja V. Effect of Socio-economic characteristics of farmers on their adoption of organic farming practices. In P. Sharma, and V. Abrol (Eds.), Crop Production Technologies; 2012.
Baskaur, RashmiTyagi, VinodKumari. Knowledge and adoption level of organic vegetable farmers in Haryana. The Pharma Innovation Journal. 2021;10(5S): 07-11.
Monikha CR, Jansirani R. Adoption of organic farming practice among certified organic farmers in western zone of Tamil Nadu. J PharmacognPhytochem. 2019; 8(4):658-660.
Singh Bhagwan, Sharma AK.Factors affecting adoption of organic farming technology in Arid Zone.Annals of Arid Zone. 2019;58 (3&4):1-5.
Singh Bhagwan. Association between farmer's characteristics and adoption of moth bean production technology in arid zone.Indian Journal of Extension Education and Rural Development.2015;23:15-18.

*Assistant Professor,
School of Agriculture,
Bharath Institute of Higher Education and Research, Selaiyur, Tambaram, Chennai
** UG Student, Pushkaram College of Agriculture Sciences, Thiruvarankulam,
Pudukkottai-Tamil Nadu
email : manivannan.agri@bharathuniv.ac.in

7. Contribution of Teacher-Education in Environment Preservation

Neeraj Mohan Puri* and Dr. Rashmi Tyagi**

Abstract

This research paper is an attempt to discuss the contribution of teacher education to preserve the environment. Environment is an imperative feature of Planet Earth which distinguishes it and makes it unique from rest of the planets. The word Environment has its roots in the French word environment which means to encircle or surround. Demographics of India shows that youth constitute 28.6 % of the entire Indian Population, which comes out to nearly 1\4 of the population. They are the custodians of the future. Hence, teachers have gargantuan task to sensitize students, educate them and spread awareness in society to keep this planet cleaner greener for the generations yet to come. The purpose of this study is **to define the role of a teacher as environment ambassadors and to identify ways and means to be followed by teachers to conserve environment.** Data for this study is collected through primary source that is observations from daily life and secondary data is taken from the digital or print media. Study will have some managerial implications in the form of processes and techniques to be followed by various schools to conserve environment and underpinning the role of teachers to make our children more responsible and environment conscious students.

Keywords : Environment, Preservation, Teacher's role, Sustainable Development.

Introduction

Environment is an essence of life. We cannot imagine life without environment. The word Environment has its roots in the French word environment which means to encircle or surround. As the civilizations progressed population explosion took place, demand for all the natural and manmade resources started increasing. In order to maintain equilibrium in demand and supply agriculturists, industrialists and real estate tycoons started exploiting the resources to the extent possible. Eventually, this led to degradation of environment resulting to water, air, land pollution, melting of glaciers, deforestation, rising temperature, unabated increase in the level of pesticides and excessive use of fertilizers. At present times, Environment Preservation is a pressing global issue. To prevent further deterioration of the environment is a hurricane task which no Government can do alone. This is a collaborative responsibility and umpteen duty of every native of this planet.

India in particular has one fourth of its population under 15 years, hence schools and teachers at large has a mammoth role to play in this direction. Youth and every citizen has to come forward to join the mission of Sustainable development if we want to contain this unchecked menace. Our callous and damn care attitude will lead to extinction of human race. Insatiable nature of human being has deprived Mother earth from its salubrious beauty. Environment degradation has acquired monstrous proportions. Environmental education, awareness, conservation is only way forward to mitigate the intolerable loss. We all have witnessed that during CORONA lockdown period how nature has replenished and restored itself. Environment education is not only about spreading awareness or transmitting knowledge rather it is a life skill, an attitude towards life and finally developing skills how to be rational in behaviour. Through environment education we must sensitise our young generation that resources must be used judiciously. If environment is preserved this will improve the quality and span of life and this will consequently plunge the rate of diseases.

Environment Awareness

Awareness means to stay updated with the latest trends and be aware of the prospective threats. As per the opinion of (Chaturvedi, Singh and Kumari, 2014), it is essential for the masses to visualize the potential of disaster due degradation of environment and its adverse impact on the aesthetic, social and physical aspect of environment. Awareness can also be interrelated with being informed, sensitive and responsible. As a sensitive and informed citizen everyone will use the resources religiously and understand his commitment towards the nature or environment. Education is the only potent tool to modify the reckless behaviour of the people and make them sensitive towards the environment.

Objectives

1. To define the role of a teacher as environment ambassadors.
2. To identify ways and means to be followed by teachers to conserve environment.

Role of Teacher

In modern era, teacher is considered as a harbinger of change, custodian of environment. This is a new dimension and an additional role entrusted to them. Children emulates their teachers as they are an inspiration for them. Teachers role is to promote the environment awareness cannot be undermined. They not only responsible to preserve the environment but also to enrich it. As per Blooms Taxonomy, teachers have to develop the cognitive, affective and psychomotor domains of the students to spread awareness among them. Cognitive domain covers the entire information about environment hazards. Teachers have to update students with all the possible impacts of environmental degradation, innovative ways to counter this monster. This will connect students to the nature and promote their affective domain and finally they will have an urge to protect the environment, partake in eco movements. Lastly, when the learners will be actively engaged in the recycling, planting, cleanliness, afforestation drives, seminars etc. their psychomotor development will take place.

Teachers can play a prominent role to transform behaviour of the students towards environment. They motivate learners to develop the skills and aptitude required to understand ecological issues and initiate remedial measure. Over the years environmental education is introduced as a compulsory subject in primary wing. Considering the current state of affairs, environmental education has taken a front seat. Every child should understand the significance of nature, animals, flora and fauna in our life. Educators need to engage children in several activities to enrich and conserve nature. It is rightly remarked catch the child early. Hence, young minds must be tapped at the earliest so that they understand their responsibility towards the nature. Teachers have to instil the values and ethics amongst students to protect the environment. Monumental efforts

are needed to protect the environment of planet earth. It will be deadly if we ignore the barbaric acts of human being towards environment, for an instance;
- Deforestation has led to massive reduction in biodiversity, pollution and environmental imbalance.
- Erratic weather and imbalanced rainfall are a result of climatic change
- Melting of glaciers, heat waves, sand storms and more forest fires is an outcome of rise in temperature.

Keeping into mind the alarming conditions of the environment, environmental education has become a modern-day necessity. Therefore, schools are the best place to begin environmental education, teachers have to act as crusaders of change by nurturing the age children to be respectful and sensible towards environment.

This section highlights the role teachers can play as an Ambassador of environment to mould the behavior and attitude of young generation towards the environment. Knowledge can empower any individual to take fruitful actions. The only purpose of environmental education is spread awareness among masses to care, preserve and enrich the environment. Children are like a brand-new computer in which we have to download several programmes. Teachers have to take on this task to teach children the significance of the environment. We need to educate our children how to move ahead for a sustainable life. Aim is ultimately to minimise the impact of human activities on the environment to ensure that planet heals and rejuvenate. Young children can be moulded easily so awareness from tender age is more appropriate. Tiny tots must be taught in a simple manner which is easy to understand preferably in the laps of nature, using visual and creative effects, so teaching methodology really matters a lot.

Below mentioned are few techniques which have been tested and tried with fruitful results. At Modern Sandeepni School's Eco club in Pathankot these strategies helped to create an army of eco-friendly students.

Connect with the Nature

Nature is a best teacher. Respect and love towards the nature can be created by going in the laps of nature. Children must be taken for nature walk, countryside, zoos, nature parks river side, school parks etc. This leaves indelible impact on the mind of pupils. They will be captivated with the cleanliness and beauty of nature.

Cleaning Events of Natural Areas

Practice makes man perfect. Educators should on regular basis undertake some cleaning drives natural areas like beaches, school, classrooms, home, market, public parks, forests etc either on their own or in collaboration with local NGO's. Participating students will realise how important it is to maintain cleanliness. They can easily differentiate between spic & span and filthy environment. This will not only promote values among children but also promote their aesthetic sense.

Introduce Students to Recycling

In our day-to-day life, tons of several type of waste are generated by humans which has a drastic impact on the environment. It is therefore, necessary to introduce 3 R's recycle reduce reuse to students at the earliest. This will help to put a cap on waste.

Waste Management

In order to maintain the temperature, keep our planet cool and green waste management is necessary. School's eco club and fine arts club should integrate and undertake several activities based on best out of the waste. Innovation clubs should be set up in schools where children discuss and brainstorm about better ways to dispose the waste and scheme of waste management.

Segregation of Waste

Every student may be aware about various categories of waste like dry, wet, electronic waste etc. It is vital that right from childhood kids are trained to use separate bins for disposing of waste material. This way it will be easy to proceed for recycling. Every classroom in a school must have separate bins for different kind of waste. To ensure that students follow it by heart, teachers should interact with the students about the merits of recycling and reuse.

Arrange Seminars and Debates

To sensitize students about the environmental issues, time to time quiz, seminars, debates should be held in the school. With regular participation in such events students will come to know about the exact facts and figures. Environmental talk shows can be arranged where renowned speakers share the platform and apprise students about the depleting ozone layer, melting of glaciers, deterioration in the air quality. This will definitely leave an impact over the mind of students and they may become cautious and responsible.

Gift a Sapling

School and teachers should set a culture of gifting saplings on the birthday of students. This trend will ultimately lead to afforestation at large scale.

Plant a Sapling on Birthday

Generally, we spend thousands on our children's birthday, gifts, dine out and celebrations. Teachers must encourage students to plant a sapling at home or nearby park on their Birthday. Then year on year they should nurture and preserve that tree, Record its growth. Every C

Adopt a Tree

Teachers must encourage the children to make trees as their best friend. They live long. It is Customary that every year schools do tree plantation during Earth Day, but what is important is that whether these saplings are taken care of? Are they nurtured? Children must adopt a tree either at school or in their surroundings. Enrich it, irrigate it, ensure that it grows to its optimum.

Tie A Rakhi

Plants play pivotal role in our survival. Needless to mention that there are infinite benefits which plants provide us. At Modern Sandeepni School, we do a unique activity of tying a Rakhi to the saplings or trees as they are our saviors. Knot of love, bond of affection needs to be established with the plants. Such an activity strengthens the bond of child with the nature and they feel associated with plants. They will definitely become more caring.

Attainment Points

At Sandeepni School we have gone a mile forward. We have clubbed plantation and preservation drive with examination system. Any student who plants a tree and nurture it for 6 months during an academic year is given 10 attainment points for academic improvement. These points can be redeemed to upgrade the academic performance of any weakest academic subject. This novel scheme has made children dedicated and devoted towards their ecological duties.

Apart from above teachers being the social change agents can perform following tasks:

(i) Discuss with the children in classrooms about the local environment changes and problems.
(ii) Let children be made competent enough to classify between living and non-living things.
(iii) Creating awareness on renewal and non-renewal resources.
(iv) Providing ample knowledge and skill regarding Gandhian concept of development.
(v) Educational excursions to environment related places.
(vi) Research based projects should be assigned to students based on Environmental issues.

Conclusion

Modern age teachers are entrusted with an additional role to instruct and guide students to have caring and responsible attitude towards the environment. Teachers have to plan several activities through which they can foster love towards the nature among students. Educators should bring youth closer to the nature, provide adequate information about the repercussions of degradation of the environment, all types of pollution, kind of diseases which will breed with the degradation of the environment, possible future threats like extinction of several resources, pure air, potable water etc. Draw their attention towards the global environment crisis and engage students into numerous cultural, co-curricular activities to spread awareness among masses to conserve nature.

Managerial Implications

This study will be beneficial for the teachers as they will get an insight about various best practices they can adopt to inculcate eco friendly habits. The activities suggested in this paper will be a cornerstone to make children more responsive, cautious, nature lover and sensible to the environment. Eventually, this will make students environment conscious and they will watch their actions to ensure sustainable development.

References
Bloom, B.S. (1956). Taxonomy of Educational objective Hand Book: The Cognitive Domain, New York: Long Mans, Green and Co.
Chaturvedi, A., Kumari, R. and Singh, S. (2014). Environmental awareness Through Education.. Shaikshik Parisamvad (An International Journal of Education). Vol. 4 (2), pp 9-13.
Singh, H. (2014). Environmental preservation: A path towards sustainability and economic sustenance.
https://www.earthreminder.com/role-of-teacher-in-environmental-education/

*Principal
Modern Sandeepni School, Pathankot
email : Victoriousleader.1@ gmail.com
**Director
Bharati Vidyapeeth English Medium High School, Mumbai
email : tyagirashmi02@gmail.com

8. Environmental Impacts of Tourism Industry

Girdhari Lal Meeena

Abstract

Tourism, in simple terms, is an activity that involves people visiting places of interest, both local and international, and exploring new different activities and experiences for leisure or business. Countries such as the Maldives, British Virgin Islands, China, and Seychelles including many others across the world, depend highly on the tourism sector as a source of income generation The global tourism sector is the largest industry, contributing up to USD 2.9 Trillion to GDP with France, the USA, Spain, China, and Italy being the world's top destinations. And on a global scale, tourism generates income as one of the fastest growing industries for many countries. But in as much as mass international as well as local inbound tourism has numerous positive impacts on the environment, it also comes with its downsides. As such, investment in sustainable tourism options can put in place policies or a framework that can help protect the environment as well as boosting the tourism industry at a global level. This article particularly sheds light on both the positive and negative impacts of tourism on the environment. The positive impacts of tourism on the environment include

Keywords : Tourism, Impacts, Environment, Industry, Sustainable

Introduction

In the developing countries like India, tourism has been one of the major sectors of the economy, contributing to a large proportion of the National Income and generating number of employment opportunities. Tourism has the capacity to help support communities and instigate positive environmental change when done with the right approach towards the long-term sustainability in regions and complying with the UN's 17 sustainable development goals that range from eradicating hunger from eradicating hunger, gender equality to addressing climate actions based on the specific regional needs.

Aftermath of Climate Change

We can see the rise of the positive trend in the last years. Ecotourism and sustainable tourism have gained popularity in the industry but there are still many areas where improvements need to be done. If the Number of tourists in a given area is greater than the capacity of the local environment of supporting infrastructure (which is the case of many popular destinations), negative impact quickly arise and can become overwhelming for the system.

As we embark on new adventures in foreign countries it's important to realize what environmental impacts our presence poses to local ecosystems and resources. According to the United Nations Environments programme, The three negative environmental impacts of tourism are the depletion of natural resources. Pollution and physical degradation of ecosystem. This environment may be man-made (ancient monuments, cultural buildings, resorts, etc.) or it could be natural (areas of natural beauty, climate, wildlife etc.) but as we said in the previous step, the negative effects of tourists on the very environment that drew them often outweigh the positive, so we will focus on these first.

There are two main ways that tourism negatively impacts on the environment :
- Through the development of the area
- Through the behaviour of tourists

The development of an area results in the construction of facilities, not only attractions and hotels but also buildings, roads, parking lots, facilities etc. These are often situated near tourism activities, which depend on destinations' natural resources, which can result in damage to the surrounding area.

Such infrastructure developments might impact biodiversity and ecological habitats, damage original visual resources, and weaken the destination's regional resilience to natural disasters in extreme weather conditions, which in turn may result in negative phenomena, such as soil erosion and landslides. The negative impacts also include the overuse of water resources and deforestation.

The behaviour of tourists, and their use of facilities, can result in environmental pollution through an increased number of people. As well as air pollution from an increase in the use of fossil fuels, pollution of the land and sea swells in tourist areas and in tourist seasons.

Tourism's Three Main Impact Areas

Negative impacts from tourism occur when the level of visitor use is greater than the environment's ability to cope with this use within the acceptable limits of change. Uncontrolled conventional tourism poses potential threats to many natural areas around the world. It can put enormous pressure on an area and lead to impacts such as soil erosion, increased pollution, discharges into the sea, natural habitat loss, increased pressure on endangered species and heightened vulnerability to forest fires. It often puts a strain on water resources, and it can force local populations to compete for the use of critical resources

Depletion of Natural Resources

Tourism development can put pressure on natural resources when it increases consumption in areas where resources are already scarce.

Water Resources

Water, and especially fresh water, is one of the most critical natural resources. The tourism industry generally overuses water resources for hotels, swimming pools, golf courses and personal use of water by tourists. This can result in water shortages and degradation of water supplies, as well as generating a greater volume of waste water..In dryer regions like the Mediterranean, the issue of water scarcity is of particular concern. Because of the hot climate and the tendency of tourists to consume more water when on holiday than they do at home, the amount used can run up to 440 litters a day. This is almost double what the inhabitants of an average use.

Water pollution due to recreational boating activities has equally been reported. According to estimates by Ocean Conservancy, for instance, records an estimate of 70,000 tons of wastewater produced per year from cruise ships in the Caribbean, which affects the natural habitat of marine life. Golf course maintenance can also deplete fresh water resources. In recent years golf tourism has increased in popularity and the number of golf courses has grown rapidly. Golf courses require an enormous amount of water every day and, as with other causes of excessive extraction of water, this can result in water scarcity. If the water comes from wells, over pumping can cause saline intrusion into groundwater. Golf resorts are more and more often situated in or near protected areas or areas where resources are limited, exacerbating their impacts.

Natural Resources Depletion

When the number of tourists visiting an area over time surpasses the level to which the area can sustain, it subsequently leads to an overuse of the available local resources causing a **strain on the environment**. Food, fresh water, and power usage in hotels and resorts increase to a high capacity when tourist numbers increase, which also affects the access of local dwellers to such services or resources. In most cases, tourism puts a strain on the already scarce local **natural resources** owing to over-consumption.

Improper development of infrastructures such as extensive paving and sand and beach mining, unplanned construction of resorts, hotels, roads, airports, power plants, reservoirs, and waste disposal systems brought about as a result of tourist visits has led to congestion within areas that are fragile and sensitive like **natural habitats** for wildlife, wetlands, coral reefs, lakes, forests, minerals, oceans, fertile soils, and riverbed basins.

Encroachment into the natural habitat of plant and animal species to build hotels, roads, and beaches poses a great risk to the **endangered species** and often push wildlife to migrate in search of less congested areas or deeper into the forest that may have unfavourable breeding, preying, camouflaging, and feeding environments.

And on instances where marine tourists taking part in recreational fishing are not properly controlled, the outcome is the endangerment to some of the aquatic species – causing an imbalance in aquatic ecological functions.

Land degradation

Important land resources include minerals, fossil fuels, fertile soil, forests, wetland and wildlife. Increased construction of tourism and recreational facilities has increased the pressure on these resources and on scenic landscapes. Direct impact on natural resources, both renewable and non-renewable, in the provision of tourist facilities can be caused by the use of land for accommodation and other infrastructure provision, and the use of building materials.

Besides pushing wildlife far interior into the wild, development projects most of the time affect the scenery and aesthetic nature of natural habitats, thereby destroying the quality that makes it a tourist attraction site in the first place.

Forests often suffer negative impacts of tourism in the form of deforestation caused by fuel wood collection and land clearing. For example, one trekking tourist in Nepal - and area already suffering the effects of deforestation - can use four to five kilograms of wood a day.

Pollution

Tourism can cause the same forms of pollution as any other industry: air emissions, noise, solid waste and littering, releases of sewage, oil and chemicals, even architectural/visual pollution.

Air Pollution and Noise

Transport by air, road, and rail is continuously increasing in response to the rising number reported that the number of international air passengers worldwide rose from 88 million Improper development of infrastructures such as extensive paving and sand and beach mining, unplanned construction of resorts, hotels, roads, airports, power plants, reservoirs, and waste disposal systems brought about as a result of tourist visits has led to congestion within areas that are fragile and sensitive like **natural habitats** for wildlife, wetlands, coral reefs, lakes, forests, minerals, oceans, fertile soils, and riverbed basins.

Encroachment into the natural habitat of plant and animal species to build hotels, roads, and beaches poses a great risk to the **endangered species** and often push wildlife to migrate in search of less congested areas or deeper into the forest that may have unfavourable breeding, preying, camouflaging, and feeding environments.

Transport emissions and emissions from energy production and use are linked to acid rain, global warming and photochemical pollution. Air pollution from tourist transportation has impacts on the global level, especially from carbon dioxide (CO_2) emissions related to transportation energy use. And it can contribute to severe local air pollution. Some of these impacts are quite specific to tourist activities. For example, especially in very hot or cold countries, tour buses often leave their motors running for hours while the tourists go out for an excursion because they want to return to a comfortably air-conditioned bus.

Noise pollution from airplanes, cars, and buses, as well as recreational vehicles such as snowmobiles and jet skis, is an ever-growing problem of modern life. In addition to causing annoyance, stress, and even hearing loss for it humans, it causes distress to wildlife, especially in sensitive areas. For instance, noise generated by snowmobiles can cause animals to alter their natural activity patterns.

Solid Waste and Littering

In areas with high concentrations of tourist activities and appealing natural attractions, waste disposal is a serious problem and improper disposal can be a major despoiler of the natural environment - rivers, scenic areas, and roadsides. For example, cruise ships in the Caribbean are estimated to produce more than 70,000 tons of waste each year. Today some cruise lines are actively working to reduce waste-related impacts. Solid waste and littering can degrade the physical appearance of the water and shoreline and cause the death of marine animals.

Tourisms as a whole and some of the actions by tourists have over time adversely affected the destination areas through various kinds of environmental pollution including air, land, water, and soil. Some tourists, for example, will litter and leave behind garbage or waste like plastic wrappers and cigarette butts in the surrounding environment thereby causing land pollution, plastic pollution, and cigarette pollution respectively.

In mountain areas, trekking tourists generate a great deal of waste. Tourists on expedition leave behind their garbage, oxygen cylinders and even camping equipment. Such practices degrade the environment with all the detritus typical of the developed world, in remote areas that have few garbage collection or disposal facilities. Some trails in the Peruvian Andes and in Nepal frequently visited by tourists have been nicknamed "Coca-Cola trail" and "Toilet paper trail".

Sewage

Construction of hotels, recreation and other facilities often leads to increased sewage pollution. Wastewater has polluted seas and lakes surrounding tourist attractions, damaging the flora and fauna. Sewage runoff causes serious damage to coral reefs because it stimulates the growth of algae, which cover the filter-feeding corals, hindering their ability to survive. Changes in salinity and siltation can have wide-ranging impacts on coastal environments. And sewage pollution can threaten the health of humans and animals.

Aesthetic Pollution

Often tourism fails to integrate its structures with the natural features and indigenous architectural of the destination. Large, dominating resorts of disparate design can look out of place in any natural environment and may clash with the indigenous structural design.

A lack of land-use planning and building regulations in many destinations has facilitated sprawling developments along coastlines, valleys and scenic routes. The sprawl includes tourism facilities themselves and supporting infrastructure such as roads, employee housing, parking, service areas, and waste disposal.

Physical Impacts

Attractive landscape sites, such as sandy beaches, lakes, riversides, and mountain tops and slopes, are often transitional zones, characterized by species-rich ecosystems. Typical physical impacts include the degradation of such ecosystems.

An ecosystem is a geographic area including all the living organisms (people, plants, animals, and microorganisms), their physical surroundings (such as soil, water, and air), and the natural cycles that sustain them. The ecosystems most threatened with degradation are ecologically fragile areas such as alpine regions, rain forests, wetlands, mangroves, coral reefs and sea grass beds. The threats to and pressures on these ecosystems are often severe because such places are very attractive to both tourists and developers.

Physical impacts are caused not only by tourism-related land clearing and construction, but by continuing tourist activities and long-term changes in local economies and ecologies.

Physical Impacts of Tourism Development

The development of tourism facilities such as accommodation, water supplies, restaurants and recreation facilities can involve sand mining, beach and sand dune erosion, soil erosion and extensive paving. In addition, road and airport construction can lead to land degradation and loss of wildlife habitats and deterioration of scenery.

In Yosemite National Park (US), for instance, the number of roads and facilities have been increased to keep pace with the growing visitor numbers and to supply amenities, infrastructure and parking lots for all these tourists. These actions have caused habitat loss in the park and are accompanied by various forms of pollution including air pollution from automobile emissions; the Sierra Club has reported "smog so thick that Yosemite Valley could not be seen from airplanes". This occasional smog is harmful to all species and vegetation inside the Park. (Source: Trade and Environment Database)

- **Deforestation and intensified or unsustainable use of land**
Construction of ski resort accommodation and facilities frequently requires clearing forested land. Coastal wetlands are often drained and filled due to lack of more suitable sites for construction of tourism facilities and infrastructure. These activities can cause severe disturbance and erosion of the local ecosystem, even destruction in the long term.

Physical impacts from tourist activities

- **Trampling** Tourists using the same trail over and over again trample the vegetation and soil, eventually causing damage that can lead to loss of biodiversity and other impacts. Such damage can be even more extensive when visitors frequently stray off established trails.
- **Anchoring and other marine activities** In marine areas (around coastal waters, reefs, beach and shoreline, offshore waters, uplands and lagoons) many tourist activities occur in or around fragile ecosystems. Anchoring, snorkelling, sport fishing and scuba diving, yachting, and cruising are some of the activities that can cause direct degradation of marine ecosystems such as coral reefs, and subsequent impacts on coastal protection and fisheries.

- **Alteration of ecosystems by tourist activities** Habitat can be degraded by tourism leisure activities. For example, wildlife viewing can bring about stress for the animals and alter their natural behaviour when tourists come too close. Safaris and wildlife watching activities have a degrading effect on habitat as they often are accompanied by the noise and commotion created by tourists as they chase wild animals in their trucks and aircraft. This puts high pressure on animal habits and behaviours and tends to bring about behavioural changes. In some cases, as in Kenya, it has led to animals becoming so disturbed that at times they neglect their young or fail to mate.

Conclusion

To sum up, environmental sustainability is an issue of utmost concern even when promoting tourism. From the discussions herein, it is correct to conclude that in regards to the environment, tourism has both advantages and probable threats that ought to be examined.

This calls for the need of practicing healthier and sustainable tourism practices, especially ecotourism. It desperately requires everyone's involvement and initiative to always conserve and protect the environment when travelling or in a foreign land as it has been proven that it is possible to ensure a mutually beneficial co-existence between tourism and the surrounding ecosystems as well as natural resources.

Efficient management and proper planning with the aid of strict legislation and proper interpretation are also key to creating ecological awareness for both the local and visiting tourists.

References :

- Sharma K (2014) Introduction to Tourism Management, McGraw Hill Education (India) Private Limited, India.
- Farrell B, Twining-Ward L (2005) Seven steps towards sustainability: Tourism in the context of new knowledge. Journal of Sustainable Tourism 13: 109-122.
- Mir S (2016) Role of tourism in development of Jammu and Kashmir: possibilities for new set up. 3: 108.

- Hardy AL, Beeton RJS (2001) Sustainable tourism as maintainable tourism: Managing resources for more than average outcomes. Journal of Sustainable Tourism 9: 168-192.
- Hunter C (1995) On the need to re-conceptualise sustainable tourism development. Journal of Sustainable Tourism 3: 155-165.
- Kuhn TS (1970) The structure of scientific revolutions. (2ndedn), University of Chicago Press, Chicago, USA.
- "The Impacts of Tourism "This content is taken from Coventry University online course, An assessment of environmental impacts of tourism in the Lower Mekong Basin. (2010).Mekong River Commission. Retrieved May 19, 2017 from http://www.mrcmekong.org/assets/Publications/technical/Tech-No28-An-essessment-of-Env.pdf
- Dayananda, K.C. (2016). Tourism and It's Impact on Indian Economy. *IOSR Journal Of Humanities And Social Science, 21(6),* 24-28. Retrieved May 19, 2017 from http://www.iosrjournals.org/iosr-jhss/papers/Vol.%2021% 20Issue6/Version-4/E02106042428.pdf
- Rath, N., Singh, N., & Lopes, S.A. (n.d.). Impact of Tourism on Indian Economy. *Tactful Management Research Journal,* 76-79. Retrieved May 20, 2017 from http://tmgt.lsrj.in/SeminarPdf /307 .pdf
- Sunlu, U. (2003). Environmental Impacts of Tourism. *CIHEAM Options* Mediterranean's, 263-270. Retrieved May 20, 2017 from http://om.ciheam.org/om/pdf/a57/04001977.pdf
- Tourism and the Environment. Faulted Ireland's Environmental Action Plan 2007-2009. (2007). Retrieved May 20, 2017 from http://www.noticenature.ie/files/Tourism-and-the-Environment .pdf
- Venkatesh, M., & Raj, P.S. J. M. (2016). Impact of Tourism in India. *InternationalJournal of Scientific Engineering and Applied Science, 2(1),* 167-184. Retrieved May 19, 2017 from http://ijseas.com/volume2/v2i1/ijseas20160119.pdf
- Raina A. K., Dr. S. K. Agarwal (2004), "The Essence of Tourism Development: Dynamics, Philosophy, and Strategies", Sarup & Sons Publications, New Delhi,

- Satish Babu (2008), "Tourism Development in India: A Case Study", A.P.H. Publishing Corporation, New Delhi.
- Akhtar, Javed (1991), "Tourism management in India" Ashish New Delhi, (p.p 44-47)
- जीएस 3 ||अर्थव्यवस्था || उद्योग || प्रमुख उद्योग
- www.ecotourism.org/what-is ecotourism
- www.tourismconcern.org.u/content /2014
- www.researchgate.net/publication
- www.statista.com/statistics/732406/overningt-tourist-arrivals

Assistant Professor,
Department Of Business Administration,
Seth RL Saharia Government P.G. College,
Kaladera, Jaipur (RAJ.)

9. Environmental Concern : A Facilitator for Practicing Sustainable Production Techniques in Textile and Garment Industries

Dr.Ritu Gupta* and Dr.Rachana Asopa**

The story of man's interaction with natural environment dates back to the dawn of man's emergence as the dominant species on our planet Earth, which very well implies that our existence, survival and growth are dependent on the quality of environment. Nowadays we are facing unprecedented challenges of globalization and industrialization namely climate change, diminishing resources and biodiversity, increasing waste, contamination of water, energy and deterioration of resources. The environmental issues are reaching crisis point and are rightly, major topical issue. All of these issues have been compounded by population growth, magnifying human impact on the planet, and all will have disastrous consequences if they continue to be unchecked. Textile and Garment industry is a major contributor to environmental damage, where textile and fashion designers can be well placed to mitigate the issues through designing and persuing Sustainable textiles and garments. The sustainable Garment Production design concepts and techniques such as use of materials which are recycled, renewable and can be reused in Production Industries and can help address various environmental issues which plays a marginal but critical role towards averting major ecological crisis. The major purpose of the study was to know whether environmental factor was considered to be a facilitator for practicing sustainable product designs. The findings of the study revealed that environmental concern was found to be a crucial facilitator for Textile and Garment Industries. This in turn promotes the use of renewable products. renewable energy and recycled material which helps in preserving earth's resources for future generation. The findings would help the community to become more environmentally sensitive which would sparkle the context and need for sustainable textiles and garments leading towards better health and well-being of the global ecosystem.

Aftermath of Climate Change

Keywords : Sustainability, Textiles, Garment Production, Designer, Facilitator, Environmental Concern

Introduction

Recent public awareness of the escalating problems due to diminishing natural resources are helping focus attention on the need to adopt sustainable and healthy lifestyles. Even Wal-Mart, the Sultan of PR hype and hyperbole, has undertaken a major campaign to introduce organic foods and organic clothing along with sustainable business practices. Sustainable clothing and green eco fashion have entered mainstream consumer consciousness with a barrage of recent media attention. But what really is sustainable clothing and is it different from organic clothing?

While concepts of "sustainable clothing" and "organic clothing" share many similarities, they have different roots and history. Where organic clothing grew and evolved out of the organic agriculture movement, sustainable clothing is a product of the environmental movement. They are both working towards the same ends but one has the feel of the farm and the other has the feel of the lab. One of the most apparent differences between the organic approach and the sustainable approach is the emphasis that the sustainable approach places on reuse and recycling of manufactured products.

Frei Designs-Eco Friendly Fashion Designs

Although sustainable resources have been a trend for some time now, fashion is having its green push right now, and Frei Designs is on the forefront of eco-friendly fashion. Frei Design's seamlessly combines skilled artistry with a social conscious creating a product that is both fashionably forward and eco-friendly. Frei Designs is a wholesale apparel business specializing in high-end women's garments with an emphasis on sustainable fabrications and practices. More than just fashion or style, Frei Designs seamlessly blends impeccable design with personal responsibility, creating beautiful clothing with a high attention to fit and detail, all with an emphasis on leaving a smaller footprint on the Earth. Three factors are essential in the production of Frei's garments: style, quality, and sustainability. Frei Designs' garments are produced locally with a tight quality control process that ensures a well-made product from start to finish. Fabrics are purchased from farms and mills associated with ecologically sensitive practices, and dyes used are non-toxic. Also, production facilities used by Frei Designs must pay the employees fair and living wages. On the style end, Frei Designs are created through sophisticated and tailored pattern making, unique hand-dying methods, and one-of-a-kind fabric selections, ensuring that the final products are just as unique as the individuals wearing the garments. Boasting an exceptional sense of wear-ability, excellent craftsmanship, and an artisan attention to detail, the garments cater to an underserved market for sustainable clothing that retains a signature sense of style.

Conventional Garment Production Techniques :
- Designing and Sampling of the garment.
- Receiving and finalization of the ORDER between buyer and manufacturer.
- Procuring of raw materials.
- Pattern making and the grading.
- Cutting of fabric
- Garment assembly
- Sewing Operations
- Embroidery
- Fixing of pockets, collars, cuffs, lining, inter lining & other accessories
- Sewing of the garment Finishing of the garment-labeling
- Quality control
- Packaging & forwarding
- Transportation of the finished goods

Sustainable Production Techniques:Emerging Standards

Improving a corporation's sustainability footprint and reducing environmental impact is about more than just recycling materials. It requires a more holistic corporate approach that includes reusing environmentally-friendly packaging, reducing manufacturing and operational waste and pollution, improving building energy efficiency and reducing energy consumption, moving towards the use of renewable energy, improving shipping and transportation efficiencies, and designing sustainability into the products and services that are sold to the public. **Never Too Late To Follow the Right Path.**

The MTS Unified Sustainable Textile Standard examines garment sustainability in five areas of sustainability :

1. Safe for Public Health & Environment,
2. Renewable Energy & Energy Efficiency,
3. Material, Biobased or Recycled,
4. Facility or Company Based,
5. Reclamation, Sustainable Reuse & End of Life Management. To achieve For each of these five areas of sustainability, the sustainable impact of the garment is monitored across 12 categories :

1. Intake, Solid and Hazardous Waste
2. Global Warming.
3. Acidification
4. Ozone Depletion,
5. Eutrophication,
6. Photochemical Smog
7. Human Health,
8. Ecological Toxicity,
9. Fossil Habitat Alteration,
10. Habitat Alteration,
11. Criteria Air Pollutants
12. Fuel Depletion,

The level of sustainability that a textile product achieves is determined by an elaborate point system that allocates points based upon degree of achievement for the different categories within the different areas of sustainability. Textile manufacturers and suppliers conduct their own testing and supply MTS with the testing and certification results.

McDonough Braungart Design Chemistry (MBDC) and Green Blue are two other organizations on a mission to introduce sustainable design, manufacturing and business practices MBDC is a process and design consulting company dedicated to helping manufacturing companies incorporate environmental awareness and sustainability into all aspects of their product designs and manufacturing processes, Green Blue, originally a part of MBDC and then spun-off as a separate non-profit organization, has developed a comprehensive Sustainable Textile Standard based upon the "cradle-to-cradle" approach developed at MBDC. According to Green Blue, conventional industrial design has been based upon the "cradle-to-grave" approach. A company harvests raw materials, combines them in the manufacturing process giving birth to a new product, sends it out into the world where it does its job, and the product eventually becomes old and used up and is then thrown into the rubbish heap where it is buried in one of the ten's of thousands of landfills infecting the land near all cities and towns.

Sustainable Technology Education Project (STEP)

Many companies, organizations and educational programs have evolved to promote and give shape to sustainable textiles and clothing. One of these is the Sustainable Technology Education Project (STEP), a nonprofit organization that "aims to increase people's awareness of sustainable technology, enabling them to recognize the economic, environmental and social impacts of their own technology choices. "STEP defines eco-fashion as sustainable clothing that is grown and produced without harming the environment and that supports Fair Trade and the rights and working conditions of all peoples involved in the growing, production and manufacturing of clothing at all lifecycle stages. According to the Sustainable Technology Education Project guidelines, eco-fashion and sustainable clothing are generally made from organically grown natural fibers such as cotton, wool

and hemp, but they can also be made from recycled petroleum-based materials such as plastic soda bottles and other re-used synthetic fibers. For many, recyclability equals sustainability.

Global Organic Teextile Standards (GOTS) is a tool for an international understanding of environmental friendly production systems and social accountability in the textile sector. It covers the production, processing, manufacturing, packaging, labeling, Export , Import and distribution of all natural fibers. That means, for example: use of certified organic fibers, prohibition of all GMOs and their derivatives and prohibition of a long list of synthetic chemicals. During production Formaldehyde and aromatic solvents are prohibited ,dyestuffs must meet strict requirements (ie: threshold limits for heavy metals, no AZO colorants or aromatic amines) and PVC cannot be used for packaging. A fabric that is produced to the GOTS standards is more than just the fabric. It's a promise to keep our air and water pure and our soils renewed; it's a fabric, which will not cause harm to you or your descendants. An organic fiber fabric processed to GOTS standards is the most responsible choice possible in terms of stewardship of the earth, preserving health, limiting toxicity in the load to humans and animals.

Norm Thompson

The casual clothing company with the tag line "Escape from the Ordinary", has developed a Sustainability Toolkit and Scorecard designed to evaluate and rank a wide variety of products mostly related to garment and textiles and their production and manufacturing environmental impacts. The Norm Thompson Sustainability Toolkit helps producers, manufacturers and consumers understand how different growing, production, manufacturing, shipping and transportation decisions affect a product's sustainability ranking and environmental impact. Curiously enough, they do not directly define sustainability but rely upon the reader to infer their definition from their evaluation criteria and content. After searching through the hundreds of garments on the Norm Thompson,only 10 garments that could be considered sustainable or organic clothing and 6 of those were varying styles of organic cotton bras. For a clothing company concerned about sustainability, synthetic fibers outnumber natural fiber garments and most of the natural fiber clothing is made from conventional, pesticide grown and chemically finished manufactured cotton. Many schools, universities and institutes have created courses and curriculums for sustainability as part of their design and environmental studies programs.

Measures to be Taken by the Garmrnt Manufacturers to make Production Techniques more Sustainable :

Environmentally friendly practices are not generally synonymous with the latest fashion. Many schools, universities and institutes have created courses and curriculums for sustainability as part of their design and environmental studies programs The consortium represents every aspect of the production process, from design to yarn-spinning, textiles to garment production. Garment manufacturing has a "definite impact" on the environment at every level of production, from the amount of energy it uses to the mounds of scrap fabric that end up going to waste. One garment house alone, he noted, uses more than 91 million metres of fabric. About 18 million metres-enough to cover 6,000 football pitches-end up as waste.

One of the first initiatives is to recycle scrap fabric by turning it into 30 per cent recycled denim. Another is converting factories into more energy-efficient plants. It is feasible to cut energy use by 20 per cent with current technology available. That means a medium-sized factory, which on average uses 35 million kilowatt hours of energy annually, can save seven million kilowatt hours per year, that's enough to power 1,750 households, SFBC is also devising a carbon accounting standard in concert with WWF Hong Kong This would allow manufacturers to add labels to clothing, informing consumers about the carbon footprint that went into producing the garment. To share information and devise new ways to make the trade more environmentally friendly. Manufacturers should be committed to make all aspects of production process socially and environmentally sustainable over time.

The Use of Water in A Dry World

In consideration of environmental and social impact, the use of water in growing and processing cotton is of major concern. Conventional cotton requires on average 3000 cubic litres more water per acre than organic cotton to grow due to the repeated application of pesticides, herbicides and chemical fertilizers. Careful use of water through the utilization of efficient irrigation schemes and, where possible, rain fed crops helps to make organic cotton a sustainable agriculture. Sustainable textile production relies on minimizing social and environmental exposure to harmful chemicals so that only a very limited and highly regulated number of chemicals (such as caustic soda) are used. Thus water usage is minimized with correct procedures for recycling/cleaning waste water. Farm and factory workers are not exposed to hazardous chemicals, and local communities do not end up with a sick environment and ill population. **"Sustainable clothing products means fair trade for a fair world."**

*Associate Professor,
Garment Production and Export Management,
Government G.D College for Women, Alwar.
email : ritug1972.rg@gmail.com
**Associate Professor,
Department of Chemistry,
Government G.D College for Women, Alwar.
email : rasopa67@gmail.com

10. Environment Protection : A New Dimension in Sustainable Tourism Development in India

Dr. Beena Sharma

Abstract

Sustainable tourism is a positive approach intended to reduce the tension and friction created by the complex interactions between the tourism industry, visitors, the environment and the communities which are host of holiday makers. It is an approach, which involves working for the long term viability and quality of both natural and human resources. The definition of sustainable development in elusive. It is a concept whose definition will undoubtedly continue to evolve over the period of time.

The sustainable tourism is define as the management of tourism resources in such a way that fulfills economic, social and aesthetic needs while maintaining integrity, essential ecological processes, biological diversity and life support system.

Keywords : Sustainable, Environment, Human Resources, Tourism

Introduction

Sustainable tourism is "envisaged a leading to management of all resources in such as a way that economic, social and aesthetic needs can be fulfilled maintaining cultural integrity, essential ecological process, biological diversity and life support system". A clear distinction should be made between the concepts of ecotourism and sustainable tourism, the term ecotourism itself refers to a segment within the tourism sector, while the sustainability principles should apply to all types of tourism activities, operations, establishments and projects, including conventional and alternative forms.

Objects :

To develop a sustainable tourism programme with sustainable principles at the core of the decision making process. The programme should also points the way to the future by identifying what actions are needed to achieve sustainable development. To study how to minimize negative impact upon the natural and social cultural environment. To find out about the challenges of sustainable tourism development.

Methodology

The methodology used in this research paper is secondary data analysis. This paper covers the concept of sustainable tourism development, its role and challenges in India. Only secondary data from some authentic government sources and research papers of eminent researcher, books are used.

Importance Of Sustainable Tourism Development

Sustainable tourism development is included the ecological social, cultural, economical developments. Ecological sustainability ensures that development is compatible with the maintenance of essential ecological processes, biological diversity and biological resources, social and cultural sustainability ensures that development increases people's control over their lives is compatible with the culture and value of people affected by it, and maintains and strengthens community identity. Economical sustainability ensures that development is economically efficient and that resources are managed so that they can support future generation.

Sustainable tourism make fine balance between the requirements of tourism and ecology. On one hand and the need of local communities for jobs, new skills, income generating employment and a better status for women on the other hand.

The global importance of eco-tourism and its impact was recognized with the launching ofthe year 2002 as the international year of Eco – tourism (IYE) by the United Nations general Assembly. In India, eco – tourism as a concept has gained momentum recently in India, but as a way of life Indians have practiced eco – tourism since times immemorial by their traditional approach to native and rich cultural heritage. It has a vast potential for eco – tourism that needs to be tapped for economic benefits as well as for healthy conservation and preservation of nature.

In India, tourism is second largest net earning of foreign exchange. The main strength of Indian tourism at present is its cultural attractions, particularly movement and archeological remains, fairs and festivals, wild life and beaches. The aim of the tourism policy now is to diversify and tourism product in such a way that the development of ecotourism and nature based tourism is promoted to attract environmentally conscious tourists.

Challenge Of Sustainable Tourism Development

In India tourism industry is facing various challenges due to lack of strategic business plans, lack of well – trained local native, guides, lack of suitable marketing techniques, lack of methods for gaining community consensus on development project and lack of infrastructure etc.

It is becoming evident that increased tourism to sensitive natural areas, in the absence of appropriate knowledge, information, planning and management can become a threat to the integrity of both ecosystems and local cultures.

Tourism promotions is bound to have a series of socio-cultural, socio-economic, physical and environmental impacts on the habits which would require a systematic evaluation and analysis, using scientific techniques before development decisions are taken. Therefore, a scientific approach to tourism planning would require analytical studies related to

1. Likely impact of development on the local environmental and the hill habitat.
2. Evaluating the tourist resources and infrastructure needs.
3. Establishing certain development thresholds consistent with carrying capacity of thearea and similar aspects.

Conclusion

Since environment has always been an important aspect of life. The quality of environment is taken as the barometer of success of the society today. The government from time to time has been framing various legislation and the society has been responding accordingly. Tourism by its very nature is a very complex multidisciplinary service industry that requires strong partnership and well coordinated efforts and programmes between various institutions. This issue acquires importance as ultimately when the government cannot assume management responsibility of tourism destinations. Therefore, it becomes essential first to identify major stakeholders, their interest, power and influence in order to clearly define their roles in supporting the goal of sustainable tourism development. Clearly a central tourism agency at the highest level of the government must be formed to be the catalyst for continuous planning, implementation and monitoring of sustainable tourism development.

References
1. Gulab Nabi, "Socio – Economic impact of tourism", 2000.
2. Bhatia A.K., "Tourism Development, Principles and Practices", 2005.
3. Ranga Mukesh, Nigam Devesh, "Tourism management", 2003.
4. Sustainable Tourism Development, https : //en.wikipedia.org.
5. Sharma K.K., "Tourism in India", 2002.
6. Singh Ratandee, "Tourism in India", 2006.
7. Dr. Aswal Pawan, "Tourism Development", 2005.
8. Kumar Mannel, "Tourism Today", 2004.
9. Raheja Banwari Lal, "Tourism Development Strategies", 2006.

**Assistant Professor,
ABST Govt. College Sambhar Lake,
Rajasthan
email : sharmabeena25092014@gmail.com**

11. Economic Growth and Sustainable Development

Dr. Meghna Meena

Abstract

Economic growth and environmental sustainability are important issues for a country'sprosperity. Sustainable development strives for moderate and responsible use of the limitedavailableresources within the economic activity. The change in climate is not due to economic growth,but it is mainly due to the absence of effective policies designed to reduce greenhouse gasemissions. However, the Current trends of population and economic growth in many sucheconomies have increased pressures on their natural resources and environment. In thecontext the importance of green growth comes in place. Green growth means fosteringeconomic growth and development, while ensuring that natural assets continue to provide theresources and environmental services on which our well-being relies. This paper deals with thedetails of how the focus shifted to economic growth and how to maintain balance between economic growth and environmental sustainability.

Keywords : Economic Growth, Sustainable development, Economy, green growth.

Introduction :

From times immemorial the focus of the state has been on increasing economic productivity. To achieve the same, the Man initially focused on inventing new technologies and innovation like invention of wheel, manufacturing steam engines and eventually development of production line at shop floor level. All this innovation and invention brought about industrial revolution in eighteenth and nineteenth century. The per capita income of the countries increased and thereby increasing gross domestic product (GDP) of the countries. But in this phase of economic development the major emphasis has always remained on economic growth with least focus on sustainable development.

What is Sustainable Development?

Sustainable Development means the development which meets the requirements of the present without compromising the ability of future generations to meet their own needs. This most commonly accepted definition of Sustainable Development was given by the Brundtland Commission in the report Our Common Future (1987). Sustainable development demands for concerted efforts towards building an inclusive, sustainable and resilient future for the people and planet.

Three essential elements of sustainable development are social inclusion, economic growth, and environmental protection. It is very important to harmonize them. Sustainable economic growth, living in harmony with nature, achieving sustainable livelihood and appropriate technology are important for sustainable development.

Why There is Need of Sustainable Development?

As discussed in above the focus in earlier times has been on economic growth, where little emphasis has been on sustainable development, this has led to many economic, social, environmental and political issues.

In terms of economic issues as per Oxfam International report, the top 10% of the Indian population holds **77%** of the total national wealth. 73% of the wealth generated in 2017 went to the richest 1%. Thereby increasing economic inequality this has led to the unequal distribution of income and opportunity between different groups in society.

Similarly, Social issues like Rural-Urban Divide Migration from Rural to Urban areas and Reverse migration these days from Urban to rural areas, increasing slums in urban areas due to migration in search of job, increasing growth of nuclear family which is away from joint family system thereby leading to higher divorce rate, increasing urban population and development of new satellite towns, increasing accidents on road as per road safety report around 151,113 persons were killed and 451,361 injured in road. Also due to Globalisation the intake of junk food has increased thereby leading to increase in lifestyle diseases as per a report, more than 7 million people die of cancer each year and 30% of those diseases are attributed to lifestyle choices. Thus economic Development had a drastic impact on social parameters of life.

Moreover, the major impact of economic Growth has remained on ecology and environment. The environmental impact of economic growth comprisesof the increased consumption of non-renewable resources, higher levels of pollution, global warming and the potential loss of environmental habitats. ThisInverted-U relationship between environmental degradation and economic growth came to be known as the "Environmental Kuznets Curve," by analogy with the income-inequality relationship postulated by Kuznets. Along with this issues like Biodiversity loss e.g. Cheetah species going extinct, Ocean Acidification, Pollution, Ozone Layer depletion, Climate Change, as per a report, in last 100 years the temperature has increased by 2 degrees Celsius. Thus economic growth has led to degradation of ecology and environment.

Lastly with respect to Political issues, the faster pace of economic growth in the North has led to North-South divide leading to formation of groups like G77. Also Many issues like Subsidies in developing Countries has remained long standing rift in WTO between Developing and Non developing countries. Along with this the High growth rate of china and India has alarmed the western countries therby leading to many anti-evasion duties on their products.

Economic Factors Affecting Environmental Sustainability

- Lack of Environmental Compliance: Negligence of environmental principles is one of the main reason why natural hazards end up causing a significant number of avoidable casualties.Any exercise to scientifically ascertain the risk from natural hazards to a region are barely applied in the right spirit.
- Ill-effects of Subsidies: For the welfare and development of vulnerable sections of society, the government is providing many subsidies. Subsidised nature of services such as energy and electricity leads to their overuse and undermines environmental sustainability.Subsidies undermine the revenue base and further limit the government's capacity to invest in new, cleaner technologies.
- No Cost to Environmental Resources: Easy access to natural resources is open entirely and no individual user bears the full cost

of environmental degradation and as a result resources are overused.
- Complexity of Population Dynamics: The continuous increasing population tends to exacerbate the linkages between underdevelopment and environmental degradation.

Why Sustainable Development is Important and how can it be Achieved?

Sustainable development brings about development which is sustainable in nature thereby it talks about economic growth along with environmental sustainability. For example, if economic development means production of plastics and earning income from it, sustainable development means recycling of e-waste and thereby using the product again hence its impact on environment reduces. So sustainable development is important as it talks about economic growth which can be sustained for long period of time without having drastic impact on ecology and social inclusion.

Sustainable development can be achieved from efforts in the direction of Technological developments, social inclusion, political intervene-tion, environmental regulation, legal control etc.

In terms of technological developments, the focus should be on developing technologies which leads to lower pollution levels like hydrogen based engines and e-vehicles, recycling of waste technologies, technology to control the acidification of oceans, Sprinkler technology along with drip irrigation to control economical usage of water. Shift towards solar energy away from hydrocarbon based energy production. Focus on service sector led growth as done in India.

In terms of Social inclusion, the economic growth would be sustainable if all section of society is included in the growth plan, Gender based development is the major topic of discussion in post-modern era. along with this inclusion of weaker section of society in planning process is much needed. The equitable growth is the future for which innovative taxation policy should be thought which is regressive for the rich and thereby fruits if growth should be shared with poor as well in terms of reformist policies like MNREGA, Universal basic income, basic health facilities, good learning outcomes etc.

In terms of environmental regulation, Good foreign practices like odd-even scheme practices in France and recently in Delhi can be altered appropriately to fit in local conditions, along with this "Har ghar vrakhsa" like schemes could be promoted, more focus on Infrastructure development which is sustainable for e.g New projects should be developed after consulting NGOs , Environmental experts etc, along with environmental norms on vehicular pollution should be made more firm with outgo of petrol and diesel vehicles till 2030 .Industrial pollution should be controlled with stricter emission norms along with surprise checks and heavy penalties imposed . the recent cheetah project of India will go long way in conserving bio-diversity in India. Along with this the Paris climate targets should be taken seriously and each country should strive to achieve the SDG goals.

Recent Steps Taken by Indian Government for Sustainable Development

India follows a holistic approach towards its Sustainable Development Goals (SDGs) 2030by launching various schemes. India's SDG Index Score ranges between 42 and 69 for States and between 57and 68 for UTs.

Several schemes such as Swachh Bharat mission, Beti Bacho Beti Padhao, Pradhan Mantri AwasYojana, Smart Cities, Pradhan Mantri Jan Dhan Yojana, Deen Dayal Upadhyay Gram Jyoti Yojana and Pradhan Mantri UjjwalaYojana, among others. Has been undertaken by the government to achieve SDG goals.

Along with these schemes like Namami Gange Mission which aims to achieving the SDG 6 - was launched as a priority programme with a budget outlay of Rs. 20,000 crores for the period 2015-2020. Major components compriseof urban and rural sanitation, sewerage project management, tackling industrial pollution, water use efficiency and quality improvement, ecosystem conservation and Clean Ganga Fund, among others.

National Clean Air Programme in 2019 was launched as a pan India time bound national level strategy for prevention, control and abatement of air pollution besides augmenting the air quality monitoring network across the country.Along with this Coal Tax to promote clean energy and the "National Clean Energy Fund" to promote environmentally sustainable projects. India also hasNational Adaptation Fund for Climate Change.This fund aims to assist "national and state level measures" to address theclimate change.

Way Forward

The Main emphasis in the future should be to develop a National Policy on Resource Efficiency (RE**),** building upon the existing policies to address multiple sectors should be devised for mainstreaming Resource Efficiency approach in the development pathway for achieving Sustainable Development Goals.

India's positive engagement at COP 24 in 2018 negotiations in Katowice, Poland resulted in protection of key interests, comprising recognition of different starting points for developed and developing countries; flexibilities for developing countries and consideration of principles including equity and common but differentiated responsibilities and respective capabilities. This should be strived by other countries as well to meet the intended outcomes of SDG.

Efforts should be also taken to do away with the impasse on many issue which are lying with the appellate body of WTO in relation to subsidies so that litigation free environment of growth could be foreseen.

Crypto-currency is the future and the pollution related to it should be controlled and managed by means of greater technological innovation. Along with these policy frameworks should be drawn on global level for climate resilient growth which can withstand global warming issues and erratic rainfall as seen in western Rajasthan this year thereby impacting farmers output and well-being.

To promote sustainable development, governments will need to **form coherent cross-sectoral policies** – with respect to the environment, agriculture, energy, economy, trade, foreign affairs and development cooperation – that will improve integrated water resources management and governance.

Conclusion

Implementing India's Nationally Determined Contributions as per Paris climate deal requires investments of scale and size which is unprecedented. This essentially means that along with domestic public budgets, international public finance and private sector resources would have to be mobilized from a variety of sources.

The developing countries like India will endeavour to do the best possible within their own domestic resources, keeping in mind the sustainable development imperatives. It is time for the global community to exhibit the requisite momentum to act upon their responsibilities on establishing the enabling environment for climate action.

Lastly, Sustainable development is the pathway to the future we want for all. It offers a framework to generate economic growth, achieve social justice, exercise environmental stewardship and strengthen governance.

– **Ban-ki-Moon**

References

Arti, P., & Leua, A. (2015). Farm Specific Technical Efficiency and Potential Output of Banana Crops in South Gujarat. *Indian Journal of Economics and Development, 18*(2), 445-449

Distribution Technology Ltd. (2015, May 19). *Dynamic planner risk profiler.*

Grewai, P., Bains, A., Gill, J.S., Grover, K., Singh, M., Mann, B.S., & Bains, K.K. (2015). Farm specific technical efficiency and potential output of banana crops in South Gujarat.

Kumar, R., Jain, S., Meena, L.K., & Sen, C. (2015). Resource use efficiency and constraints in production and marketing of tissue culture and sucker propagated banana in Uttar Pradesh (India). *International Journal of Agricultural Science and Research, 5*(5), 1-10.

IBEF. (2019, June 19). *Indian economy.* IBEF India brand equity foundation.

**Assistant Professor,
Department of E.A.F.M.,
Govt. M.S. College for Women, Bikaner,
Rajasthan**

12. Ecological Restoration : Planning, Evaluation, Outcomes and Hurdles

Pragya Dadhich[1], Anita Malav[2] and Poonam Jaiswal[3]

Abstract

Human greed is inevitable, and so does its effects on the environment. In ancient times the damage caused by a human was balanced by natural restoration, but it's not the scenario anymore; the rate of forest exploitation has exceeded the rate of natural regeneration a long time ago. That's the whole reason why the recovery process of nature should be assisted by using different interventions and techniques. Restoration ecology is an emerging science; with a very limited amount of literature available to guide the process of planning and evaluation. Both planning and evaluation of the restoration must consider the biotic- abiotic conditions of the site, restoration techniques, objectives, etc. While planning a restoration, it should be kept in mind that each site is different from one another, and so does the outcomes. The restoration approach can be passive or active; while passive restoration tries to achieve restoration by simply accelerating the process of natural restoration by removing hurdles, supplying nutrients, etc., active restoration offers different techniques and interventions to achieve the target. This paper reviews all aspects of restoration including planning, proper and timely evaluation, its outcomes, and major obstacles faced by restoration projects by analysing many restoration projects.

Keywords : Evaluation, policy, ecosystem, restoration.

Introduction :

Forest degradation is an inevitable consequence of the population blast and the ever-increasing greed of mankind. Time has long passed since when the rate of deforestation was balanced by the rate of natural regeneration; more than two third of the total land is already converted to human use like agriculture, residences, industries, etc., remaining one-third is widely threatened by fragmentation, pollution, climate change, exotic species invasion, and unsustainable exploitation (Millennium Ecosystem Assessment, 2005). Restoration is believed to be the key that can reverse the degradation caused by humans to the forests and provide resilience to biodiversity. Resilience ensures that the ecosystem is sustainable, does not need further assistance, and has adaptability i.e., able to adjust and maintain functions in face of environmental challenges. Restoration aims to guide a degraded ecosystem to conditions resembling its past structure; and is generally based on the successional concept of smooth turnover time, followed by the establishment of a stable climax community (Matthews, et al., 2009).

SER defines restoration as "The process of assisting the recovery of an ecosystem that has been degraded, damaged, or destroyed" (SER, The SER International Primer on Ecological Restoration, 2004). A proper definition, basic guidelines for restoration planning along with a list of key attributes of successful restoration were given by 'The Society of Ecological Restoration i.e., SER. In most cases, ecological outcomes such as vegetation structure, species diversity and abundance, and ecological processes are used as restoration attributes as these are the most commonly used indicators of the ecological condition of any system (Aronson & Floc'h, 1996; Ruiz-Jaen & Aide, 2005). The ultimate and often exclusive goal of any restoration project is to create an ecosystem that can support itself and is resilient i.e., does not need further assistance (Urbanska, et al., 1997; SER 2004).

As time passes awareness about nature has increased; and there are many global commitments from recent history to support forest restoration as, a commitment to the restoration of 15% of degraded ecosystems worldwide by 2020 at the meeting of the Convention on Biological Diversity, 2010 in Nagoya, Japan (Biodiversity, 2010); at United Nations Conference on Sustainable Development (Rio+20 conference),2012 (Rio+20 Dialogues, 2012); a commitment is launched to restore 150 million hectares of lost and degraded forests globally by 2020, its worth's US$ 85 billion per year (Restoring lost forests, 2012). The Restoration Initiative (TRI) is a program approved by The Global Environment Facility (GEF) council to help 10 countries define and achieve a commitment to restoring 150 million hectares of degraded land and 350 million hectares by 2030 (IUCN Press release, 2016). The biodiversity conservation strategy of Australia set a 5-year goal for the restoration of 1000km^2 of fragmented landscape and aquatic systems to improve connectivity.

Active restoration v/s natural restoration

Passive or natural regeneration is the spontaneous recovery of native plant species on an abundant land, it can be assisted by human interventions such as control over some biotic and abiotic factors like control over grazing, weeds, fire protection, etc. (Zahawi, et al., 2014); while on the other hand, active restoration requires the planting of nursery-grown seedlings, direct seedlings, and control over disturbance regime to speed up recovery process usually at a higher cost to establish vegetation structure, reassembling local species, and to catalyze the recovery (Chazdon & Guariguata, 2016).

Active restoration is preferred in areas where natural restoration is hindered; like as isolated and extensively degraded sites, low rainfall, long history of extensive disturbance, soil degradation, weed infestation, and loss of seed banks (Crouzeilles, et al., 2017). Active restoration was believed to be more effective and is preferred by practitioners, but recent research prove it wrong and found that active restoration may have higher (Shoo, et al., 2015) or similar (Gilman, et al., 2016; Meli, et al., 2017) results as passive restoration in terms of plant biodiversity. In the Australian wet tropics uplands, the study site achieve a regrowth level comparable to the reference site after 30 years with natural restoration and after 10 years while using active restoration (Shoo, et al., 2015). The widely held notion, that justifies active restoration supremacy over passive restoration was due to a lack of control over biotic and abiotic factors in the past time.

Restoration Planning :

While planning restoration it is important to understand when and where we can rely on passive or natural restoration, when extensive interventions are needed; and whether chosen targets represent unrealistic expectations (Holl & Aide, 2011). Minimum interventions and maximum results i.e., use of passive restoration as much as possible believes to be the most effective and should be the first approach on sites where possible (Prach & Walker, 2011). The odds of any restoration project success should be estimated briefly before the program beings, as the future gain is uncertain but the immediate loss is permanent (Moilanen, et al., 2009). Site specific planning is key to success in ecological restoration. While restoring a forest, selection of appropriate planning and designing, selection of native plant species and proper monitoring is necessary to accelerate the process of restoration (Dadhich and Jaiswal, 2022).

Menz et al. suggested a four-point plan to ensure the sustainability of restoration while enhancing ecological values (Menz, et al., 2013); (a) Identification of focal areas demanding restoration, (b) Identification of knowledge gaps and prioritization of research needs, (c) Restoration knowledge hubs to aggregate knowledge at the science- practice interface and (d) Ensuring Political viability of restoration.

Identification of focal areas that demands restoration: Goals concerning a program must be realistic and ecosystems should be identified where resources are present to achieve maximum ecosystem services and biodiversity gain in the most cost-effective manner (Hobbs, 2007). The Global Partnership on Forest Landscape Restoration (GPFLR) is a program launched by IUCN and its partners. It has already identified 2 billion hectares around the world with high opportunities for restoration.

Gaps in knowledge of restoration ecology must be identified, capacities should be developed and later on, research should be translated into policy and practice. Restoration approaches must be developed according to the conditions of the site being restored. Restoration initiatives must be tuned with evolving knowledge, it will allow cost-effective inventions to be developed (Hobbs, et al., 2011; Valentine, et al., 2020). Knowledge about site-specific restoration processes can be improved when Science and practice merge. Restoration patterns, as well as restoration techniques used, vary according to site conditions; not even two sites can be the same. Two sites having the same restoration history can differ in abiotic factors, landscape conditions, or even disturbance history. Evidence-based literature and information repositories must be developed for future referencing (Sutherland, et al., 2004). The political viability of any restoration project should be checked to make the attempt successful. Scientists should shift their focus from journal writing and professional conferences to reach a broader community and political audience, who will help in restoration funding. Net benefits of sustainable, ecologically resilient restoration must be communicated in a compelling way to policymakers and practitioners if longer-term funding opportunities are to be realized, particularly support for science programs to fill knowledge gaps (Biggs, et al., 2012).

Evaluation of restoration :

Evaluation of the success of different restoration projects is necessary as it justifies the role of restoration; gives ground for further projects by understanding the cause of problems, overcoming the hurdles, understanding the strategy and requirements according to different sites, and avoiding repeating costly mistakes. Our understanding of the success of any restoration program is often hindered by imprecise targets, lack of quality monitoring systems, and lack of transfer of information concerning project outcomes (Miller & Hobbs, 2007; Mcdonald & Williams, 2009; Parkes, et al., 2012; Tischew, et al., 2010). Thus an empirical assessment of forest restoration can justify the involvement of restoration in ecological resource management policies and provide a strong base for the development of effective practices (Wortley et al., 2013). Evaluation of restoration success is not as easy as it seems, as there is considerable debate among ecologists regarding the characters and measurements of successful restoration (Hobbs & Norton, 1996; Hull & Gobster, 2000; Choi, 2004; Burke & Mitchell, 2007; Thorpe & Stanley, 2011; Le, et al., 2012).

Ecological processes are rarely measured because they are slower to recover (Morgan & Short, 2002), and require multiple measures which can increase the time and cost utilized in evaluation (Herrick, 2000). Vegetation structure is the most common indicator of restoration projects to evaluate project success, followed by faunal diversity and ecological processes. Measures associated with vegetation structure are easy and rapid to measure, and usually, there is little seasonal variation in these measures. For animals invertebrates are commonly used because they represent many functional groups like pollinators and decomposers; and (Longcore, 2003); and have a critical role in the nutrient cycle (Tian, et al., 1997). Vertebrates are used in cases where wildlife recovery is the prime objective of the restoration project and in conservation biology projects (Nichols & Nichols, 2003).

Despite the variation in indicators used in the evaluation, each project has a common goal to restore the ecosystem to its previous and non-degraded form; as exact information about the past structure and composition of any ecosystem is hard to obtain, we use reference sites for comparison; reference sites resemble project sites in environ-mental conditions and range of variability. The second type of comparison is with unrestored degraded sites, which provides a no-action baseline. Over time different ecologists suggest various approaches to achieve the target reference level, one such approach is to minimize "dark species", which are species absent from an ecosystem but present in surrounding ecosystems i.e., belong to the same species pool (Partel, et al., 2011).

Based on short-term assessments, it is usually difficult to predict the result of a project; sometimes project seems to go perfectly meet fails in the end due to non-native species or other factors (Matthew & Spyreas, 2010). On the other hand, in some other cases, projects initially seem to be unsuccessful end up meeting the expected goals, as the conditions become more favourable with time (Clements, et al. 2010).

Restoration Outcomes :

Relying upon only ecological outcomes to evaluate restoration status is not sufficient, some ecologists argued that additional attributes like the importance of socioeconomic aspects with social and cultural values should be added to the SER primer of restoration success (Shackelford, et al., 2013). Some ecologists highlighted the benefit of assigning an economic value to ecosystem services recovered through restoration (Benayas, et al., 2009; Bullock, et al., 2011); on the other hand, some others focused on social influences in achieving restoration goals (Miller & Hobbs, 2007; Le, et al., 2012). In a remarkable example from Latin America, values of dry forest restoration like tourism, timber, non-timber resources, and carbon sequestration were first quantified and then compared with costs of restoration like loss of livestock production, fencing, and tree establishment (Birch, et al., 2010)

Outcomes of the restoration projects vary widely; a restoration project can be successful, and results in complete and quick recovery; it can be partially successful by improving the degraded land to a degree, or it can yield only a little or no recovery. Total recovery relative to the reference site is often possible on the sites where colonization by native and desired species is still possible by simple and mostly natural restoration and soil and other physical factors are relatively intact. For instance, in oak depressional wetlands in Ohio, a complete recovery to the relative reference site was noted (Martin & Kirkman, 2009); and in Argentina, grassland recovery was noted after 4 years of invasive pine removal (Cuevas & Zalba, 2010). A more typical result of all restoration projects is that even though most of them do not result in complete recovery but the results are always more effective than no action (Benayas, et al., 2009). For instance, in the Bawangling Forest region in Hainan Island, China; after logging and shifting cultivation significant recovery was noted after restoration (Ding, et al., 2012).

In some cases of successful restoration, natural constraints inhibiting the establishments, are reduced with the course of restoration and result in a complete restoration like the initial lack of recovery in river macro invertebrates affected by historical mine pollution was followed by rapid changes toward a target goal once water quality reached a certain level (Clements, et al., 2010); but in other cases, these constraints do not self-correct over time and partial recovery is relatively permanent. For example, in the Midwestern united states wetland potholes, several barriers to recovery of an ecosystem like isolation, infrequent flooding, and invasive species present; and they did not weaken over time (Aronson, et al., 2010). A similar case was noted by Ballantine and Schneider in restoring depressional wetlands constraints to soil development remaining after 55 years (Ballantine & Schneider, 2009).

A complete lack of recovery can also occur, and mostly is related to strong biotic-abiotic feedback which hinders the restoration actions (Suding, et al., 2004). Like in the Dutch Wadden sea seagrasses extinct in the 1930s and even after every restoration attempt, have never recovered. Later after some research, it was found that recovery was prohibited by the high turbidity of suspended sediments, and the presence of seagrasses is necessary to reduce turbidity (Heide, et al., 2007).

Outcomes of different restoration approaches may vary considerably. Rey benayas et al. found that although the project did not reach the level of the assigned reference system ecosystem services increased notably in terms of biodiversity (Benayas, Newton, et al., 2009). Worm et al. found a four-fold increase in ocean productivity after the restoration of biodiversity (Worm, et al., 2006). In some other cases, restoration of ecosystem services was found to be more feasible than the restoration of biodiversity as in the case of the New Zealand island system, where ecosystem variables like isotopic carbon signatures and marine-derived nitrogen levels recovered within 22 years of rat eradication (Jones, 2010).

Sometimes restoration of one ecological service costs you another ecological service; in such a scenario, the tricky task is to ensure multi-functionality in both the long and short term. As an example, growing short-lived and fast-growing grasses is a common approach for carbon offsets in the initial phase of restoration projects but these plants neither approach the diversity of naturally occurring forests nor guarantee success (Wuethrich, 2007). On contrary, the inclusion of slow-growing and long-lived tree species would better promote long-term carbon sequestration and biodiversity (Chazdon R. L., 2008).

Ideally, restoration projects would eventually achieve a self-sustaining ecosystem without the need for future human intervention. If restoration sites across time are compared, it is important to note where these constraints self-correct over time or need further assistance.

Restoration Hurdles :

In most of the cases of restoration problem of "leakage" is noted i.e., restoration of any area leads to degradation of another area as in restoring areas degrading activities are prohibited. For example, when AES planted forests on 40,000 small holdings in Guatemala, residents were forced to cut other forests for fuelwood (Environmental Audit Committee, 2007). Recovery in both terrestrial and aquatic ecosystems is slowed or even stopped by the local extinction of native species and the dominance of exotic species has a strong impact on ecological processes (Florens, et al., 2010; Tanentzap, et al., 2009). This is also noted in the recovery process of indigenous butterflies at the black river Gorges national park, Mauritius (Florens, et al., 2010).

Sometimes the introduction of species in the initial phase of restoration does nothing but delay the colonization of native species (Cox & Anderson, 2004). Sometimes initially established species prevent further colonization of the desired species and lower the eventual diversity of the final community (Galatowitsch, 2009). It has also been noted that the genetic structure of an introduced population can affect the local adaptation and genetic diversity of desired species (Vander, et al., 2010). Legacies of land i.e., damage caused by current as well as past disturbances influence the restoration pattern more than restoration actions; as noticed in the case of Sandrivier valley, lies in the ranches of Argentina and Tierberg (Seymour, et al., 2010). Mostly the non-native species removal projects result in replacement with another non-native species (Reid, et al., 2009).

The partnership between managers and policymakers is a must for a restoration program (Gonzalo-Turpin, et al., 2008), and also requires the participation of scientists in the on-the-ground restoration project and decision-making while acknowledging their value system (Arlettaz, et al., 2010). Community involvement, transfer of knowledge among scientists, practitioners, community members, and administrative organizations; and inclusion of a broad range of stakeholders in the decision-making process are some of the key characteristics of a successful restoration project (Bernhardt, et al., 2007). The majority of restoration research is skewed towards economically strong countries, which are not areas of highest deforestation (Aronson, et al., 2010).

Most of the policies made in the field of restoration ecology are based on cases, where outcomes of similar restoration techniques on different sites are the same i.e., show simple, rapid, and predictable progress towards the target. It is most likely the situation when abiotic conditions are relatively uniform, shifting with biotic changes and the species pool is relatively intact (Pickett, et al., 2009). But unfortunately, it is not the case most often in most scenarios despite using the same techniques restoration outcomes of different sites diverge from each other due to abiotic factors (Baer, et al., 2010). In some cases, a different restoration dynamic is observed, where restorations coverage towards a predictable outcome but not the target goal. This is the clearest sign of failure of the techniques used in restoration (Tanentzap, et al., 2009; Matthew & Spyreas, 2010).

Restoration needs a multidisciplinary approach; it includes applications of microbiology (Harris, 2009), seed science (Merritt & Dixon, 2011), pollination ecology (Menz, et al., 2011) along with socioeconomic expertise. Successful science-practice communication is paramount to achieving the greatest benefits in the field of restoration ecology; practitioners hold a key role in identifying knowledge gaps and guiding further research.

Conclusion :

It must be realized that prevention of degradation and damage of any ecosystem in the first place is a far better investment than restoring it after degradation (Menz, et al., 2013). Restoration can be made a success by identifying and mitigating disturbance or degradation causing factors, eliminating them with judicious intervention in restoring and removing limiting factors for vegetation development, and by accelerating the natural process of nutrient cycling. Ecological restoration target can be achieved by proper planning, timely implementation, and careful evaluation cum management. The restoration ecology is emerging science and there is a lot to experience yet.

Bibliography :

Arlettaz, R., Schaub, M., Fournier, J., Reichlin, T. S., & Sierro, A. (2010). From publications to public actions: when conservation biologists bridge the gap between research and implementation . Bioscience, 60:835-42.

Aronson, J., & Floc'h, E. L. (1996). Vital Landscape Attributes:

Missing Tools for Restoration Ecology. Restoration Ecology, 377-387.
Aronson, J., Blignaut, J. N., Milton, S. J., Maitre, D. L., Esler, K. J., Limouzin, A., . . . Lederer, N. (2010). Are Socioeconomic Benifits of Restoration Adequately Quantified? A Meta-analysis of Recent Papers (2000-2008). Restoration Ecology, 143-154.
Assessment, M. E. (2005). Ecosystem and human well-being. Washington DC : Island Press.
Baer, S., Meyer, C. K., Bach, E. M., Klopf, R. P., & Six, J. (2010). Contrasting ecosystem recovery on two soil textures: implications for carbon mitigation and grassland conservation. Ecosphere, 1-22.
Ballantine, K., & Schneider , R. (2009). Fifty-five years of soil developmentin restored freshwater depressional wetlands. Applied Ecology , 1467-1480.
Benayas, J. M., Newton, A. C., & Bullock , J. M. (2009). Enhancement of Biodiversity and Ecosystem Services by Ecological Restoration: A Meta- Analysis . Science , 1121-1124.
Benayas, J. M., Newton, A. C., Diaz, A., & Bullock, J. M. (2009). Enhancement of Biodiversity and Ecosystem Services by Ecological Restoration: A Meta-Analysis. Science , 1121-1124.
Bernhardt, E., Sudduth, E. B., Palmer, M. A., Allan, J. D., & Meyer, J. L. (2007). Restoring rivers one reach at a time: results from a survey of US river restoration practitioners . Restoration Ecology , 15:482-93.
Biggs, R., Schluter, M., Biggs, D., Bohensky, E. L., BurnSilver, S., Cundill, G., . . . West, P. C. (2012). Towards Principles for Enhancing the Resilience of Ecosystem Services . Annual Review of Environment and Resources , 421-448.
Biodiversity, S. P. (2010). Strategic plan for Biodiversity . Nagoya, Japan.
Birch, J. C., Newton, A. C., Aquino, C. A., Cantarello, E., Echeverria, C., Kitzverger, T., . . . Garavito, N. T. (2010). Cost-effectiveness of dryland forest restoration evaluated by spatial analysis of ecosystem services. National Library of Medicine .
Bullock, J. M., Aronson, J., Newton, A. C., Pywell , R. F., & Rey-Benayas, J. M. (2011). Restoration of Ecosystem Sevices and biodiversity: conflicts and opportunities . Trends in Ecology and

Evolution , 541-549.
Burke, S. M., & Mitchell, N. (2007). People as Ecological Participants in Ecological Restoration . Restoration Ecology , 348-350.
Chazdon, R. L. (2008). Beyond Deforestation: Restoring Forests and Ecosystem Services on Degraded Lands. Science, 1458-1460.
Chazdon, R. L., & Guariguata, M. R. (2016). Natural regeneration as a tool for large-scale forest restoration in the tropics: prospects and challenges . Biotropica, 716-730.
Choi, Y. D. (2004). Theories for ecological restoration in changing environment: Toward 'futuristic restoration. Ecological Research , 75-81.
Clements, W. H., Vieira, N. M., & Sonderegger, D. L. (2010). Use of ecological thresholds to assess recovery in lotic ecosystems . North America Benthological society , 29:1017-23.
Committee, E. A. (2007). Environmental Audit Report. Retrieved from House of Commons: https://publications.parliament.uk/pa/cm200607/cmselect/cmenvaud/cmenvaud.htm#reports
Cox, R. D., & Anderson , V. J. (2004). Increasing native diversity of cheatgrass-dominated rangeland through assisted succession . Range Management , 57:203-10.
Crouzeilles, R., Ferreira, M. S., Chazdon, R. L., Lindenmayer, D. B., Sansevero, J. B., Monteiro, L., . . . Strassburg, B. B. (2017). Ecological restoration success is higher for natural regeneration than for active restoration in tropical forests. Applied Ecology, 1-7.
Cuevas, Y. A., & Zalba, S. M. (2010). Recovery of Native Grasslands after Removing Invasive Pines. Restoration Ecology , 711-719.
Ding, Y., Zang, R., Liu, S., He, F., & Letcher, S. G. (2012). Recovery of woody plant diversity in tropical rain forests in Southern China after logging and shifting cultivation. Biological Conservation , 225-233.
Ehrenfeld, J. G. (2000). Defining the Limits of Restoration: The Need for Realistic Goals. Restoration Ecology, 2-9.
Florens, F. B., Mauremootoo, J. R., Fowler, S. V., Winder, L., & Baider , C. (2010). Recovery of indigenous butterfly community

following control of invasive alien plants in a tropical island's wet forests. Biodiversity Conservation , 19:3835-48.

Future Earth. (2015). Retrieved from International Council of Science: https://council.science/what-we-do/affiliated-bodies/future-earth/

Galatowitsch, S. M. (2009). Carbon offsets as ecological restoration . Restoration Ecology , 17:563-70.

Gilman, A. C., Letcher, S. G., Fincher, R. M., Perez, A. I., Madell, T. W., Finkelstein, A. L., & Corrales-Araya, F. (2016). Recovery of floristic diversity and basal area in natural forest regeneration and planted plots in a Costa Rican wet forest. Biotropica, 798-808.

Gonzalo-Turpin, H., Couix, N., & Hazard , L. (2008). Rethinking partnerships with the aim of producing knowledge with practical relevance: a case study in field of ecological restoration. Ecological Society.

Harris, J. (2009). Soil Microbial Communities and Restoration Ecology: Facilitators or Followers? Science, 573-574.

Heide, T. v., Nes, E. H., Geerling, G. W., Smolders, A. J., Bouma, T. J., & Katwijk, M. M. (2007). Positive Feedbacks in Seagrass Ecosystems: Implimentations for Success in Conservation and Restoration . Ecosystems , 1311-1322.

Herrick, J. E. (2000). Soil quality: an indicator of sustainable land management? Applied Soil Ecology , 75-83.

Hobbs, R. J. (2007). Setting Effective and Realistic Restoration Goals: Key Directions for Research. Restoration Ecology, 354-357.

Hobbs, R. J., & Norton, D. A. (1996). Towards a conceptual Framwork for restoration ecology. Restoration Ecology, 93-110.

Hobbs, R. J., Hallett, L. M., Ehrlich, P. R., & Mooney, H. A. (2011). Intervention Ecology: Applying Ecological Science in the Twenty-first century . Bioscience, 442-450.

Holl, K. D., & Aide, T. M. (2011). When and where to actively restore ecosystems? Forest Ecology and Management, 1558-1563.

Hull, B. R., & Gobster, P. H. (2000). Restoring forest ecosystem: the human dimension. Journal of Forestry , 32-36.

Institute, w. R. (n.d.). Retrieved from https://www.wri.org/initiatives/global-restoration-initiative/forest-landscape-restoration-principles

International, B. L. (2010). Restoration Model Set to Transform Indonesia's forest sector. News release.

Jones, H. P. (2010). Seabird islands take mere decades to recover following rat eradication. Ecological applications, 2075-2080.

Le, H. D., Smith, C., Herbohn, J., & Harrison, S. (2012). More than just trees: Assessing reforestation success in tropical developing countries. Journal of Rural Studies, 5-19.

Longcore, T. (2003). Terrestrial Arthropodes as Indicators of Ecological Restoration Success in Coastal Saga scrub (California, U.S.A.). Restoration Ecology, 397-409.

Martin, K. L., & Kirkman, L. K. (2009). Management of ecological thresholds to re-establish disturbance-mantained herbaceous wetlands of the south-eastern USA. Applied Ecology, 906-914.

Matthew, J., & Spyreas, G. (2010). Convergence and divergence in plant community trajectories as a framework for monitoring wetland restoration progress. Applied Ecology, 47:1128-36.

Matthews, J. W., Peralta, A. L., Flanagan, D. N., Baldwin, P. M., Soni, A., Kent, A. D., & Endress, A. G. (2009). Relative influence of landscape vs. local factors on plant community assembly in restored wetlands. Applied Ecology, 2108-2123.

Mcdonald, T., & Williams, J. (2009). A perspective on the evolving science and practice of ecological restoration in Australia. Ecological Management & Restoration, 113-125.

Meli, P., Holl, K. D., Benayas, J. R., Jones, H. P., Jones, P. C., Montoya, D., & Mateos, D. M. (2017). A global review of past land use, climate, and active vs. passive restoration effects on forest recovery. PLOS ONE.

Menz, M. H., Dixon, K. W., & Hobbs, R. J. (2013). Hurdles and Opportunities for Landscape-Scale Restoration. Science, 526-527.

Menz, M. H., Phillips, R., Winfree, R., Kremen, C., Aizen, M. A., Johnson, S. D., & Dixon, K. (2011). Reconnecting plants and pollinators: Challenges in the restoration of pollination mutualisms. Trends in Plant science, 4-12.

Merritt, D. J., & Dixon, K. W. (2011). Conservation. Restoration seed banks--a matter of scale. Science, 424-425.

Miller, J. R., & Hobbs, R. J. (2007). Habitate Restoration- Do We Know What We're Doing? Restoration Ecology, 382-390.

Moilanen, A., Teeffelen, A. J., Ben- Haim, Y., & Ferrier, S. (2009).

How Much Compensation is Enough? A Framework for Incorporating Uncertainty and Time Discounting When Calculating Offset Ratios for Impacted Habitat . Restoration Ecology , 470-478.

Morgan, P. A., & Short, F. T. (2002). Using Functional Trajectories to Track Constructed Salt Marsh Development in the Great Bay Estuary, Maine/New Hampshire, U.S.A. Restoration Ecology, 461-473.

Nichols, O. G., & Nichols , F. M. (2003). Long- Term Trends in Faunal Recolonization After Bauxite Mining in the Jarrah Forest of Southwestern Australia . Restoration Ecology, 261-272.

Parkes, T., Delaney, M., Dunphy, M., Woodford, R., Bower, H., Bower, S., . . . McDonald, T. (2012). Big Scrub: A cleared landscape in transition back to forest? Ecological Management & Restoration, 212-223.

Partel, M., Szava-Kovats, R., & Zobel, M. (2011). Dark Diversity: Shedding light on absent species. Trends in Ecology & Evolution , 124-128.

Pickett, S., Cadenasso, M. L., & Meiners, S. J. (2009). Ever since Clements: from succession to vegetation dynamics and understanding to intervention . Applied Vegetation Science , 12:9-21.

Prach, K., & Walker, L. R. (2011). Four opportunities for studies of ecological succession. Trends in Ecology and Evolution , 26:119-23.

Reid, A. M., Morin, L., Downey, P. O., French , K., & Virtue, J. G. (2009). Does invasive plant management aid the restoration of natural ecosystems? Biological Conservation , 142:2342-49.

release, I. P. (2016, June 14). IUCN and partners lauch global effort to boost restoration of degraded forests. Retrieved from IUCN: https://www.iucn.org/news/forests/201606/iucn-and-partners-launch-global-effort-boost-restoration-degraded-forests

Restoring lost forests. (2012). Retrieved from IUCN: https://www.iucn.org/content/leaders-define-pathway-restoring-150-million-hectares lostforests#:~:text=%E2%80%9CThe% 20 restoration%20of%20lost%20forests%20will%20increase%20carbon,Global%20Partnership%20on%20Forest%20%26%20Landscape%20Restoration%20%28GPF

Rio+20 Dialogues. (2012). Retrieved from Rio+20: https://www.ituc-csi.org/rio-20-dialogues-demands-concrete

Ruiz-Jaen, M. C., & Aide, T. M. (2005). Restoration Success: How Is It Being Measured? Restoration Ecology, 569-577.

SER. (2004). The SER International Primer on Ecological Restoration. Retrieved from Society for Ecological Restoration International Science: https://cdn.ymaws.com/www.ser.org/resource/resmgr/custompages/publications/ser_publications/ser_primer.pdf

SER. (n.d.). Restoration Resource Center Project Database. Retrieved from SER: https://www.ser-rrc.org/project/chemical-free-farming-by-restoring-soil-water-table-conserve-local-biodiversity/

Seymour, C. L., Milton, S. J., Joseph, G. S., Dean, W. J., Ditlhobolo, T., & Cumming, G. S. (2010). Twenty years of rest returns grazing potential, but not palatable plant diversity, to Karoo rangeland, South Africa . Applied Ecology , 47:859-67.

Shackelford, N., Hobbs, R. J., Burgar, J. M., Erickson, T. E., Fontaine, J. B., Laliberte, E., . . . Standish, R. J. (2013). Primed for change: Developing Ecological Restoration for the 21st century . Restoration Ecology, 297-394.

Shoo, L. P., Freebody, K., Kanowski, J., & Catterall, C. P. (2015). Slow recovery of tropical old- field rainforest regrowth and the value and limitations of active restoration. Conservation Biology, 121-132.

Suding, K. N., Grass, K. L., & Houseman, G. R. (2004). Alternative states and positive feedbacks in restoration ecology. Trends in Ecology & Evolution , 46-53.

Sutherland, W. J., Pullin, A. S., Dolman, P. M., & Knight , T. M. (2004). The need for evidence-based conservation . Trends in Ecology & Evolution , 305-308.

Tanentzap, A. J., Burrows, L. E., Lee, W. G., Nugent, G., Maxwell , J. M., & Coomes, D. A. (2009). Landscape-level vegetation recovery from herbivory: progress after four decades of invasive red deer control . Applied Ecology , 46:1064-72.

Thorpe, A. S., & Stanley, A. G. (2011). Determining appropriate goals for restoration of imperilled communities and species. Journal of Applied Ecology, 275-279.

Tian, G., Brussaard, B., Kang, B., & Swift, M. (1997). Soil fauna-meditated decomposition of plant residues under constrained environmental and residue quality conditions. Environmental

Sciences, 125-134.

Tischew, S., Baasch, A., Conrad, M. K., & Kirmer, A. (2010). Evaluating restoration success of frequently implemented compensation measures: results and demands for control procedures. Restoration Ecology, 18:467-80.

Urbanska, K. M., Webb, N. R., & Edwards, P. J. (1997). Restoration ecology and sustainable development. Cambridge, U.K.: New York Cambridge University Press.

Valentine, L., Shackelford, N., Johnson, B. A., Craig, M. D., Perring, M. P., Hulvey, K., . . . Standish, R. J. (2020). How one ecologist has influenced the way we think about restoration ecology. Restoration Ecology.

Vander, K. M., Bischoff, A., & Smith, B. (2010). A question of origin: where and how to collect seed for ecological restoration. Basic Applied Ecology, 11:300-11.

Worm, B., Barbier, E. B., Beaumont, N., Duffy, J. E., Folke, C., Halpern, B. S., . . . Watson, R. (2006). Impacts of biodiversity loss on ocean ecosystem services. National Library of Medicine.

Wortley, L., Hero, J.-M., & Howes, M. J. (2013). Evaluating Ecological Restoration Success: A Review of Literature. Restoration Ecology, 537-543.

Wuethrich, B. (2007). Reconstructing Brazil's Atlantic Rainforest. Science, 1070-1072.

Zahawi, R. A., Reid, J. L., & Holl, K. D. (2014). Hidden Costs of Passive Restoration. Restoration Ecology, 284-287.

Dadhich Pragya and Jaiswal Poonam (2022). Restoration of Forests: Human Concern. International Journal for Research in Applied Sciences and Biotechnology, Volume-9, Issue-3, 85-89, doi.org/10.31033/ijrasb.9.3.15

Research Scholar,
J. D.B. Govt Girls College, Kota
Pragyadadhich225@gmail.com
[2] **Assistant Professor,**
J.D.B. Govt Girls College, Kota
[3] **Associate Professor,**
J.D.B. Govt Girls College, Kota

13. Sustainable Development and Industrialization

Dr.Dev Karan

Abstract

Sustainable Development is a process of development that promotes economic growth through increased capacity of produced goods, introduce the process that is environment friendly and also provide services that are improving the live hoods of peoples without compromising the needs of future generation.

Sustainable Development is the organizing principals for meeting human development goals while at the same time sustaining the ability of natural systems to provide the natural resources and eco system service upon which the economic and society depends. This is the state of society where living condition and resources uses continue to meet human needs without undermining the integrity and stability of natural system. Sustainable Development can be classified as development that meets the needs of the present without compromising the ability of future generation. As the concept development, it has shifted to focus more on economic social and environmental protection for future generation.

The economic growth is environmental friendly, sustainable for long period and responsible towards society. The human activities are become much selfish, they do not care about the environment so the society suffered with negative impact of human activities like – heap of waste material (mechanical, chemical and many other type of waste) and all type of pollution. So the study of Sustainable Development by industrialization become inevitable for all type of disciplines.

Keywords : *Development,* economic growth , industrialization

Sustainable Development is a process of development that promotes economic growth through increased capacity of produced goods, introduce the process that is environment friendly and also provide services that are improving the live hoods of peoples without compromising the needs of future generation.

Sustainable Development is the organizing principals for meeting human development goals while at the same time sustaining the ability of natural systems to provide the natural resources and eco system service upon which the economic and society depends. This is the state of society where living condition and resources uses continue to meet human needs without undermining the integrity and stability of natural system. Sustainable Development can be classified as development that meets the needs of the present without compromising the ability of future generation. As the concept development, it has shifted to focus more on economic social and environmental protection for future generation.

Object of this Study :

The economic growth is environmental friendly, sustainable for long period and responsible towards society. The human activities are become much selfish, they do not care about the environment so the society suffered with negative impact of human activities like – heap of waste material (mechanical, chemical and many other type of waste) and all type of pollution. So the study of Sustainable Development by industrialization become inevitable for all type of disciplines.

The main key objectives of the paper are:

- Economic and social security – sustainable growth and inclusion by overcoming poverty and inequality and equal opportunity for all
- Environmental security – low carbon green growth and environmental protection with industrialization
- Physical and personal security – protection of individuals, institutions, nation and advancement of peace

Research Methodology :

This paper is based on historical, descriptive and analytical method. For this researcher has used secondary sources like books, journals, articles, e- resources, news paper articles and reports of several international organisations.

Why Sustainable Development and Industrialization is Important

- The business concerns are only body who can change the behavior of consumers or all stake holders. It's a common question that why Sustainable Development is important? The answer is very simple and common and well known that increasing much production and wrong business activities are polluting the natural environmental and damages the people's health, crop, wild life and all eco system. Due to unlimited human wants and greed destroy the limited and precious natural resources.

It is necessary to prevent the unwanted use of natural resources and reduces the wastage of resources, be adopt the concept of Sustainable Development and achieve the business object by using of valuable natural resources efficiently. Due to government rules and regulations and by social awareness activities the common interest develop among people that protection of natural environment is necessary. All over the world people are much concerned for environmental issues and changing their behavior for the protection of environment.

Object of Sustainable Development and Industrialization

- By reducing the unemployment by industrial development means there is no poverty
- By the removing the poverty made the task of zero hunger
- By the Sustainable Development and industrialization achieve the target of good health and well being
- Increases the educational institutions, that institutions have a quality for education
- Sustainable Development creates the gender equality by improving the industrialization and employment opportunities
- Industries also help to provide clean water and sanitation
- Industries provide renewal energy like – wind, solar, water energy, that will be affordable for all
- The energy production system also save the environment
- Industries do the decent or sustainable work for economic growth
- Efforts for developing the green industries
- Do the innovation in processing, manufacturing, packaging, transporting and all activities are in green way for Sustainable Development
- Infrastructure is also develop in sustainable way

- Industries are produce the responsible products for consumption and create the Brand – image.
- Save the climate like – save the life on land and also below water and at the sky.
- For peace, justice make strong institution.
- Public private partnership for the Sustainable Development and industrialization.

Reasons for Adopting Sustainable Development by Industrialization :
- For conserving scares natural resources
- Fulfill the corporate social responsibility of company
- Increase the good-will of company
- To capture the available opportunities
- To get the competitive advantage
- To follow the government rules and regulations
- Environment conscious consumer products
- Fight healthy competition with well known companies

Advantages of Sustainable Development :

Company's who develop new and improved products and services who's features are environment friendly. This provides opportunity to a good place in new markets as well increase their profit, get sustainability and enjoy competitive advantage over the other companies that are not concern with the environment. Some advantages are mentioned below –
- Companies get sustainability for long period and enjoy with profitability
- Environment friendly companies enjoy with long term growth
- It reduces the variable cost in long run, although its initial fixed cost is more
- It helps the company in marketing of products and services
- It helps in competition in new markets
- It help in making a powerful, attractive and message full advertisement copy
- It promotes corporate social responsibility (CSR)

Its employees also feel proud to working with environment friendly company

Threats of Industrialization :
- Population growth and urbanization
- Unlimited human needs
- Energy use and warming
- Excessive waste and subsequent pollution of soil, air and water
- Poverty, climate change and unemployment conditions
- Lake of awareness of mass

Challenges and Future of Sustainable Development :

Currently Sustainable Development evolution is in its initial stage hence facing many difficulties and challenges like –

- There is lack of regulatory body for standardization. Customer how to believe that the campaign of green and organic product is true because there is lack of authentic labeling / standardization of product. A standard quality control board is very necessary for licensing and labeling .
- It is new concept for Indian consumer (rural and urban both) although both are aware about it but it is still a new concept.
- To introducing the consumers with green concept and Sustainable Development efforts are necessary. Indians faith in "Ayurvedic and Desi herbal treatment" so they are familiar with the herbal and green products. They are already using the herbal items in their kitchen, beauty treatment and in many diseases. They also use the natural fresh food items in their routine lifestyle and also believe in "yoga and pranayam." So Indian customers are already aware about organic food items so its future is bright.
- Green product by corporate sector is a new term, so it take some time for adopting. It is a long term investment matter for business but its future is bright.
- The marketers focusing on customers and introducing them that why they are using green products or shift from other branch by green products/ organic products. If they satisfy the customers, the customer also ready to adopt the green new products.
- Produce reusable items
- Give the protection to recycling industries

Aftermath of Climate Change

- Protection the environment within the framework of legislation
- Research to solve the problems of environmental issues
- Creation of environmental awareness among all sectors of population

Solutions for environment friendly industrialization

There is a need for the adoption of new technologies in the industry. The new technology open the door of new and growing economies and their impact is also positively on economies but there is some threats is also.

There are some examples that are the solutions of environment friendly industrialization like –

- For the continued growth, protect the environment by their commercial activities.
- Adopt the environment friendly process.
- Reducing the impact of social pressure by satisfied their social environmental problems.
- Improving the management of change.
- Making the long term programme for society and environment.
- Promote the recycling activities. eg -
- Production will be able to recycled.
- Production from recycled material.
- Many of products made from biodegradable material eg.– bamboo .
- Products being repairable and not like through away.
- Not contain the depleting substances in production process. Etc
- All process of manufacturing is in sustainable way.

By the awareness of government and consumers more efforts are implemented for sustainable business.

Manufacturers are able to make the product attractive for consumer by their features. Now a days companies are trying to shift towards sustainable development. Eg – they start to using biodegradable packaging material and trying reduces the transportation, energy, water etc.

Conclusion :

As a conclusion first the marketers being genuine about protection of environment and fulfill their green campaign and Sustainable Development. Companies all business policies and manufacturing process are consist with green concept or environment friendly activities. Marketers are not only do the publicity that their product are environment friendly. In other hand also educate the customers that why they run with ecological products and why they pay more for these products, How there health becoming safe and their next generation will also sustain and leave with pleasure. If marketers able to satisfy their views about green concept than this green campaign will become successful and be able to save the environment from pollution.

References

- Greg skeleton , sustainable development and the chemical industry,(1996),Contribution of the Chemical Industry to Sustainable Development ,ICCA , 2-5
- LI Yong (2015), "Director General's keynote speech at the UNIDO Seminar on Sustainable Industrialization,l", Proc. of the 8th Symposium on Operating
- System Principles , 6-7
- S. Erkman (1997), "Industrial ecology: an historical view", . Cleaner Prod. Vol. 5, No. 1-2, ELSEVIER, pp. 1-10
- Prof. Dr. Jingfu Guo and Li Cai (2011)," Research on the Comparison between Traditional Industry and Ecological Industry", Far East Research Centre.,36-42
- LI Yong (2014)," Inclusive and Sustainable Industrial Development",UNIDO, 10-40.
- L. N.

**Assistant Professor,
Deptt.of Economics,
J.N.V.University,Jodhpur
email : genwajnvu@gmail.com**

14. Sustainable Development Goals from a Gender Equality Perspective

Dr. Aruna Kumari Paliya

Abstract

The 2030 Agenda for Sustainable Development is a landmark agreement negotiated and approved by the 193 Member States of the United Nations. Comprised of 17 Sustainable Development Goals (SDGs), 169 targets and232 indicators, it aims to address the economic, social, environmental and political dimensions of sustainable development in a comprehensive and integrated way. The SDG Agenda is clear that achieving gender equality is not only an important goal in and of itself but also a catalyst for achieving a sustainable future for all. Progress on gender equality has been highly uneven across the different dimensions of the 2030 Agenda.

In some areas, such as girls' access to education, global improvement is undeniable yet insufficient, often leaving behind women and girls in the poorest households (SDG 4). In areas such as labour force participation (SDG8) and innovation and knowledge creation (SDG 9), significant gender gaps remain and progress has been minimal. In other cases, such as maternal mortality (SDG 3), progress is too slow and uneven to achieve SDG Target 3.1 by 2030. Similarly, while progress has been made towards eliminating the practice of female genital mutilation (FGM) (SDG 5), this is not enough to keep up with population growth, meaning the number of women and girls undergoing FGM is likely to rise over the next 15 years. Unless progress on gender equality is accelerated, the global community will not only fail to achieve SDG 5, it will also forgo the catalytic effect that gender equality can have for the achievement of the 2030 Agenda more broadly.

This paper shows that across countries and regions, women and girls face tremendous structural barriers that impact all aspects of their lives. Eliminating gender-specific constraints, as well as other forms of discrimination with which they intersect, is hence critical.

Keywords : *SDG, Development, Gender Equality, Issues, Challenges, India, World*

Introduction

Sustainable Development is a landmark agreement negotiated and approved by the 193 Member States of the United Nations. Comprised of 17 Sustainable Development Goals (SDGs), 169 targets and232 indicators, it aims to address the economic, social, environmental and political dimensions of sustainable development in a comprehensive and integrated way. Building on a long history of international human rights and gender equality commitments, its universal approach recognizes the common challenges faced by all countries, developed and developing alike, and reaffirms the responsibility of governments to address them. The 2030 Agenda is clear that achieving gender equality is not only an important goal in and of itself but also a catalyst for achieving a sustainable future for all.

This state of affairs presents a real test for the 2030 Agenda. At the same time, the mere fact that UN Member States have agreed to strive for a more equal world where development is based on sustainability, peace and human progress provides reason to be cautiously optimistic. The SDGs are especially important now as both a political agenda for global cooperation and a specific, time-bound set of goals for all countries.

Women and girls are half of the world's population and as a result hold half of the world's human potential. When their lives are improved, the benefits reverberate across society. Access to decent work and regular income in the handsof women, for example, contribute not only to poverty reduction (SDG 1) but also support better education, health and nutrition outcomes for women and girls and those who depend on them (SDGs 2, 3 and 4). Similarly, eliminating all forms of violence against women and girls (Target 5.2) is not only an essential component of SDG 5 but also critical to ensuring healthy lives and well-being for people of all ages (SDG 3). Women subjected to sexual or physical intimate partner violence are 1.5 times as likely to become infected with HIV (Target 3.3). They are also almost twice as likely to experience depression and alcohol use disorders (Target 3.5). The health consequences of violence against women and girls extend to their children, who may witness the abuse and suffer long-term trauma that impacts their physical, emotional and social development.

Unless progress on gender equality is accelerated, the global community will not only fail to achieve SDG 5, it will also forgo the catalytic effect that gender equality can have for the achievement of the 2030 Agenda more broadly. Thispaper shows that across countries and regions, women and girls face tremendous structural barriers that impact all aspects of their lives. Eliminating gender-specific constraints, as well as other forms of discrimination with which they intersect, is hence critical.

Sustainable Development Goals from a Gender Equality Perspective

Gender equality is a prerequisite to achieving equality between the sexes. Over the past 25 years, progress has been made through, for example, legislation prohibiting discrimination based on sex with respect to inheritance and citizenship, laws that guarantee equality within the family and laws that address domestic violence. However, while progress has been significant, discriminatory constitutional and legislative provisions remain in place in many countries, leaving women without protection or legal basis to claim their rights.

Under international human rights law and agreements, notably the Convention on the Elimination of All Forms of Discrimination against Women (CEDAW) and the Beijing Declaration and Platform for Action, States have committed to eliminating discrimination against women and promoting gender equality, including in the area of legal frameworks. The five-year review and appraisal of the Beijing Platform for Action (Beijing + 5) established 2005as the target date for the repeal of laws that discriminate against women. This deadline has come and gone and still data from 2016 show that in 18 countries husbands can legally prevent their wives from working, in 39 countries daughters and sons do not have equal inheritance rights, laws protecting women from domestic violence are lacking in 49 countries and in 37 countries rape perpetrators are exempt from prosecution if they are married to or subsequently marry the victim.

1 in 5 women and girls aged 15-49 reported experiencing physical and/or sexual violenceby an intimate partner in the previous 12

months. Available comparable data from 87 countries show that 19% of women and girls aged 15–49 have experienced physical and/or sexual violence by an intimate partner in the past 12 months.Oceania (excluding Australia and New Zealand) is the region with the highest 12-month prevalenceof intimate partner violence (IPV), with up to 40% of women aged 15–49 reporting having experienced this. Women in the same age group living in Europe and Northern America had thelowest prevalence rate, estimated at 6%.

Trend data on violence against women and girls are not widely available. Surveys are often only available for one point in time or use different methodologies, hindering comparability over time between and within countries. Comparable data for 17 countries on prevalence of physical or sexual IPV against women (aged 15–49) in the 12 months prior to the survey suggests prevalence is generally falling, especially in countries with the highest prevalence. In the Democratic Republic of the Congo, for example, there was a significant decrease from 59% (2007) to 37% (2013–2014). Despite the general downward trend, however, a statistically significant increase in IPV prevalence is observed in 5 of the 17 countries. For example, in the Dominican Republic, prevalence rose from 12% in 2007 to 16% in 2013.

Women and girls of all ages are vulnerable to violence. Based on comparable data from 50 countries, an estimated 15 million adolescent girls (aged 15–19) report experiencing forced sex in their lifetime. Data from 28 countries also show that 9 in 10 adolescent girls who have experienced forced sex report being victimized by someone close or known to them. In addition, adolescent girls and young women face the risk of violence in other settings such as in school or on university campuses. It is estimated that 246 million girls and boys globally have experienced school-related violence and one in four girls report never feeling safe using school latrines. In a survey across 27 universities in the UnitedStates in 2015, 23% of female undergraduate university students reported having experienced sexual assault or sexual misconduct.

Every year, 15 million girls under the age of 18 are forced into marriage. According to 2017 figures, an estimated 750 million women and girls were married before the age of 18. Every year, 15 million girls under the age of 18 are forced into marriage. Unless progress on this target is accelerated, the figure will grow to 16.5 millionin 2030 and to over 18 million in 2050.Amongregions with available data, Central and Southern Asia has the highest rates of child marriage, with 16 per cent of women currently aged 20–24 married before they turned 15 and 43 per cent before age 18, while Eastern and South-eastern Asia and Europe and Northern America have the lowest child marriage prevalence rates at 15% and 8%, respectively. Similarly, these regions also register the lowest rates of marriage before age 15, at 2% and 0%, respectively.

Women do 2.6 times the unpaid care and domestic work that men do. Data from 83 countries and areas show that women perform most of the domestic work, such as cooking and cleaning, and are the main caregivers of children and adults needing care. Women on average spend 18% of their day on total unpaid care and domestic work, while men allocate 7% of their day. Disaggregated by age, the time spent on unpaid care and domestic work is highest among women aged 25–44, compared to women aged 15–24 and 45–64. This peak in the care burden for women coincides with the period during which they are most likely to have young children at home. Where data are available, the evidence points to women with younger children doing more unpaid work, including care work, than those without children. Differences among women also vary by other factors including household income, whether there is access to drinking water and fuel in the home, and policies related to childcare.

The expectation that care work is women's responsibility starts at an early age. A study of 33 countries shows that girls aged 7–14 do more household work than boys the same age and perform other tasks, including care of younger siblings. The division of labour into 'women's work' and 'men's work' continues for many women as they start their own families and reverberates into the workforce (SDG 8). Gender stereotypes influence the kind of work women do outside of the home, the conditions under which that work is offered and the payment they receive. It also impacts women's ability to engage in other aspects of public life, including political participation (Target 5.5).

Despite progress, women remain under-represented in parliaments worldwide. While there has been progress over the last decade, women continue to be under-represented in parliaments worldwide. Globally, women hold 23.7% of parliamentary seats, an increase of 10 percentage points since 2000. At the country level, only in Rwanda (61%) and the Plurinational State of Bolivia (53%) do women occupy more seats in parliament than men. The use of electoral gender quotas and other temporary special measures has raised the shares of women's representation in national decision-making bodies in many countries. In sub-Saharan Africa, quotas have been shown to increase women's representation in politics, while countries in the region with few quotas experienced considerable setbacks in 2016. In Latin America, gender quotas, coupled with quotas targeting racial minorities, have increased the representation of traditional marginalized groups. Yet, despite the demonstrated impact, less than half of countries around the world have some form of legislated quota in place. While quotas and other TSMs are effective at promoting women's political representation, periodic reviews are needed to ensure they do not inadvertently impose a ceiling on women's representation.

Women are under-represented in senior and middle management positions in all countries with available data. In terms of decision-making power within government, large enterprises and institutions, women are under-represented in senior management and middle management positions. Despite some progress, the proportion of women in senior and middle management remains below 50% in all countries except the Dominican Republic, where it reached almost 53% in 2015. Globally, less than a third of senior and middle management positions are held by women. Due to break in statistical series (e.g., based on revisions to methodology), change in the female share of employment in senior and middle management is difficult to assess with certainty. Nevertheless, trend data, available for 35 countries, point to improvements in some countries but falling shares in others. Over the last decade, 11 countries have seen the proportion of women in senior and middle management increase by 7.4 percentage points on average. However, the proportion declined (by more than 3 percentage points) in 8 countries.In another 16 countries, the change in the share of women in managerial positions has not exceeded 3 percentage point.

Women and adolescent girls face many challenges and risks with respect to their sexual and reproductive health and rights. Only 52% of women married or in a union freely make their own decisions about sexual relations, contraceptive use and health careAt present, there is no comprehensive global database on laws regarding sexual and reproductive health and reproductive rights, but data on women's autonomy in decision-making regarding their sexual and reproductive health and rights are available for a subset of countries. Based on data from 45countries, mostly in sub-Saharan Africa, only 52% of women aged 15–49 there who are married or in union make their own informed decisions about sexual relations and the use of contraceptives and health services.

For adolescent girls, in addition to barriers to access, sexual and reproductive health and rights are also compromised by lack of comprehensive sexuality education and harmful practices. Complications related to childbirth and pregnancy are among the leading causes of death for girls aged 15–19. States have an obligation to provide accessible, quality and affordable sexual and reproductive health services. Yet, even when services are available, cost is often a hurdle that women find difficult to overcome. In a sample of 65 countries, cost was repeatedly identified as a factor that hampered women's ability to access health care. For example, this was the case for 11% of women in Egypt and 86% in São Tomé and Príncipe.

Data on women's role in the agricultural sector point to deep gender inequalities. Women are far less likely to be agricultural land holders: Their share ranges from0.8% in Saudi Arabia to 51% in Cabo Verde, with an overall global share of 12.8%. Available evidence shows that, when women own land, their plots are generally smaller and of lower quality than men's and their rights to the land are less secure.

Women lag behind men in Internet access and mobile phone ownership. Access to the Internet is increasing exponentially. The technology is being used to communicate and share information in school settings, in workplaces and at home. But women are not being reached at the same pace as men. In 2017, the proportion of women using the Internet globally was 5.9 percentage points lower than men's. Eastern and South- eastern Asia has the largest gender gap: Only 28% of women had access to the Internet in comparison to 42% of men. In Europe and Northern America, where Internet penetration is high for both women and men, usage among women (75%) was lower than among men (82%). Only in Latin America andthe Caribbean region were women's usage rates higher than men's: 67% compared to 65%.Despite the potential benefits, an estimated 1.7 billion women in low- and middle-income countries do not own a mobile phone: Women are 14% less likely than men to own one.

Conclusion

Progress on gender equality has been highly uneven across the different dimensions of the 2030 Agenda. In some areas, such as girls' access to education, global improvement is undeniable yet insufficient, often leaving behind women and girls in the poorest households (SDG 4). In areas such as labour force participation (SDG8) and innovation and knowledge creation (SDG 9), significant gender gaps remain and progress has been minimal. In other cases, such as maternal mortality (SDG 3), progress is too slow and uneven to achieve SDG Target 3.1 by 2030. Similarly, while progress has been made towards eliminating the practice of female genital mutilation (FGM) (SDG 5), this is not enough to keep up with population growth, meaning the number of women and girls undergoing FGM is likely to rise over the next 15 years.

A revolution in democratic governance is needed for women and girls to claim their rights and shape sustainable development. Spaces for public debate and democratic decision-making must be created to define national priorities, identify what is working well and where the gaps are, agree on pathways for transformative change and determine the roles and responsibilities of different actors.

Delivering on the gender equality commitments of the 2030 Agenda requires mobilizing and allocating sufficient resources for policies and programmes that contribute to their achievement. As countries roll out their national implementation strategies, it is paramount that investments in these and other strategic areas are prioritized. It is also important that policies and programmes are aligned with the principles of the 2030 Agenda, including human rights principles such as equality, non-discrimination and universality.

Gender-responsive processes and institutions are critical to turn the gender equality promises of the 2030 Agenda into action and to ensure that progress is monitored in a transparent and accountable way. States have committed to follow-up and review processes that are open, inclusive, participatory and transparent, as well as people-centred, gender- sensitive, respectful of human rights and focused on those who are furthest behind.

References
- Budig, M .J. and J. Misra. 2010. "How Care-Work Employment Shapes Earnings in Cross-National Perspective." International Labour Review 149 (4): 441–460.
- Budlender, D. (Ed.). 2010. Time Use Studies and Unpaid Care Work. New York and Abingdon, UK: Routledge/ United Nations Research Institute for Social Development.
- Burt, Z., K. Nelson and I. Ray. 2016. "Towards Gender Equality through Sanitation Access." Discussion Paper No. 12. UN Women, New York.
- Chen, M. A. 2016. "Expanding the Economic Potential of Women Informal Workers."Background paper for the UN Secretary-General's High-Level Panel on Women's Economic Empowerment.
- Dayringer, S. 2015. "In the 2017 High-Level Political Forum on Sustainable Development: Civil Society Plays Key Role in Voluntary National Reviews and Coherence." Global Policy Watch.
- De Henau, J. 2015. "Costing a Feminist Plan for a Caring Economy: The Case of Free Universal Childcare in the UK." Open Discussion Papers in Economics No. 79, The Open University.

- De Henau, J., S. Himmelweit, Z. Lapniewska and D. Perrons. 2016. Investing in the Care Economy: A Gender Analysis of Employment Stimulus in Seven OECD Countries. Brussels: International Trade Union Confederation.
- Duflo, E. 2012."Women Empowerment and Economic Development." Journal of Economic Literature 50 (4): 1051–1079.
- Dyson, S. 2012. "Preventing Violence against Women and Girls: From Community Activism to Government Policy."Working Paper.Partners for Prevention, Bangkok.
- Ellsberg, M., D. J. Arango, M. Morton, F. Gennari et al. 2015. "Prevention of Violence against Women and Girls: What Does the Evidence Say?" The Lancet 385 (9987): 1555–1566.
- Elson, D. 2006. Budgeting for Women's Rights: Monitoring Government Budgets for Compliance with CEDAW. New York: United Nations Development Fund for Women (UNIFEM).
- Esquivel, V. 2016. "Power and Sustainable Development Goals: A Feminist Analysis." Gender & Development 24 (1): 9–23.
- FAO. 2010. "Gender and Land Rights: Understanding Complexities; Adjusting Policies." Economic and Social Perspectives Policy Brief. FAO, Rome.
- GSMA. 2015. Connected Women 2015: Bridging the Gender Gap – Mobile Access and Usage in Low- and Middle-Income Countries. London: GSMA.
- Hansford, F. 2016. "Gender Bias in Intra-Household Resource Allocation: Who Wins and Loses, Who Decides, and How Can Public Action Help?
- ILO. 2008. "Can Low Income Countries Afford Basic Social Security?" Social Security Policy Briefing No. 3. ILO, Geneva
- IMF. 2007. World Economic Outlook: Globalization and Inequality. Washington, DC: IMF.
- Kabeer, N. 2003. Gender Mainstreaming in Poverty Eradication and the Millennium Development Goals: A Handbook for Policy-Makers and Other Stakeholders. London: Commonwealth Secretariat.

- Levien, M. 2017. "Gender and Land Dispossession: A Comparative Analysis." Discussion Paper No. 15. UN Women, New York.

Assistant Professor (Economics),
Govt. College Luni, Jodhpur
email : arunagenwa@gmail.com

15. Green and Smart Technology for Environmental Sustainability in India : An Overview

[1]Dr. Sama Jain*, [2]Dr. Varsha Saxena, [3]Dr. Neeraj Jain

Abstract

Environmental sustainability means conservation of natural resources with protection of global ecosystem by using green and smart technologies to support basic living standard of people in future. Green and Smart technology aspect is a multidisciplinary approach having a potential of energy saving idea and how to use materials in more profitable manner. By applying combination of different technologies, we can reduce 65-75% energy consumption and we can imagine that environmental friendly technology is one of the greatest challenges from engineering and social perspective.

Numerous technologies are pretend by human beings who show adverse effects on environment and civic life style. So it needs invention of new green and smart eco friendly technologies for supporting day to day activities of the present lifestyle. These new innovative technologies are more efficient due to increased consciousness and current advancement in research domains of energy and material management, which may also referred as green and clean technology. Therefore, by considering green and smart technology as the most innovatory step towards sustainable growth, this paper highlights about current latest advancement in technology along with pros and cons of these methods to create more suitable pace for moving faster and safer towards "Greener Earth" and "Greener Future"

Keywords : Green Technology, Smart Technology, Sustainability, Green Earth

1. Introduction
1.1 What is Technology
To have knowledge of combining resources to make a desired product, to solve any social problem in an economic manner can be

understood as technology. By using technical methods, we can fulfil needs and satisfy demands of common people. Technology includes technical methods, skills, processes, techniques, tools and raw resources by using machines, devices and factories. In this background, present state of technology is the use of math, science, and the arts for the benefit of life as it is known Technology.

1.2 What is Green Technology

If we combine traditional technology including science and maths concept with renewable energy resources and materials, it becomes green technology. Green Technology is an umbrella to combine technology and resources and systems which is used to conserve the natural environment and resources, which minimize and reduces the negative impact of human activities on environment. By this approach, the aim of green technology is to make environment eco-friendly and to minimize the degradation of the environment; It has zero or low greenhouse gas (GHG) emission which is safe for use and encourage healthy and better environment for all forms of life and existence; It preserve the use of energy and natural resources and capitals; It endorse the use of renewable resources of energy [1,2].

1.3 What is Smart Technology

The term "Smart" means self monitoring and analysis by using innovative machineries, mobile technology, web database techniques, wireless access, sensor technology etc. It can be also termed as clever technology to access any kind of technology which permits users to connect with internet.

Technological advances in the field of smart materials by adapting their properties due to variation of the electric or magnetic field and computational techniques have reached a point in which their synergy has a noteworthy impact on the applicability of the interdisciplinary concepts of smart technologies to real structures or smart structures. The material science has led to the theoretical and experimental development of multifunctional materials (e.g. piezoelectric stoneware, shape memory alloys, magneto rheological fluids (MRFs), and magneto attractive materials) [2,3,4]

A number of outstanding types of smart devices are smart phones, smart cars, smart thermostats, smart doorbells, smart locks, smart refrigerators, smart tablets, smart watches, smart bands, smart key chains, smart glasses, and many others are in use by using smart material concept.

2. Discussion

2.1 Pillars Of Green Technology :

Water purification, Recycling and waste management, Electric Automobiles, Solar Energy, Vertical gardens and farming, Nuclear power are some of the most important concept of green technology which are anticipated to protect environment and protect natural resources [4].

2.1.1 Water Purification :

There is an excessive and wasteful use of clean water. The Earth naturally recycles its water, but new technologies help to speed up the process. Water is the first main important need for all living being on the Earth Planet as well as for all types of industrial and agricultural growth. Our groundwater and surface water stores are at danger due to overuse in many areas. The demand is greater as compared to the amount supplied by rainwater and snowmelt. It is also observed that more than 80 percent of the wastewater generated by the public flows back into the environment without being treated or reused.

Water purification is a step by step processes used to make the water more suitable for the end users in terms of drinking water, industrial use, medical use and also for other uses by removing various pollutants. General Green methods for water purification are Settling, filtration, disinfection, coagulation are some of the basic physical and chemical processes employed for water treatment along with aerated lagoons, activated sludge or slow sand filter are some high-flying practices [5].

2.1.2 Recycling and waste management :

New advancements in green technology are designed to help manage and recycle waste material.

A waste management system is **a strategy approach of maintaining reduces, reuse, and prevent waste**. Possible waste disposal Green methods are recycling, composting, incineration, landfills, bioremediation, waste to energy, and waste minimization.

In one of the most prominent techniques of waste management, waste is converted into plastic fraction as liquid for further use as fuel. Another green method by using some chemicals is an innovative approach that uses chemicals to break down plastic waste into its valuable chemical components. These components can then be used as fuel or converted once again into new plastic products which can be further used as liquid fuel [6].

2.1.3 Electric Automobiles :

Automobile sector is one of the biggest sectors for threatening of Environmental sustainability as so many people depends on consumption of non renewable fossil fuel like petrol and diesel. To overcome this situation, alternative fuel vehicle also called as green vehicle, have been introduced by using innovative technology so that it is less harmful to the environment. The universal customer consensus is that EVs have environmental benefits because they emit a smaller amount amount of carbon dioxide than conventional vehicles; this makes them a plausible alternative. The implementation of EVs, especially battery electric vehicles, is considered a solution to the energy crisis and environmental issues. Key features regarding this technology is powerful batteries, charging methods, electric motors and control and charging infrastructure, safety parameters of EVs, reliability and efficiency of vehicle.

2.1.4 Solar Energy :

Energy received from natural resources that are replenished at a higher rate than they are consumed is termed as renewable energy resources. The main five types of such energy resources are Solar energy from the sun, Geothermal energy from heat inside the earth, Wind energy, Biomass from plants and Hydropower from flowing water. These resources are plentiful and all around us. Out of all these five resources, solar power is rapidly fetching a major competitor in the race for renewable power. About 85-90 petawatts of power is available at any given point in time to common people. There is a variety of function of solar energy. For example solar energy can be tied together for water distillation through evaporation [7]

2.1.5 Vertical gardens and farms :

This concept of vertical farming rather than horizontal farming was established to increase the food production so that rising demand can be fulfilled in an eco-friendly and more sustainable manner. Some of the vertical farms even don't necessitate soil, and decrease water use exponentially. This technology is useful in such areas, where lab availability is major trouble with high density of population to nourish overpopulated cities. Over the past few years, vertical farms have sprouted all over the world including places like Vancouver, Panama, Singapore, and cities in the UK and the U.S.

Advantages of Vertical Farming :
- It offers a map to handle future food demands.
- It permits crops to cultivate year-round.
- It utilizes considerably smaller amount water.
- No significant effect of weather condition.
- More organic crops can be developed.

Disadvantages of Vertical Farming :
- There is no effect of chemical and disease.
- It is a costly method to construct establishes such farming areas.
- Pollination would be very difficult and costly.
- It would engage higher labour costs.
- It is completely based on technology.

2.1.6 Nuclear Power :

Nuclear energy **originates from the splitting of nuclear atoms like uranium atoms by a process called fission**. This produces heat to create steam, which is used by a turbine generator to generate electricity. Nuclear power plants do not burn fissile fuel; they do not produce greenhouse gas emissions. Nuclear power has low cost of operation, as it requires initial cost of construction; Reliable and stable Source of Energy; No pollution and It Has High Energy Density. Nuclear energy cares for air quality by producing enormous amounts of carbon-free electricity [7,8].

2.2 Pillars of Smart Technology Policy :

Smart technologies are being developed, urbanized and used to decrease greenhouse gas release. Smart IoT-based services are producing green benefits. Construction of buildings with net zero carbon emissions and efficient energy usage are on get higher needs. Technologies related to smart agriculture are also helping to make the environment more sustainable. **Smart technology** is a **technology** which uses big data analysis, machine learning, and artificial intelligence to provide cognitive awareness to the objects which were in the past considered as inanimate [8,9]

2.2.1 Smart energy :

Smart energy is **the process of using devices for energy-efficiency**. It Focuses on powerful, sustainable renewable energy sources that promote greater eco-friendliness while driving down costs.

Both residential and commercial buildings in smart cities are more efficient, using less energy, and the energy used is analyzed and data collected. Smart grids are part of the development of a smart city, and smart streetlights are an easy entry point for many cities, since LED lights save money and pay for themselves within a few years.

Smart grid solutions play an important role in the development of smart cities. From prepaid energy applications to advanced metering infrastructure, there are several solutions to enhance energy services. With a smart grid, you can improve outage detection, speed of data capture, continuing and disaster recovery, field service operations and overall grid modernization techniques," [9, 10,11]

2.2.2 Smart Transportation and Mobility :

Smart transportation is **an approach that incorporates modern technologies into transportation systems by** including cloud computing, wireless communication, location-based services, computer vision, and other tools to enhance mobility. A smart transportation arrangement is clean and well-organized. It **Reduces traffic overcrowding and results in cleaner air, less waste of time and reduced energy consumption**. And cities that are functioning to provide lodgings electric and, eventually, autonomous connected vehicles can expect to realize even greater environmental benefits. The main advantages of smart transportation are Adaptive traffic signals which use timers and inductive loops to determine when the light should change as per condition, Smart pedestrian safety, Biking solutions, Parking solutions and Smart corridors etc.

2.2.3 Smart infrastructure :

Smart Infrastructures **consist of numerous operators from different domains of activity, like energy, public conveyance, and public safety**. They deploy and operate "cyber-physical systems", that are data-controlled equipment which interact with the physical world.

Top most Benefits of Smart Buildings is it Reduce Energy Consumption, show predictive Maintenance with reduced cost, Automation is possible, working on Real-Time Data available and analyzed for effective working,

2.2.4 Smart IoT devices :

The Internet of Things (IoT) is generally referred to as a smart machine or device or network of devices, **which have the capability to connect to the internet, gather information and exchange data with other devices**. There are several top devices in the market working on this technology like **Smart Mobiles, Smart refrigerators, Smart watches, Smart fire alarms, Smart door locks, smart bicycles, medical sensors, fitness trackers, smart security system**, etc

The major Advantages of IoT smart devices are it improves productivity of staff and reduced human labour. Efficiency of operation management is improves, it ensures better use of resources and assets with Cost-effective operation and safety. These devices are very much helpful to develop marketing and business development strategies by improving customer service and retention along with better business opportunities.

3. Advantages and Disadvantages of Green and Smart Technology

3.1 Advantages : Green and Smart Technology does not emit anything harmful into the air. These can bring economic benefits to almost all areas and requires less maintenance cost. The major benefit is, it is renewable which means we will never run out and can slow the special effects of global warming by reducing CO_2 Emissions [12, 13]

3.2 Disadvantages : The biggest disadvantage is high implementing costs involving advanced material and devices. Lack of information regarding alternative process technology is also a major outbreak. Skilled human resources with digital parameters is again one more need in this area [12,13, 14]

Conclusion : Attaining Environmental Sustainability via Green technologies

It is clear from above discussion that Green and Smart Technology is an essential need to achieve environmental sustainability and also to lead sustainable life as conventional technology is not satisfactory and challenging sustainability of today's environment. The development of eco-friendly and reasonable technical solution is not therefore, a question of choice, but the need of hour, which can be resolved by adopting Green and Smart technical aspects only.

Despite the negative impact of technology on environment, a fresh increase in global distress for climate change has led to the development of new environmental technology aiming to help solve some of the biggest environmental concerns that we face as a society through a shift towards a more sustainable, low-carbon economy.

6. Acknowledgements :

Authors are highly grateful to all organizers of ICMSDC-2022 for giving us this opportunity to present our paper in their esteemed conference.

Reference

[1] https://en.wikipedia.org/wiki/Technology
[2] http://www.gpnm.org/e/articles/Definition-of-Green-Technology-by-KETTHA-Ministry-of-Energy-Green-Technology-and-Water-a5.html
[3] http://mylive007.blogspot.in/2012/09/green-technology.html
[4] Recent Research in Science and Technology 2014, 6(1): 97-100 ISSN: 2076-5061 Available Online: http://recent-science.com/
[5] www.ajcebeats.com/the-**importance-of-green-technology/**
[6] www.ajcebeats.com/the-importance-of-greentechnology/
[7] Monu Bhardwaj and Neelam (2015), The Advantages and Disadvantages of Green Technology, Journal of Basic and Applied Engineering Research, 2 (22); pp. 1957-1960.

[8] http://www.gpnm.org/e/articles/Definition-of-Green-Technology-by-KETTHA-Ministry-of-Energy-GreenTechnology-and-Water-a5.html
[9] Sustainability and Green Technology, An e-book on strategies for sustainability authored by the Class of 2012 Massachusetts Academy of Mathematics and Science.
[10] http://www.wbcsd.org/plugins/DocSearch/details.asp?MenuId=NjA&ClickMenu=Lefenu&doOpen=1&type=DocDet&ObjectId=Mjc4NTc.
[11] http://www.unapcaem.org/publication/greentech.pdf
[12] http://www.nedcap.org/index_files/ Page2210.htm.
[13] http://indianexpress.com/article/india/indias-solarpower-capacity-crosses-9-gw 4510799/
[14] http://mnre.gov.in/schemes/grid-connected/solarthermal-2/

[1*]Professor,
Department of Chemistry,
Poornima Institute of Engineering and Technology, Jaipur
[2]Assistant Professor,
Department of Chemistry,
Sri Sathya Sai College for Women, Bhopal
[3]Professor,
Department of Physics,
Poornima College of Engineering, Jaipur
ISI-2, RIICO Institutional Area, Jaipur
email : *sama.jain@poornima.org*

Aftermath of Climate Change

16. भारत में जल संकट एवं सतत विकास के लिए संरक्षण के उपाय

डॉ. नीरज कारगवाल

सारांश

'जल ही जीवन है' मनुष्य सहित वनस्पति और सभी प्राणियों के जीवन का आधार जल है। लेकिन वर्तमान में जल संकट गहराता जा रहा है क्योंकि स्वच्छ पेयजल उपलब्ध नहीं हो रहा है। भारत में जल संसाधन का वितरण अपर्याप्त और असमान पाया जाता है। भारत की भूजल तालिका प्रतिवर्ष लगभग तीस सेमी की दर से घट रही है। भारत में जलसंकट अविवेकपूर्ण और अनियोजित विकास का परिणाम है तथा जनसंख्या विस्फोट, औद्योगीकरण और नगरीकरण, सिंचित क्षेत्र में वृद्धि, घटते वन क्षेत्र, जलवायु परिवर्तन और वर्षाजल संग्रहण नहीं करने के कारण भी जल संकट बढ़ता जा रहा है। रसायनिक अपशिष्ट, उर्वरक अतिप्रयोग, प्रदूषण के कारण जल की गुणवत्ता में भारी गिरावट हुई है। इस जल प्रदूषण का पारिस्थितिक तन्त्र पर नकारात्मक प्रभाव पड़ रहा है। जल स्रोतों के सूखने, भू-जल तालिका में तेजी से कमी, सूखे की पुनरावृत्ति और विभिन्न राज्यों में जल प्रबंधन सम्बंधित समस्या सामाजिक- आर्थिक चुनौतियाँ पेश कर रहे हैं। सतत विकास के लिए हमें जल संचयन प्रणालियों को पुनर्जीवित और संरक्षित करने की आवश्यकता है। भारत में नियोजित कुएँ और नहर प्रणालियाँ, जोहड़, तालाब, बावडी, टांके आदि परम्परागत जल संरक्षण विधियों का प्रचलन रहा है। जल संरक्षण प्रोत्साहन के लिए शुष्क क्षेत्रों में वर्षाजल प्रबन्धन, वाटर हार्वेस्टिंग संरचना निर्माण, जन जागरूकता और इको फ्रेंडली प्रौद्योगिकी का उपयोग भी सहायक होगा। घरेलू और औद्योगिक अपशिष्ट जल का उचित उपचार और ग्रे वाटर का प्रयोग सुनिश्चित करना भी आवश्यक है। विश्व बैंक के एकीकृत दृष्टिकोण को बढ़ावा देना, जिसका उद्देश्य जलवायु परिवर्तन के प्रभाव को न्यून करना और जल-संसाधन वितरण का सतत विकास हेतु प्रबंधन करना आवश्यक है।

मूलबिंदु : सतत विकास   जलसंकट   वर्षाजल प्रबन्धन

अनुसन्धान के उद्देश्य

➤ यह शोध लेख भारत में बढ़ते जल संकट के बारे में व्याख्यान करता है।

➤ जल संकट का समाज, कृषि एवं पर्यावरण पर प्रभाव का विश्लेषणात्मक अध्ययन करना।

➤ सतत विकास की आवश्यकता का अध्ययन करना।

➤ सतत विकास हेतु जल संरक्षण उपायों का अध्ययन करना।

अनुसंधान क्रियाविधि

यह शोध पत्र भारत में जल संकट के प्रभावों एवं सतत विकास के लिए

Aftermath of Climate Change

संरक्षण के उपाय पर अध्ययन के लिए विभिन्न पत्रिकाओं, शोध लेखों, वेबसाइटों, विभिन्न स्रोतों से प्रकाशित आंकड़ों से एकत्रित द्वितीयक आंकड़ों पर आधारित है। इंटरनेट पर उपलब्ध इस विषय पर विभिन्न अध्ययनों का भी इस शोध पत्र में उल्लेख किया गया है।

भारत में जल संकट

जल संकट देश के विकास को प्रभावित करने वाले प्रमुख कारणों में से एक है क्योंकि आज भी देश के लाखों लोगों को स्वच्छ पेयजल और सफाई के लिए साफ पानी नहीं मिल पाता है। भारत में प्रति व्यक्ति पानी की उपलब्धता काफी कम है। देश में अधिक जनसंख्या के कारण जल संसाधनों पर और अधिक दबाव पड़ा है। अविवेकपूर्ण प्राकृतिक संसाधनों के दोहन और अंधाधुन विकास की दौड़ ने इस तनाव को और बढ़ा दिया है। जल संकट प्राकृतिक कारकों के प्रभाव तथा मानव निर्मित आपदाओं का परिणाम माना जाता है। भारत के अनेक राज्य सूखा प्रभावित रहते हैं जहां जल का कूप्रबंधन, जलवायु परिवर्तन, संकट को अधिक गंभीर बना देते हैं। विगत वर्षों में देश के उत्तर पश्चिमी और मध्यवर्ती राज्यों में इसका व्यापक प्रभाव देखा गया है। यदि समय रहते जल संकट को प्रभावी ढंग से हल नहीं किया जाता, तो संभावना है कि विभिन्न राज्यों में जल संसाधन एक स्तर और नीचे चला जाएगा, जहां से प्रतिदिन दैनिक आवश्यकता पूर्ति के लिए लोगों के पास पर्याप्त जल उपलब्ध होना मुश्किल होगा। भारत के विभिन्न क्षेत्रों विशेषकर शुष्क और अर्ध शुष्क प्रदेशों में जल की गुणवत्ता बहुत अच्छी नहीं है। इन क्षेत्रों के जल में भारी धातु तत्व, रसायन, लवण, फ्लोराइड आदि पाए जाते हैं। इससे स्वास्थ्य पर प्रतिकूल प्रभाव पड़ता है साथ ही कृषि उत्पादन में भी काफी गिरावट आती है। पर्यावरण पर भी कम गुणवत्ता वाले जल का नकारात्मक प्रभाव पड़ता है। जल संसाधन की कमी का अप्रत्यक्ष प्रभाव देश के मानव संसाधन विकास सूचकांक पर भी पड़ता है केंद्र एवं राज्य की सरकारें भी समय-समय बजट आवंटन को स्वीकृति देने के बाद भी जल के मुद्दे का उचित प्रबंधन करने में असफल रही हैं। इस का कारण उचित बुनियादी ढांचे की कमी और विस्तृत क्षेत्रफल पर कार्यरूप योजनाओं को लागू करने का समयबद्ध और सतत प्रयास की कमी होना।

जल संकट का समाज, कृषि एवं पर्यावरण पर प्रभाव

भारत में कई इलाके ऐसे भी हैं जहां पानी तो है, लेकिन पाइपलाइन नहीं है। ऐसे में उन्हें विभिन्न स्रोतों से पानी लेने के लिए महिलाओं को घर से दूर जाना पड़ता है। इससे न केवल उनका सामान्य जीवन प्रभावित होता है, बल्कि लड़कियों की पढ़ाई तक छूट जाती है। ऐसा दुनिया के अन्य देशों में तो हो ही रहा है, साथ ही भारत में भी बड़े पैमाने पर होता है। जल संकट का नकारात्मक प्रभाव यह भी है कि इस समस्या ने समाज के विभिन्न वर्गों और राज्यों के मध्य तनाव तथा विवादों को बढ़ाया है।

पिछले कुछ दशकों से भारत के विभिन्न राज्यों में कृषि समुदाय को जल

की कमी ने प्रतिकूल रूप से प्रभावित किया है। लगातार जल संबंधी समस्याएं होना यथा–अनियमित वर्षा का होना, जल के कुप्रबंधन, असामान्य फसल पद्धति आदि के कारण कृषकों को काफी नुकसान हुआ है। फसलों के नुकसान और बढ़ते कर्ज ने कई किसानों को पलायन के लिए मजबूर कर दिया है। इसके साथ ही जल की कमी पशुपालन एवं दुग्ध उत्पादन पर भी प्रतिकूल प्रभाव डालती है। भारत में आज भी किसानों को फसलों की सिंचाई के लिए बड़े पैमाने पर मानसून पर निर्भर रहना पड़ता है सिंचाई परियोजनाओं पर बारिश की कमी से गंभीर प्रभाव पड़ता है। भारत में सर्वकालिक नदियां बढ़ती जनसंख्या और अत्यधिक प्रदूषण से निपटने में असमर्थ हो रही हैं। यह कारक देश हर की नदियों की कार्यप्रणाली एवं पारिस्थितिक तन्त्र को प्रभावित कर रहा है।

सतत विकास की आवश्यकता

मानव ने तकनीकी उन्नति और उर्जा संसाधनों के उपयोग की सहायता से बहुत से आविष्कार और खोज की है, जिससे उसका जीवन अधिकाधिक आरामदायक हो गया है। आज हम तकनीक, खनिज पदार्थों और उर्जा संसाधनों के बगैर जीवन के विषय में सोच भी नहीं सकते। यह बड़े पैमाने पर लगभग हर क्षेत्र में प्रवेश कर गया है चाहे वह कृषि, उद्योग, यातायात, संचार और घरेलू हो। आज की स्थिति में हमारी पारिस्थितिकी भी खतरे में है। अगर हम इसी तरह दोहन करते रहे तो अगले 100 वर्षों में अधिकतर खनिज और संसाधन समाप्त हो जाएगें।मानवीय लापरवाही और स्वार्थ के कारण ये प्राकृतिक संसाधन इस सीमा तक विकृत हो गए हैं कि इनका नवीनीकरण बहुत कठिन है। संयुक्त राष्ट्र पर्यावरण और विकास आयोग द्वारा 1987 में तैयार की गई, रिपोर्ट का शीर्षक था ''हमारा साझा भविष्य''। प्रारंभ में विश्व दो समूहो में विभाजित था–विकसित और विकासशील देश और इन्होंने आपस में एक दूसरे पर दोषारोपण करना शुरू कर दिया। विकसित देशों ने विकासशील देशों पर तीव्र जनसंख्या वृद्धि, गरीबी और प्रदूषण फैलाने वाली आदिम तकनीक के लिए दोष दिया। विकासशील देशों का तर्क था कि विकसित देशों की खर्चीली जीवन शैली ने उपलब्ध संसाधनों पर अत्यधिक दवाब डाल दिया है। लेकिन काफी जोरदार चर्चाओं और तर्कों के बाद यह अनुभव किया गया कि कुछ ऐसे समान आधार होने चाहिए जिनकी भविष्य में रक्षा करने पर विश्व एकमत हो। यह अनुभव किया गया कि पारिस्थितिकी, अर्थशास्त्र और तकनीक में संतुलन होना चाहिए। इसलिए ब्रुटलेंड आयोग ने सतत् पोषणीय विकास को इस प्रकार परिभाषित किया– ''भविष्य की पीढ़ियों की अपनी आवश्यकताओं की पूर्ति करने की क्षमता से बिना समझौता किए वर्तमान पीढ़ी की आवश्यकताओं की पूर्ति।'' दशकों पहले महात्मा गाँधी ने जिस रणनीति का सुझाव दिया उसे अब संसार में भी विकास के विशेषज्ञ अधिकाधिक स्वीकार करने लगे हैं। गाँधीजी की विकास की धारणा इस पर आधारित है कि प्रकृति लोगों की जरूरत को पूरा कर सकती है, उनके लालच को नहीं।

सतत् टिकाउ अथवा स्थाई विकास के अंतर्गत भावी पीढ़ियों के लिए

आवश्यकताओं की पूर्ति की क्षमताओं से समझौता किए बिना वर्तमान पीढ़ी की आवश्यकताओं को पूरा किया जाता है। अतः के बिना विकास और पर्यावरण सुरक्षा के साथ स्थाई संतुलन बनाए रखना ही निर्वहनीय या टिकाऊ विकास है। इसके पश्चात् पूँजी, कुशल श्रमिक एवं तकनीक आदि के प्रयोग के बावजूद यदि अधिकतम विकास का प्रयास किया जाए तो पर्यावरण को स्थाई रूप से क्षति पहुँचने लगती है। इस प्रकार विकास का यह स्तर लम्बे समय तक नहीं चल सकता। सतत् विकास की इस अवधारणा में पर्यावरण के अनुरूप विकास के साथ ही संसाधनों को भावी पीढ़ियों के लिए बचाए रखने पर भी ध्यान रखा जाता है। वर्तमान में यह विकास का एक भूमंडलीय दृष्टिकोण बन गया है। 1992 में पृथ्वी सम्मेलन में घोषित एजेंडा–21 (रियो घोषणा) में इसके प्रति पूर्ण समर्थन व्यक्त किया गया। 2002 ई. जोहांसबर्ग सम्मेलन का मूल मुद्दा ही सतत् विकास था।

सतत् विकास हेतु जल संरक्षण उपायों एवं जल प्रबन्ध

वार्षिक वर्षा जो हमारे देश में होती है, वह एक अनमोल संसाधन है। जल संचयन न केवल सूखे और बाढ़ों की संभावना को घटाता है, बल्कि वह समुदाय की भूमिगत जल पर निर्भरता को भी कम करता है, परन्तु भूमिगत जल के विपरीत, वर्षा का पानी अत्यन्त स्वच्छ है, जिसमें किसी भी प्रकार का खारापन या कृत्रिम तत्व नहीं पाये जाते हैं। इस कारण वर्षाजल सिंचाई, वाष्पीकरण, कूलरों, कपड़े धोने व अन्य कई कार्यों के लिये उपयुक्त हैं। सबसे पुरानी जल संचयन व्यवस्थाओं में एक हमारे ही देश के पश्चिमी घाटों के निकट स्थित पुणे शहर के पास पायी जाती है यहाँ पर पहाड़ी के पत्थरों में पेयजल प्रदान करने के लिये कई जलाशयों को खोद लिया गया था। रायगढ़ जैसे किलों में पानी के संरक्षण व संचयन के लिये टैंकों, तालाबों, इत्यादि का निर्माण हुआ था। ये जलाशय और कुएँ अभी भी प्रयोग में लाये जाते हैं, सिंधु घाटी सभ्यता की मोहनजोदड़ो और हड़प्पा नगरों के खंडहर शहरी पानी की आपूर्ति और नालियों की एक सुनियोजित व्यवस्था को दर्शाती है। वनों के पेड़–पौधे (वनस्पति) पानी को भूमि में रिस जाने में सहायक हैं। इस प्रकार वे जल तालिका का पुनःभरण करते हैं। वर्षाजल के संचयन की दो मुख्य तकनीकें हैं:– भूमि की सतह पर भविष्य में प्रयोग के उद्देश्य से किया गया वर्षा जल का संग्रहण और दूसरी तकनीक भूमिगत जल का ही पुनःभरण करना।

वर्षा के पानी को सतह पर ही संग्रहित कर लेना एक पारंपरिक तकनीक है और इसके लिये टैंकों, तालाबों, चौक–बांध, बैयरो जैसे जल कोषों का प्रयोग किया जाता था। भूमिगत जल का पुनःभरण वर्षा के पानी के संचयन की एक नयी संकल्पना है और प्रायः इसके लिये विभिन्न प्रकार के संरचनाओं (ढांचों) का प्रयोग किया जाता है। भारत के मरुस्थल अथवा अर्ध–मरुस्थल क्षेत्रों में, टांके और जोहड़ या टैंक प्रणाली की व्यवस्था पारंपरिक रूप से पेयजल तथा कृषि उत्पादन का आधार है। टैंकों का निर्माण भूमि में खुदाई करके, वर्षा जल का संग्रहण करके किया जाता है। राजस्थान के मरुस्थल प्रदेश में थोड़ी सी ही वर्षा होती है, परन्तु

Aftermath of Climate Change

यहाँ के लोगों ने इधर की जटिल परिस्थितियों में भी वर्षाजल एकत्रित करने का प्रयास किया। बड़े-बड़े जलाशय जिन्हें खादीन (झींकपद) कहते हैं, बांध जिन्हें जोहड़ कहते हैं एवं अन्य विधियों का प्रयोग जल प्रवाह को रोकने एवं एकत्रित जल प्रवाह के लिये प्रयोग किया जाता है। मानसून मौसम के अंत में, इन जलाशयों का पानी पौधों को सींचने के काम के प्रयोग में लाया गया। घरेलू स्तर पर जल संचयन अपनी संपत्ति पर गिरते वर्षा के पानी का संग्रहण है, जिसको बाद में अपने ही घर या उसके आँगन में किसी उपयोग में लाया जाता है। हमारे देश के कई घरों के मालिक वर्षा के पानी का पेड़ों, बागों इत्यादि को सिंचित करने में प्रयोग करते हैं।

शुष्क क्षेत्रों में जल अभाव एक प्रमुख समस्या है इसलिए कृषि कार्य हेतु ड्रिप इरिगेशन यानी बूंद सिंचाई प्रणाली का जल संरक्षण के लिए किया जाना लाभकारी है। इस प्रणाली की उत्पादकता और लाभ को देखते हुए सरकार ने अनुदान देने की घोषणा भी की है। इस सिंचाई प्रणाली में जल सीधे जड़ों में उपलब्ध कराया जाता है जिससे लगभग साठ प्रतिशत तक जल की बचत होती है। खरपतवार कम, श्रम की बचत, भूमि के पोषक तत्वों का अधिक उपयोग तथा पौधों की तीव्र वृद्धि में यह विधि बहुत उपयुक्त होती है। इसी प्रकार वाटर हार्वेस्टिंग जल प्रबंधन की ऐसी तकनीक है जिसके द्वारा हम वर्षा जल को अधिक से अधिक मात्रा में पौधों के लिए उपयोगी बनाते हैं। वर्षा का जल गड्ढों में एकत्र कर लिया जाता है और उसको वाष्पोत्सर्जन से बचाया जाता है। जिस समय पौधों को जल की अधिक आवश्यकता होती है तब उस पानी को उपलब्ध कराया जाता है। काजरी यानी केंद्रीय मरु क्षेत्र अनुसंधान संस्थान जोधपुर के अनुसार कम ढाल वाले केचमेंट एरिया के साथ जल वर्षा जल का समुचित प्रयोग में लाने के लिए और उसके संरक्षण के लिए वाटर हार्वेस्टिंग बहुत उपयुक्त होती है। यह मिट्टी में नमी की मात्रा वृद्धि करके उत्पादकता बढ़ाती है।

शुष्क क्षेत्रों में किसान अपने जीविका उपार्जन के लिए मोटे अनाज वाली फसलों की खेती करने को बाध्य है क्योंकि आर्थिक रूप से अधिक लाभप्रद नहीं होती और ना ही उत्पादक होती है। अतः अब आवश्यकता है कि किसान समय के साथ उपयोगी तथा जलवायु के अनुकूल खेती के तरीकों में परिवर्तन करें। शुष्क एवं अर्ध शुष्क क्षेत्रों में बागवानी फसलों विशेषकर फल उत्पादन द्वारा आर्थिक स्थिति में सुधार के लिए महत्वपूर्ण कार्य हो सकता है क्योंकि वृक्षों ने जल की कमी तथा सूखा सहन करने की क्षमता अनाज फसलों से अधिक होती है। वृक्षों में फसलों की अपेक्षा कीट आदि का प्रतिकूल प्रभाव भी कम रहता है। इसमें उर्वरक सिंचाई तथा अन्य निवेश की आवश्यकता भी कम होती है। इस प्रकार बागवानी फसलों से एक और बढ़ती हुई जनसंख्या को संतुलित आहार प्रदान करने में मदद मिलती है वहीं दूसरी ओर यह रोजगार के अवसर ज्यादा से ज्यादा उपलब्ध करा कर ग्रामीण अर्थव्यवस्था में सुधार का साधन बनती है।

निष्कर्ष एवं सुझाव

कृषि क्षेत्र में जल संकट की चुनौतियों से निपटने में देश की सहायता के

Aftermath of Climate Change

लिए वैज्ञानिकों और लोगों की संयुक्त भागीदारी पर बल दिया जाना चाहिए। किसानों के सहयोग से दशकों के उनके अनुभव और समग्र दृष्टिकोण से खेती को सुगम और सन धारणीय बनाया जा सकता है। भारत ने अगले पचास वर्षों में जीरो कार्बन उत्सर्जन का लक्ष्य निर्धारित किया है। पर्यावरण की सुरक्षा और जलवायु परिवर्तन से निपटने के लिए महत्वपूर्ण पृथ्वी ग्रह हितैषी जन आंदोलन चलाने की आवश्यकता है। इस अमृत काल में देश उच्च कृषि विकास के साथ-साथ समग्र विकास पर भी ध्यान केंद्रित कर रहा है। भारत में कृषि क्षेत्र के अंतर्गत लगी बड़ी जनसंख्या को गरीबी से बाहर निकालने और उन्हें बेहतर जीवन प्रदान करने की क्षमता कृषि विकास में मौजूद है। देश में किसानों को जलवायु परिवर्तन की समस्या से बचाने के लिए सरकार द्वारा प्राकृतिक कृषि और डिजिटल खेती पर जोर दिया जा रहा है। डिजिटल खेती के क्षेत्र में काफी संभावनाएं देखी जा रही है। युवाओं का इस आशय हेतु आह्वान किया जाना चाहिए कि वे नवीन तकनीको और नवाचार से किसानों की सहायता करें जिससे कृषि लागत कम हो सके तथा उत्पादकता बढ़ाई जा सके। प्रौद्योगिकी और आर्टिफिशियल इंटेलिजेंस (कृत्रिम बुद्धिमत्ता) के इस्तेमाल से ड्रोन के जरिए फसलों के अनुमान भूमि रिकॉर्ड के डिजिटल करण और कीटनाशकों तथा पोशाक उर्वरकों के छिड़काव का उल्लेखनीय प्रयास किया जा रहा है।

जल संरक्षण के लिए बड़े क्षेत्रों में सिंचाई की व्यवस्था की जा रही है और बड़े वाटर शेड में सर प्लस जल को दूसरे क्षेत्रों तक पहुंचाने की संभावनाओं पर कार्य योजना बनाई जा रही है। इसी आशय में भारत में विभिन्न नदियों को जोड़ा जा रहा है। इस प्रकार भारत में संधारणीय अर्थात सतत विकास के उद्देश्य की प्राप्ति के लिए जल संरक्षण के विभिन्न उपाय करके अभीष्ट की प्राप्ति की जा सकती है। पेरिस समझौते पर हस्ताक्षर करके भारत में स्थाई विकास के रास्ते पर आगे बढ़ने हेतु कदम उठाया है, इससे वर्तमान पीढ़ी के लिए ही नहीं बल्कि आगे आने वाली वीडियो के लिए भी देश में सुरक्षित स्वस्थ वातावरण बनाने में मदद मिलेगी। भारत में विकास निश्चत रूप से जल संकट निवारण करके ही संभव हो सकता है और इसके लिए जल की बचत, राज्य व केंद्र सरकार के सहयोग एवं समय रहते प्रभावी कदम उठाने की आवश्यकता है। स्वच्छ जल अथवा किसी भी प्राकृतिक संसाधन की कमी से राष्ट्र के समय, धन व श्रम का अधिकांश निवेश इनकी पूर्ति करने में करना पड़ता है। आज हमें अगली पीढ़ियों के लिए प्राकृतिक संसाधनों को बचाए रखने का अवसर प्राप्त हुआ है, इसके लिए स्थानीय और वैश्विक स्तर पर हमें पर्यावरणीय तथा प्राकृतिक संसाधनों के उपयोग को समानता, न्याय और पारिस्थितिक संतुलन ही तर्ज पर रखते हुए, विकास हेतु सर्वोत्तम प्रयास करने चाहिए। साथ ही हमें पर्यावरण से जुड़े कार्यक्रमों को बढ़ावा देने के अतिरिक्त, व्यक्तिगत, कानूनी तथा प्रबंध किए स्तर पर संगठित प्रयास क्यों पारदर्शी नवाचारों, जवाबदेह और मजबूत राजनीतिक इच्छाशक्ति के द्वारा इस विकट संकट से उबरने में हम कामयाब हो सकते हैं।

सन्दर्भ सूची

- शुष्क क्षेत्र – जल संग्रहण एस.सी. महनोत और पी.के. सिंह
- महाराष्ट्र और राजस्थान में जल संकट– वैभव चक्रवर्ती
- शोध कार्य डॉ. अल्पना शर्मा (वैज्ञानिक) ,भागवत प्रसाद पंड्रे (कार्यक्रम सहायक) कृषि विज्ञान केन्द्र, शहडोलज. ने. कृषि विश्व विद्यालय, जबलपुर
- योजना मासिक पत्रिका, भारत सरकार, नवम्बर 1998
- Faunal Heritage of Rajasthan, India: Conservation and Management of water*ISBN* 3319013459. SEP. 2017.
- Climate Change Modelling, Planning and Policy for Agriculture. ISBN 8132221575.
- Rajasthan Development Report. *P-306.* 2017.
- Climate Change and Agriculture Over India. ISBN 9788171884643.
- Talab Kahe Pukar Ke. *P- 177.* OCT. 2017.
- Geography of Rajasthan. ISBN 9781156482056.
- Plant Geography and Flora of Rajasthan. *P- 162.*
- New Dimensions in Agricultural Geography: Landuse and agricultural planning. ISBN 8170224047.

Websites :

https://hindi.indiawaterportal.org/content/
https://www.cgiar.org/cgiar-at-50/innovation-explorer/?innovation-category=climate
https://www.mygkbook.com/rajasthan-ka-bhugol/water-conservation-in
https://www.hindi.rajras.in/rajasthan/jal/paramparagat-jal-prabandhan/

सहायक आचार्य–भूगोल,
राजकीय महाविद्यालय बीबीरानी, अलवर।
email : neeraj.karagwal@gmai.com

17. Effects of Fluoride Water (5.8 ppm) on Essential Biochemical Parameters, Histology of Testis and Reproductive function of Male Albino Rats (*Rattus norvegicus*)

Mamta Solanki

Abstract

The present study was undertaken to evaluate the effect of fluoride toxicity on the reproductive system of male rats. Sexually mature male Wistar (*Rattus norvegicus*) rats were exposed to fluoride (5.8ppm F) contaminated drinking water for 180 days (6 months) *ad libitum*. The body and organ weights, Sperm motility and density in cauda epididymis were assessed, fertility, circulating level of testosterone, biochemical and histological analysis were performed in reproductive organs. Fluoride treatment brought about a significant decrease in body and reproductive organs weights (testis, cauda epididymis, seminal vesicle and coagulating gland) as compared to control group. The cauda epididymal sperms were decapitated (29.33%) and sluggishly motile sperms. The cauda epididymal spermatozoa motility and sperm density of testis and cauda epididymis, testosterone level, fertility% and litter size diminished significantly in fluoride water exposed rats' group. The concentration of protein, sialic acid, fructose, ascorbic acid, and glycogen declined in all the reproductive organs studied. However, the cholesterol concentration of testis was found to be increased significantly following fluoride water treatment revealing non-utilization of cholesterol by the system hence reduced level of testosterone was observed. The histoarchitecture of testis was found to be altered as compared to control rats. There was a marked reduction in the number of primary spermatocytes, secondary spermatocyte, and spermatids. In conclusion, fluoride contaminated drinking water of 5.8 ppm concentration for 180 days to male rats adversely affected their fertility, histoarchitecture of testis and overall reproduction.

Keywords : Fluoride contaminated water, spermatozoa density, spermatozoa motility, fertility, antiandrogenic, antifertility.

Introduction

Fluorine is a highly active environmental element and exists widely in the environment as inorganic or organic compounds due to its great reactivity. Fluoride toxicity is a condition in which there are elevated levels of the fluoride ion in the body. Although fluoride is safe for dental health at low concentrations, sustained consumption of large amounts of soluble fluoride salts is dangerous. Ingestion of fluoride can produce gastrointestinal discomfort at doses at least 15 to 20 times lower (0.2–0.3 mg/kg or 10 to 15 mg for a 50 kg person) than lethal doses (Bradford *et al* 1994), chronic ingestion of fluoride in large amounts interferes with bone formation. In this way, the most widespread examples of fluoride poisoning arise from consumption of ground water that is abnormally fluoride-rich (Pearce 2006). World Health Organization recommends a level of fluoride from 0.5 to 1.0 mg/L, depending on climate (WHO, 1994).

Around one-third of the world's population drinks water from groundwater resources. Of this, about 10 percent, approximately 300 million people, obtains water from groundwater resources that are heavily contaminated with arsenic or fluoride (Eawag, 2015). These trace elements derive mainly from leaching of minerals (Rodriguez *et al.*, 2013).

A lot of studies have shown that excessive fluoride not only could damage the bones and teeth (Long *et al.*, 2009; Shivarajashankara *et al.*, 2002), but also was harmful to other tissues and systems, such as nervous, immune, respiratory, digestive and reproductive system (Chinoy and Sequeira, 1989; Gupta *et al.*, 2007; Long *et al.*, 2009). Recently, a lot of investigations have proved the male reproductive toxicity due to the excess ingestion of fluoride with slat, which showed that the long-term exposure to excessive fluoride decreased the counts and mobility of the sperm, increased the rate of sperm deformity and abnormal sperms, changed the histological structure (Lu *et al.*, 2014; Li *et al.*, 2016; Wan *et al.*, 2006; Sun *et al.*, 2014), and suppressed the levels of serum testosterone (T) (Dong *et al.*, 2016) and luteinizing hormone (LH) (Zhou *et al.*, 2013).

However, most of studies done by using fluoride salt with combination of other electronegative elements, there is paucity of literature on long term exposure of fluoride contaminated drinking water, "the water which was used by residing population of human and animals" on reproduction of male rats, therefore the present investigation has been undertaken to highlight the effects of naturally occurring fluoride contamination in water on reproductive organs of male albino rats.

Materials and Methods

The fluoride contaminated drinking water samples were collected from Watika village of Sanganer Tehsil and subjected for fluoride analysis using standard technique (APHA. AWWA, and WPCF, 1976). The water sample containing fluoride (5.8-ppm) was used for experiment in rats. Healthy adult male albino rats (*Rattus norvegicus*) weighing between 200- 250 gm. were divided into two groups. Group- I, control animals received tap water (1.0 ppm) and in Group-II, rats were exposed to 5.8 ppm fluoride contaminated drinking water for 180 days. The animals were maintained under standard husbandry conditions on a standard diet (Ashirwad Ltd., Chandigarh) and water *ad libitum*. Further, the animals were kept under air-cooled condition and exposed to 14 h daylight. After completion of the treatment, half of the animals were kept for fertility test and rest of the animals were used for biochemical study.

On day 181st the animals were weighed and autopsied. The blood was extracted through cardiac puncture. The reproductive organs viz testis, cauda epididymis, vas deferens, seminal vesicle, ventral prostate and coagulating gland, were excised, blotted free of blood, weighed and used for tissue biochemistry. The fresh testis was fixed in Bouin's fluid for histopathological study. The parameter studied were sperm count and motility (Prasad *et al.*, 1972), serum testosterone level, tissue biochemistry for protein (Lowry *et al.*, 1951), sialic acid (Warren., 1959), glycogen (Montgomery., 1957), cholesterol (Zlatkis *et al.*, 1953), ascorbic acid (Roe and Kuether., 1943), and enzyme activity of acid and alkaline phosphatases (Oser., 1965).

A minimum of six replicates were done for each tissue and parameter. The results were analyzed statistically using student's 't' test.

Results and Discussion

The data revealed that the fluoride (5.8 ppm F) water treatment to rats for 180 days reduced body and reproductive organ weights of testis, seminal vesicle and coagulating gland, (P< 0.001) cauda epididymis significantly (P< 0.01) as compared to control group (Table – 1). The reduced body and organ weights may be attributed to lowered androgen level in circulating blood. As structural and functional integrity of reproductive organs depends on circulating level of androgen, therefore any change in it leads to altered physiology of reproductive organs (Chinoy *et al*, 1982). Boros *et al.* (1984) and Pillai *et al.* (1988) observed the reduction in the body weight with voluntary reduction of food intake in fluorotic animals. According to Chinoy (1991) fluoride might reduce food intake and protein metabolisum, which ultimately hamper body growth.

The fluoride water exposure to rats changed internal milieu of cauda epididymis hence decapitated spermatozoa and sluggishly motile sperms were observed. However, the reduced sperm density (testis and cauda) due to fluoride water ingestion may be attributed to lowered testosterone level. Further fertility rate and average number of litters declined significant (P<0.001) as compared to control rats (Table –2). In the present study declined level of serum testosterone was noted in fluoride water treated rats, therefore diminished sperm motility and density (cauda, testis) can be explained. However further reduced sperm motility and density contribute to inhibition of fertility and number of litters. Follicle stimulating hormone (FSH) and testosterone are the main hormones required in maintaining normal spermatogenesis in rats (Rea *et al.*, 1986) therefore, lowered testosterone level in treated rats indicative of impaired testicular and cauda epididymal sperm motility following fluoride treatment have been reported by Kumar and Susheela (1994).

The androgen dependent parameters (protein, ascorbic acid, sialic acid, fructose, acid and alkaline phosphatases) declined significantly (P<0.001) in reproductive organs (testis, cauda epididymis, vasdeferens, ventral prostate, seminal vesicle) following long term exposure of fluoride water may be attributed to diminished serum testosterone level (Table-3, 4) in fluorotic rats. The protein synthesis, content and concentration of accessory sex organs are androgen dependent (Podesta *et al*, 1975). Ascorbic acid concentration was decline in testis and vas deferens. The animal study reported in ICMR Bulletin (1979) indicated considerable reduction in cellular ascorbic acid content indicated that fluoride ions interfered with vitamin synthesis pathway of gland.

Nag et al. (1977) has reported that an optimal level of sialic acid in reproductive organs is essential for functional integrity of spermatozoa, therefore, declined sialic acid concentration may alter the normal physiology of spermatozoa. Fructose has a vital role in providing energy to the sperm (Curry and Arherton 1990). Reduced level of fructose after the treatment may be due to the direct suppression in the testicular androgen secretion (de Cassia de, sesa et al., 2000; Sarkal et al; 2000).

The glycogen concentration of testis was also decline significantly (P<0.001) following fluoride treatment. Chinoy and Mehta (1999) reported that feeding a protein deficient diet to male mice treated for 30 days with NaF (10, 29 mg/kg/b.wt.) caused a significant decrease glycogen concentration in the vas deferens. A significant decrease in (p<0.001) enzyme activity of acid and alkaline phosphatases in testis, cauda epididymis and ventral prostate were observed after fluoride water treatment (Table-4). The decreased acid and alkaline phosphatases enzyme activity in testis, cauda epididymis and ventral prostate may be due to increased lysosomal activity and antiandrogenic manifestation of fluoride water. This observation is in agreement with the finding of Narula and Jacob (1992) they reported a general decline in the AIP content of the various reproductive and accessory organ of male mouse after androgen estrogen therapy.

However, the cholesterol concentration of testis enhanced significantly (P<0.001) following fluoride water exposure in rats. Cholesterol is one of the most important precursors in the synthesis of steroid hormones (Dorfman et al, 1963). Androgens are synthesized from cholesterol, but increase concentration may result in the reduction of fertility (Eik-Nes and Hall, 1962). The increased cholesterol concentration in testis is indicative of non-utilization by the system leading to a fall in circulatory androgen in rats due to androgen suppressive activity of the test substance.

In control rats testis, seminiferous tubules showed normal

spermatogenesis and lumen filed with spermatozoa. The interstitum contained leydig cells. The fluoride water treatment for 180 days induced histopathological changes in rat testis as compared to control group. The seminiferous tubular and leydig cells diameter diminished significantly. The spermatogenesis was arrested with destroyed germinal epithelium. The lumen was devoid of spermatozoa completely as compared to control rat (Figs 1 to 4).

Bataineh and Nusier, (2006) reported histological alteration in testis with 100 and 200 ppm NaF to rats. Chinoy *et al.* (2005) found alteration in histology of testis with NaF (10 mg/kg b.wt.) exposure to mice with disorganized germinal epithelium, denudation of cells in the lumen, and formation of giant cells. According to Chinoy *et al.* (2004) arrest spermatogenesis in testicular histology in male mice treated with sodium fluoride might be the lack of available proteins necessary for cell division, growth, and differentiation of germ cells. Fluoride exposure decreases the level of testosterone, which is essential for the initiation of spermatogenesis according to (Zhang *et al*. 2006).

Conclusion :

The long-term fluoride contaminated drinking water to rats induced diminished body growth and reproductive organ weights. The serum testosterone level declined significantly causing reduced androgen dependent biochemical parameters, fertility, litter size and altered testis histoarchitecture. The data suggest that long term fluoride water exposure caused antiandrogenenic and antifertility effects in male rats.

Table-1: Body and organ weights of control and fluoride water (5.8 ppm) treated rats.

Parameter		Control	Fluoride water (5.8 ppm for 180 days)
Body wt. (gm)	**Initial**	206.00 ± 2.30	239.31± 5.81
	Final	221.87^b±2.81	215.00^b± 5.84
Organ wt. (mg/100 gm b.wt.)	Testis	615.05± 13.88	486.97^a± 11.0
	Cauda epididymis	88.49± 2.73	78.84^b± 1.03

	Vas deferens	46.19± 1.60	47.02± 1.02
	Seminal vesicle	241.67± 2.76	168.89^a± 5.16
	Ventral prostate	95.89± 1.56	95.94± 1.87
	Coagulating gland	28.48± 0.85	22.31^a± 0.60

Values are mean ± SE, a=p<0.001, b=p<0.01

Table-2: Level of serum testosterone, spermatozoa motility, spermatozoa density, decapitated spermatozoa, fertility and litters of control and fluoride water (5.8 ppm) treated rats.

Parameter	Tissue	Control	Fluoride water (5.8 ppm for 180days)
Testosterone (ng/ml)	Serum	1.88± 0.09	1.12^a± 0.05
Spermatozoa motility (%)	Cauda epididymis	66.00± 2.42	24.55^a± 0.98
Spermatozoa density (million/ml)	Testis	5.27± 0.38	1.04^a± 0.01
	Cauda epididymis	61.64± 1.93	12.16^a± 0.28
Decapitated spermatozoa (%)	Cauda epididymis	Nil	29.33^a
Fertility (%)		100	33.33
Litter size/rat		8.50± 0.42	1.83^a± 0.56

Values are mean ± SE, a=p<0.001

Table-3: Concentration of protein, sialic acid and fructose of Control and fluoride water (5.8 ppm) treated rats.

Parameter	Tissue	Control	Fluoride water (5.8 ppm for 180 days)
Protein (mg/gm)	Testis	216.50± 6.04	135.00^a± 1.29
	Cauda epididymis	172.70± 4.16	127.67^a± 0.39

	Vas deferens	182.67± 1.70	153.00^a± 2.05
	Seminal vesicle	238.83± 3.11	137.17^a± 0.82
	Coagulating gland	23.57± 0.99	24.26± 0.46
Sialic acid (mg/gm)	**Testis**	5.99± 0.17	3.43^a± 0.02
	Cauda epididymis	6.29± 0.31	3.65^a± 0.05
	Vas deferens	6.36± 0.11	3.15^a± 0.02
Fructose (mg/gm)	**Vas deferens**	5.68± 0.20	1.23^a± 0.02
	Seminal vesicle	6.93± 0.12	1.39^a± 0.04

Values are mean ± SE, a=p<0.001

Table-4: Glycogen, ascorbic acid, cholesterol, enzymic activity of acid and alkaline phosphatase of control and fluoride water (5.8 ppm) treated rats.

Parameter	Tissue	Control	Fluoride water (5.8 ppm for 180 days)
Glycogen (mg/gm)	Testis	6.38± 0.28	5.02^b± 0.12
Ascorbic acid (mg/gm)	Testis	3.92± 0.32	1.50^a± 0.02
	Vas deferens	4.05± 0.15	1.00^a± 0.02
Cholesterol (mg/gm)	Testis	6.40± 0.08	19.39^a± 0.24
Acid Phosphatase (mg^{Pi}/gm/hr.)	Testis	3.48± 0.12	0.91^a± 0.02
	Cauda epididymis	4.58± 0.22	1.67^a± 0.03
	Ventral prostate	3.46± 0.13	0.7± 0.01
Alkaline Phosphatase (mg^{Pi}/gm/hr.)	Testis	5.93± 0.06	2.10^a± 0.02
	Cauda epididymis	8.41± 0.20	3.48^a± 0.09
	Ventral prostate	6.71± 0.2	1.93^a± 0.02

Values are mean ± SE, a=p<0.001, b=p<0.0

Histoarchitecture of testis of control and fluoride water treated rats

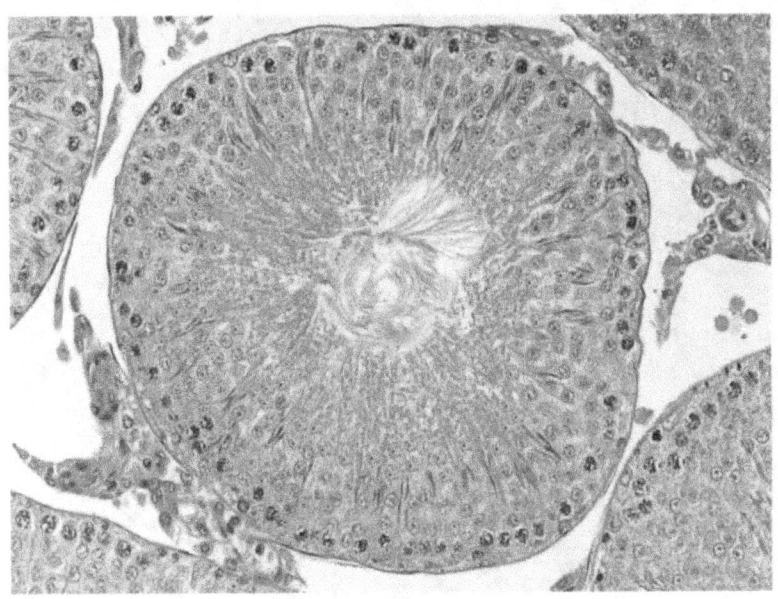

Fig.1- T.S of Testis of Control rat (x200)

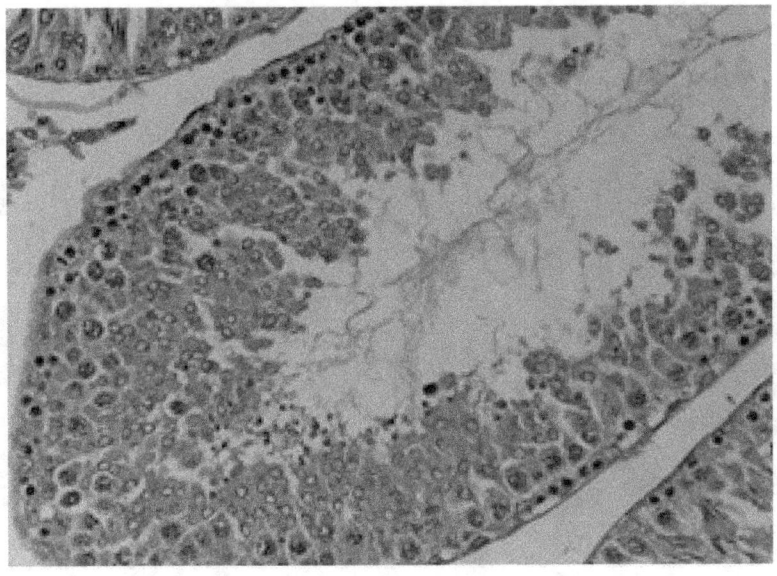

Fig.2- T.S of Testis of 180 days FW treated rat (x200)

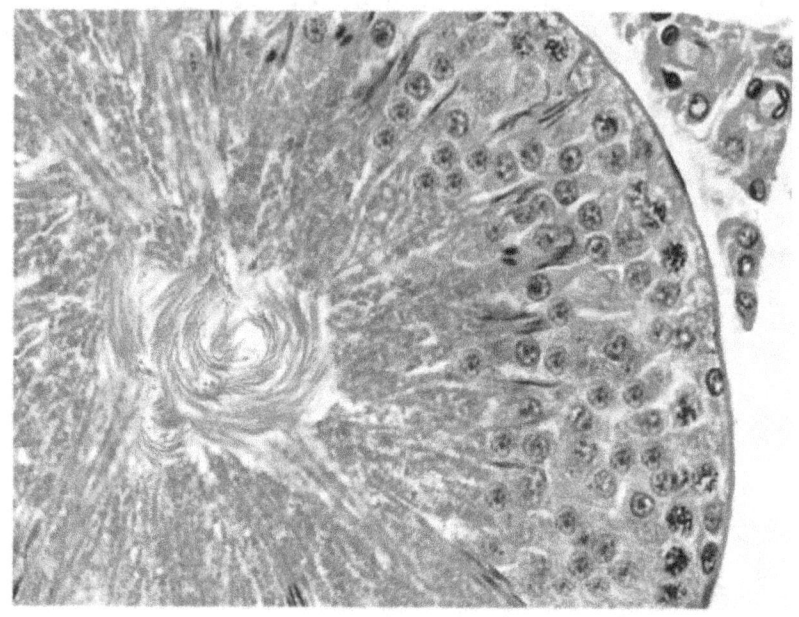

Fig.3- T.S of Testis of Control rat (x400)

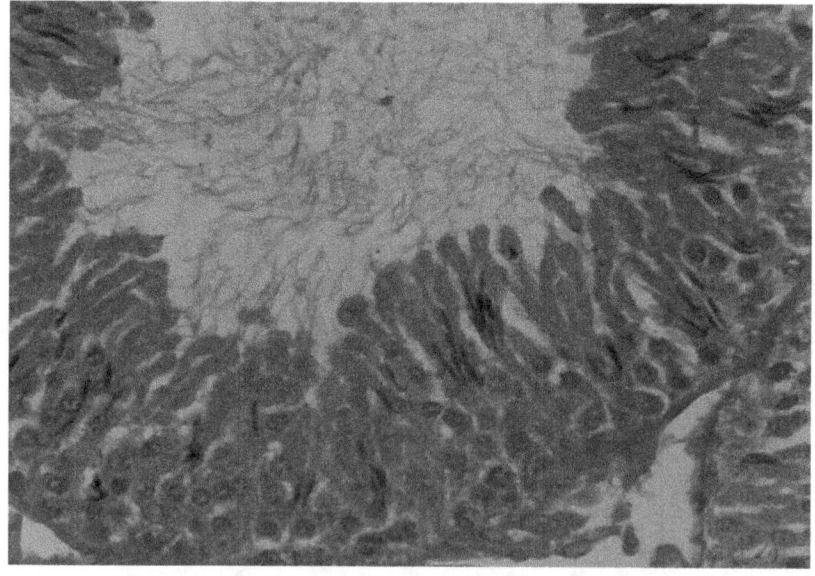

Fig.4- T.S of Testis of 180 days FW treated rat (x400)

References :
APHA, AWWA and WPCF. 1976: Standard methods for examination of water and waste water *(14th edn.)*. American Public Health Association, Washington, DC.
Bataineh, N.H. and Nusier, M.K. 2006: Impact of 12- week ingestion of sodium fluoride on aggression, sexual behavior, and fertility in adult male rats. *Fluoride*, 39 (4): 293-301.
Boros, I., Vegh, A., Schaper, R., Keszler, P. and Ritlop, B. 1984: Fluoride levels in sera and hard tissues of rats consuming F-via drinking water. *Fluoride,* 17: 183-192.
Gessner, BD., Beller, M., John, P., Middaugh, J.P., Gary, M. and Whitford, G.M. 1994: Acute fluoride poisoning from a public water system. *New England J. of Medicine*, 330 (2): 95-99.
Chinoy, N.J. and Sequeira, E. 1989: Effects of fluoride on the histoarchitecture of reproductive organs of the male mouse. *Reprodu. Toxicol.*, 3 (4): 261-267.
Chinoy, N.I., Seth, K.M., Seethalakshmi, L., Parmar, P.Y., Sanjeevan, A.G., Rao, M.V., Sharma, J.D., Chinoy, M.R., Maithidi, R.S., Trivedi, D.G., Ashok Kumar, R., and Ranga, G.M. 1982: Studies on reproductive physiology of animals with special reference to fertility control. Comp. *Physio Ecol.* 7:325-345.
Chinoy, N. J., Sheth, K. M., Seethalakshmi, L., Parmar, P.Y., Sanjeevan, A. G., Rao, M. V., Sharma, J. D., Chinoy, M. R., Maithili, R. S. Trivedi, D. G., Ashok Kumar R., and Geetha Ranga 1982: Studies on reproductive physiology of animals with special references to fertility control. *Comp. Physiol. Ecol.* 7: 325 – 345.
Chinoy, N.J. 1991: Effects of fluoride on physiology of some animals and human beings. *Indian J. Env. Toxicol.,* 1(1): 17-32.
Chinoy, N.J. and Mehta, D. 1999: Effects of protein supplementation and deficiency on fluoride induced toxicity in reproductive organs of male mice. *Fluoride*, 32(4): 204-214.
Chinoy, N.J. and Sequeria, E. 1989a: Effects of Fluoride on the histoarchitecture of the reproductive organs of the male mouse. *Reprod. Toxicol.*, 3:261-267.
Chinoy, N.J. and Sequeria, E. 1989b: Fluoride induced bio-chemical changes in reproductive organs of male mice. *Fluoride,* 2(2): 78-85.
Chinoy, N.J., Sorathia, H.P. and Jhala, D.D. 2005d: Fluoride +

aluminium induced toxicity in mice testis with giant cells and its reversal by vitamin C. *Fluoride,* 38 (2), 109-114.

Chinoy, N.J., Tewari, K. and Jhala, D.D. 2004c: Fluoride and/ or arsenic toxicity in mice testis with formation of giant cells and subsequent recovery by some antidotes. *Fluoride,* 37 (3); 172-184.

Curry, P.T and Arherton, R.W. 1990: Antispermatogenic activity of *Solanum xanthocarpum.* S and W root Arch. *Androl.,* 25-107.

Dong, T., He, J., Wang, S., Wang, L., Cheng, Y., Zhong, Y. 2016: Inability to activate Rac1-dependent forgetting contributes to behavioral inflexibility in mutants of multiple autism-risk genes. *Proc. Natl. Acad. Sci.* U.S.A. 113(27): 7644--7649.

Dorfman, R. I., Forchielli, E. and Gut, M. 1963: Androgen biosynthesis and related studies. *Recent Prog. Horm. Res.* 19: 251–273.

Eawag 2015: *Geogenic Contamination Handbook – Addressing Arsenic and Fluoride in Drinking Water* Archived at the Wayback Machine. C. A. Johnson, A. Bretzler (eds.), Swiss Federal Institute of Aquatic Science and Technology (Eawag), Duebendorf, Switzerland.

Eik-Nes, K.B. and Hall, P.E. 1962: Isolation of dehydroepiandrosterone C^{14} from dogs infused with cholesterol 4-C^{14} by the spermatic artery. *Proc. Soc. Exp. Biol, Med.,* 111: 280-282.

Ghosh, D., Das Sarkar, S., Maiti, R., Jana, D. and Das, U. B. 2002: Testicular toxicity in sodium fluoride treated rats: association with oxidative stress, *Repro. Toxicol.,* 16: 385–390.

Gupta R.S., Khan, T.I., Agrawal, D., and Kachhawa, J.B.S., 2007: The toxic effects of sodium fluoride on the reproductive system of male rats. *Toxicol Ind Health,* 23(9):507-513.

ICMR Bulletin 1979: Recent advances in research on fluoride toxicity and fluorosis, 3: 1-4.

Kumar, A. and Susheela, A.K. 1994: Ultra-structural studies of spermiogenesis in rabbit exposed to chronic fluoride toxicity. *Int. J. Menopausal Stud.,* 39(3): 164-171.

Li, Y., Bian, S., Wang, J. and Wang J. 2016: Effects of fluoride and chitosan on the gene expressions of bone morphogenic protein 2 and collagen type-1 alpha1 chain in the mouse femur. Fluoride, 49:47–

55.
Long, HU., Ying Jin., Lin, M., Sun,Y., Zhanga, L., Clinch, C. 2009: Fluoride toxicity in the male reproductive system. *Fluoride* 42(4):260–276.
Lowry, O.H., Rosebrough, N.J., Farr, A.L. and Randall, R.J. 1951: Protein Measurement with the Folin – Phenol reagent. *J. Bio. Chem.,* 193: 265-275.
Lu, Z., Wang, S.,Zilong Sun, Z.,Ruiyan Niu, R and Wang, J. 2014: In vivo influence of sodium fluoride on sperm chemotaxis in male mice. *Reprodu. Toxicol.,* 88, 533–539.
Montgomery, R. 1957: Determination of glycogen. *Arch. Biochem. and Biophys,*67 (2): 378-386.
Nag, S., Sarkar, D. and Ghosh, T.T. 1977: Sialic acid and sialidase activity in rat testis and epididymis in relation to age and action of different antifertility agents. *Indian J. Exp.Biol.,* 15:510-512.
Narayana, M.V. and Chinoy, N.J. 1994: Effect of fluoride on rat testicular steroidogenesis. *Fluoride,* 27(1): 12-17.
Narula, A. and Jacob, D. 1992: Regulation of fertility in the male mouse after simultaneous androgen estrogen therapy. *J. Adv.,* 3 (1 & 2): 11-15.
Ortiz-P´erez, D., Rodríguez-Martínez, M., Martínez, F., Borja-Aburto, V.H., Castelo, J., Grimaldo, J.I., De la Cruz, E., Carrizales, L., Díaz-Barriga, F., 2003. Fluoride-induced disruption of reproductive hormones in men. *Environ. Res.* 93, 20–30.
Oser, B.L. 1979: In; Hawk's Physiological Chemistry, 14th Edn., Mc Grawhill, New York, London, 763.
Pearce, Fred 2006: When the Rivers Run Dry: Journeys Into the Heart of the World's Water Crisis. Toronto: Key Porter. ISBN 978-1-55263-741-8.
Pillai, K.S., Mathai, A.T. and Desmukh, P.B. 1988: Effect of sub acute dosage of fluoride on male mice. *Toxicol. lett.,* 44: 21-29.
Podesta, E.J., Calendra, R.S., Rivarola, M.A. and Blaquier, J.A. 1975: The effect of castration and testosterone replacement on specific proteins and androgen levels of the rat epididymis. *Endocr.* 97: 399-405.
Prasad, M.R.N., Chinoy, NJ, and Kadam, KM. 1972: Changes in succinic dehydrogenase levels in rat epididymis under normal and

altered physiological condition. *Fertil. Steril.*, 23:186.

Rea, M.A., Weinbauer, G.E., Marshall, G.R. and Nieschlag, E. 1986: Testostetrone stimulates pituitary and serum FSH in GnRH antagonist-suppressed rats. *Acta Endocrinol*, 113(4): 487-492.

Rodríguez-Lado L., Sun, G., Berg, M., Zhang, Q., Xue, H., Zheng, Q., Johnson, C.A. 2013: Groundwater arsenic contamination throughout China". *Science.* 341 (6148): 866-868.

Roe, J.H. and Kuether, C.A. 1943: The determination of ascorbic acid in whole blood and urine through the 2, 4- dinitrophenyl hydrazine derivative of dehyro ascorbic acid. *J. Biol. Chem.*, 147: 399- 407.

Sarkar, M., Gangopadhyay, P., Basak, B., Chakrobarty, N., Banerji, J., Adhikary, P. and Chatterjee, A. 2000: The reversible antifertility effect of *Piper betle* Linn. On Swiss albino male mice. *Contracep.*, 62(5): 271-301.

Shivarajashankara, Y.M., Shivashankara, A.R., Bhat,P.G. and Raoc, S.H. 2002: Brain lipid peroxidation and antioxidant systems of young rats in chronic fluoride intoxication. *Fluoride,* 35(3): 197-203.

Sun, F., Li, X., Yang,C., Lv, P., Li.,G Xu, Z. 2014: A role for PERK in the mechanism underlying fluoride-induced bone turnover. *Toxicol.*, (5) 52-66.

Susheela, A.K. and Jethanandani, P. 1996: Circulating testosterone levels in skeletal fluorosis patients. *J. Toxicol. Clin. Toxicol.*, 34(2): 183-189.

Susheela, A.K. and Kumar, A. 1991: A study of the effects of high concentrations of fluoride on the reproductive organs of male rabbits, using light and scanning electron microscopy., *Repro.* and *Ferti.* 92: 353 -360.

Wan, S. X., Zhang, J. H. and Wang, J. D. 2006: Effects of high fluoride on sperm quality and testicular histology in male rats. *Fluoride.* 39: 17-21.

Warren, L. 1959: The triobarbituric acid assay of sialic acids. *J. Biol. Chem.*, 234: 1971.

W.H.O., 1994: Expert Committee on Oral Health Status and Fluoride Use Fluorides oral health. WHO. 92(94):120846-5.

Zhang, J.H., Liang, C., Ma, J.J., Niu, R.Y. and Wang, J.D. 2006a:

Effects of sodium fluoride and sulfur dioxide on oxidative stress and antioxidant defenses of testis in male rats. *Fluoride*, 39:185-190.

Zhou, Y., Zhang, H., He, J., Chen, X., Ding, Y., Wang, Y., Liu, X., 2013: Effects of sodium fluoride on reproductive function in female rats. *Food and chemi. Toxicol.*, 56:297-303:

Zlatkis, A., Zak, B. and Boyle, A.J. 1953: A new method for direct determination of serum cholesterol. *J. Lab. Clin. Med.*, 41(3):486-92.

Assistant professor (Zoology)
Samrat prithviraj chauhan government college, Ajmer, Rajasthan
email : **9116426636mamta@gmail.com**

18. Green Chemistry and their Twelve Principles for Sustainable Development of Environment

D.T. Sakhare

Abstract

This paper provides an overview of applicabilitytwelve principles and future trends of Green Chemistry. Green or Sustainable Chemistry is a term that refers to the creation of chemical products and processes that reduce or eliminate the use and production of harmful substances. They are used exclusively chemicals and chemical processes that do not have negative consequences for the environment. It is based on twelve principles that can be used to initially create or recreate molecules, materials, reactions and processes that are safer for human health and the environment. The processes of the Green Chemistry that have been developed to date include almost all areas of chemistry, including organic, inorganic, biochemistry, polymer, toxicology, environmental, physical, technological, etc. Through the several prevailing trends of the green program such as catalysis, biocatalysis and the use of alternative: renewable feedstock (biomass), reaction media (water, ionic liquids and supercritical fluids), reaction conditions (microwave irradiation) and new synthetic pathways (photocatalytic reaction), the dual goals – environmental protection and economic benefit can be achieved. This article shows examples of the prevailing trends in ways that Green Chemistry reduces the impact of chemical processes and technologies on the environment.

Keywords : Green Chemistry, Biocatalysis, Biomass, Ionic Liquids, Supercritical Fluids, Microwave Irradiation, Photocatalysis.

1. Introduction :

Green Chemistry is defined as the "design of chemical products and processes to reduce or eliminate the use and generation of hazardous substances."[1,2]. This definition and the concept of Green Chemistry were first formulated at the beginning of the 1990s nearly 20 years ago [3]. In the years since, there has been international adoption that resulted in the creation of literally hundreds of programs and governmental initiatives on Green Chemistry around the world with initial leading programs located in the U.S., United Kingdom, and Italy [4]. These have played a significant role in informing sustainable design [5] Important early programs include the US Presidential Green Chemistry Challenge Awards established in 1995 [6]. the Green Chemistry Institute founded in 1997 [7] and the publication of the first volume of the now well-established Green Chemistry journal of the Royal Society of Chemistry in 1999 [8].

The most important aspect of Green Chemistry is the concept of design. Design is a statement of human intention and one cannot do design by accident. It includes novelty, planning and systematic conception. The Twelve Principles of Green Chemistry are "design rules" to help chemists achieve the intentional goal of sustainability. Green Chemistry is characterized by careful planning of chemical synthesis and molecular design to reduce adverse consequences. Through proper design one can achieve synergies—not merely trade-offs.

The Green Chemistry approach strives to achieve sustainability at the molecular level. Because of this goal, it is not surprising it has been applied to all industry sectors. From aerospace, automobile, cosmetic, electronics, energy, household products, pharmaceutical, to agriculture, there are hundreds of examples of successful applications of award winning, economically competitive technologies [9].

The concept of Green Chemistry has had this large impact due to the fact that it goes beyond the research laboratory in isolation and has touched industry, education, environment, and the general public. The field of Green Chemistry has demonstrated how chemists can design next generation products and processes so that they are profitable while being good for human health and the environment. Following the scientific enthusiasm of Green Chemistry, teaching initiatives, governmental funding, and the establishment of Green Chemistry Research Centers have multiplied in the past two decades. Many universities now offer classes on Green Chemistry and Green Engineering. Some institutions offer degrees in the field. Governmental funding has also increased in several countries around the world [10].

1.1 Importance of Green Chemistry : Prevents pollution at the molecular level. Is a philosophy that applies to all areas of chemistry, not a single discipline of chemistry. Applies innovative scientific solutions to real-world environmental problems. Results in source reduction because it prevents the generation of pollution. Reduces the negative impacts of chemical products and processes on human health and the environment. Lessens and sometimes eliminates hazard from existing products and processes. Designs chemical products and processes to reduce their intrinsic hazards.

1.2 Chemistry & Society Pharmaceutical : Drugs (pain killers, antibiotics, heart and hypertensive drugs), disinfectants,vaccines, dental fillings, anesthetics, contraceptives. **Agriculture:** Fertilizers, pesticides. **Food:** Preservatives, packaging and food wraps, refrigerants. **Transportation:** Petrol and diesel, catalytic converters to reduce exhaust emissions. **Clothing:** Synthetic fibres, dyes, waterproofing materials. **Safety:**Polycarbonate materials for crash helmets. Sports:Composite materials for rackets, all weather surfaces Office inks, photocopying toners. **Homes:** Paints, vanishes and polish, detergents, pest killers.

1.3 History Of Green Chemistry :

1. In 1990 the Pollution Prevention Act was passed in the United States. This act helped create a modus operandi for dealing with pollution in an original and innovative way. This paved the way to the green chemistry concept.
2. Paul Anastas and John Warner coined the two letter word "green chemistry" and developed the twelve principles of green chemistry.
3. In 2005 Ryoji Noyori identified three key developments in green chemistry: use of supercritical carbon dioxide as green solvent, aqueous hydrogen peroxide for clean oxidationsand the use of hydrogen in asymmetric synthesis.

1.4 Global Recognition Of Green Chemistry : Australia: The Royal Australian Chemical Institute (RACI) presents Australia's Green Chemistry Challenge Awards. Canada: The Canadian Green Chemistry Medal is an annual award given to any individual or group for promotion and development of green chemistry Italy: Green Chemistry activities in Italy centre on inter-university consortium known as INCA. In 1999, INCA has given three awards annually to industry for applications of green chemistry. Japan: In Japan, The Green & Sustainable Chemistry Network (GSCN), formed in 1999, is an organization consisting of representatives from chemical manufacturers and researcher. UK: In the United Kingdom, the Crystal Faraday Partnership, a non-profit group founded in 2001, awards businesses annually for incorporation of green chemistry. USA: United States Environmental Protection Agency (EPA).

1.5 Nobel Prize in Green chemistry :
1. The Nobel Prize Committee recognized the importance of green chemistry in 2005 by awarding Yves Chauvin, Robert H. Grubbs, and Richard R. Schrock the Nobel Prize for Chemistry for "the development of the metathesis method in organic synthesis.
2. Frances Arnold won in 2018, it for the directed evolution of enzymes, a technique she has pioneered over the past 25 years and has used to pursue new avenues within green chemistry and to engineer reactions completely new to nature.

1.6 Green chemistry and Sustainable development : The UN defines sustainable development as 'meeting the needs of present without compromising the ability of future generation. Green chemistry focuses on how to achieve sustainability through science and technology. To better understand and solve the issue of environmental pollution, many approaches and models have been developed for environmental impact assessments. Some of these approaches and models have been successful in predicting impacts for selected chemicals in selected environmental settings. These models have joined air and water quality aspects to point and nonpoint sources and have been very useful for the development of emission control and compliance strategies. However, some of the approaches and models were aimed primarily at evaluating the quantity of pollutants that could be discharged into the environment with acceptable impact, but failed to focus on pollution prevention. However, some of the approaches and models were aimed primarily at evaluating the quantity of pollutants that could be discharged into the environment with acceptable impact, but failed to focus on pollution prevention. The concept of end-of-pipe approaches to waste management decreased, and strategies such as environmentally conscious manufacturing, eco-efficient production, or pollution prevention gained recognition.

2. Green Chemistry

(Green color is the color of chlorophyll and the color of the dollar. Being a green series of years is a battleground of environmental activists, and becoming a green becoming a trend in product marketing. And for chemists it becomes imperative to be green in applying the principles of green chemistry in all aspects of chemical sciences, in fundamental and applied research, production and education. [11].

2.1 Definition of Green Chemistry

According to the EPA definition, green chemistry is defined as a chemistry that designs chemical products and processes that are harmless to the environment, thus preventing the formation of pollution. Chemical products should be made so that they do not remain in the environment at the end of their application and that they are broken down into components that are harmless to the environment. Saving based on efficient synthesis without the use of "exotic" reagents, reducing the required energy, and replacing organic solvents with water are significant even at the laboratory level, while in industrial scale possible millions of savings [12].

Green chemistry is not a separate scientific discipline, but a responsible interdisciplinary approach to science, based on chemical, ecological and social responsibility, which enables creativity and the advancement of innovative research [13]. As a propulsive area of research, it tries to find and maintain a balance between the use of natural resources, economic growth and environmental conservation.

2.2 Trends in Green Chemistry

Green chemistry "program for the design, development and application of chemical products and processes that reduce or eliminate the use or production of substances that are hazardous to human health and the environment" and to achieving the main goals of the green program comes through several dominant trends [14] :

a. Research in the field of catalytic and biocatalytic reactions in order to obtain highly selective, pure compounds without the

formation of toxic byproducts;
b. Seeking new raw materials, harmless and renewable, such as biomass;
c. Designing less toxic eco-compatible chemicals;
d. Finding and testing new alternative, non-toxic and renewable reaction media such as water, ionic liquids and supercritical fluids
e. Finding and testing new alternative reaction conditions, such as microwave, ultrasound and light reacting
f. Exploration of alternative routes for the purification of poisoned air and water to improve their quality, such as photocatalytic reactions [14].

Realizing the set goals, "green chemistry changes steady industrial practice-produces, pollutes, and then cleanses, and in the late twentieth century becomes the heart and soul of industrial ecology" [14].

Green chemistry is a Hippocratic oath for chemists, and in order to preserve natural resources and the environment, a new generation of scientists and technologists is being developed, which economically analyze the processes and materials used in production and development. Green chemistry or ecologically harmless, harmless and sustainable chemistry is the manufacture and application of chemical products and processes that reduce or eliminate the use and creation of hazardous substances. Instead of limiting the risk by controlling exposure to harmful chemicals, green chemistry seeks to reduce, and possibly eliminate, the danger, denying the need for exposure control. If no hazardous substances are used or produced, then the risk is zero and there is no need to worry about removing hazardous substances from the environment or limiting exposure to them or "Green chemistry is about reducing waste, raw materials, risks, energy, environmental impact and cost" [14].

3. Twelve Principles of Green Chemistry

Twelve principles of green chemistry have been developed by Paul Anastas and John Warner of EPA, and in their Green Chemistry Theory and Practice book, 1998, they explained their meaning in practice. The principles of green chemistry speak about the reduction or removal of dangerous or harmful substances from the synthesis, production and application of chemical products and thus the use of substances dangerous to human health and the environment is reduced or eliminated. When designing a green chemistry process, it is impossible to meet the requirements of all twelve principles of the process at the same time, but it attempts to apply as many principles as possible during certain stages of synthesis.

Twelve Principles of Green Chemistry :

1. Prevent Waste.
2. Atom Economy.
3. Less hazardous synthesis.
4. Design Benign Chemicals.
5. Benign Solvents and auxiliaries.
6. Design for energy efficiency.
7. Use of renewable feedstock's.
8. Reduce derivatives.
9. Catalysis
10. Design for degradation.
11. Real time analysis for pollution prevention.
12. Inherently benign chemistry for accident prevention

The twelve principles as shown in below **Fig.1**

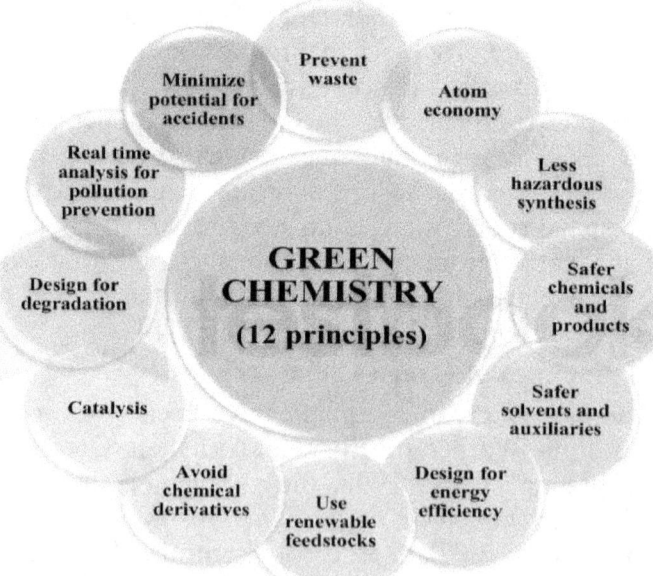

Fig. 1 Twelve Principles 0f Green Chemistry

3.1 Prevention :

It is better to check or avoid the synthesis of hazardous, toxic, explosive, bio-accumulative and waste chemical product rather than to treat or clean up [15].

For example :

(a) Check or avoid over manufacturing/synthesis of nuclear and non-nuclear weapons, explosive and harmful bio-chemical substances from various developed and developing countries because it create various type of environmental pollution and human diseases [16].
(b) Check or avoid over exploitation of natural resources like coal and petroleum because its burning produces various harmful gases like oxides of carbon and oxides of nitrogen and sulphur which result into global warming and acid rain respectively [17].
(c) Check or avoid the over production of bio-accumulative, bio-transforming, non-biodegradable substances like polythene, Aldrin, Chlordane, DDT, and methyl mercury compounds[18].

Pollution Prevention: Drive smaller, more efficient cars, Take the commuter train, Riding a bike, Fix a leaky faucet, Recycle paper or compost leaves.

3.2 Atom Economy :

Synthetic methods should be designed to maximize the incorporation of all materials used in the process into the final product. The principle of Atom Economy is logically linked to the principle of waste prevention, since it requires all raw materials used in production to maximize utilization or inclusion in the final product to ultimately reduce the amount of waste. This means that the chemical synthesis should be designed in such a way that the final product maximizes the input of raw materials or design such synthetic products that will use the entire material used for synthesis in the final product.

The principle of increasing atomic usability was defined in 1991 by Barry Trost of Stanford University. Trost believes that introducing the concept of usability atoms is essentially the prevention of waste at the molecular level. Barry Trost's concept initiated the redesign of existing synthetic reactions until then established on the principle of "making a product regardless of price". These modifications are useful and because they generally lead to increased yields.

There is a known progress in the synthesis of ibuprofen [19]. The main problem of old synthesis (boots process) is low economic cost, because the utilization of input raw materials is only about 40%. In the 1990s a new "green" method of ibuprofen synthesis was developed, involving only three steps, and almost all transitional materials were converted to the product (up to 99%) or regenerated and returned in the process and almost almost eliminated the generation of waste materials And this process is one of the processes of "green synthesis" [20, 21].

Design the chemical processes in such a way that the final product contains maximum proportion of the reactant or the starting raw materials and leaving a few numbers of atoms of raw materials[22].

Example :

Calculation of atom economy When one mole of Benzene react with 4 ½ mole of oxygen molecule then it produced one mole of maleic anhydride and 2 mole of carbon dioxide and 2mole of Water [23].

Atom economy= (mass of atom in desired product/mass of atomic reactant)*100

$$= (98/222)*100$$
$$= 44.1\%$$

3.3 Less Hazardous Chemical Synthesis :

The Less Hazardous Chemical Synthesis advocates, wherever possible, the creation of synthetic methods for the use and creation of substances that are little or no toxic to human health and the environment. Replacing harmful chemicals with biological enzymes makes many industrial processes cleaner and cheaper [24].

Design the chemical processes/product in such a way that use and generation of chemical substances should not exceed the critical limit of toxicity to avoid environmental deterioration and harmful for human being.

Example :

(a) Avoid the synthesis of chemicals like organ mercurial's compounds; which caused minamata disaster [25].
(b) Avoid the synthesis of methyl isocynate (MIC); which caused

Bhopal gas tragedy [26].

3.4 Design Benign Chemicals :

An example is the production of polymers of polyphenylene sulfone (PPSU), which is now widely used for indoor airplanes and is also introduced in underground trains where it is also important to use non-flammable materials. It is a new engineering plastic characterized by a unique combination of useful environmental, mechanical, and flame resistant properties [27]

Chemical processes and products should be designed in such a way that, it is highly selective in nature and affect their desired functions and minimizing their toxicity, bio-accumulation and bio-transformation.

Example :

2, 4-D: It is a selective pesticide which selectively kills only broad leaf weeds[28].

3.5 Benign Solvents And Auxiliaries :

The use of auxiliary substances (e.g., solvents, separation agents, etc.) should be made unnecessary wherever possible and innocuous when used.

Chromatographic separations, where large quantities of solvents are used, are problematic due to environmental pollution. Most conventional organic solvents are toxic, flammable and corrosive. Their recycling is linked to energyefficientdistillation with considerable losses and therefore the development of environmentally-friendly solvents is necessary. For now, it is promising to replace the known organic solvents with recyclable solvents, which are ionic liquids - salts at room temperature in the liquid state. Unlike volatile organic compounds, ionic liquids have low vapor pressure, do not vaporise and do so easily, resulting in safer chemical processes [29].

The use of auxiliaries substances in the form of solvents, separating agent, extractive agent should be nontoxic, non- explosive, non-hazardous, non- cancer causing, non-bio accumulated and non-mutation inducing.

Example :

Super critical Carbon dioxide is a better solvent because it is a non-toxic and non- explosive fluid [30].

3.6 Design For Energy Efficiency :

Energy requirements of chemical processes should be recognized for their environmental and economic impacts and should be minimized. If possible, synthetic methods should be conducted at ambient temperature and pressure.

The oil crisis in 1973 has initiated the development of a number of processes in which energy savings are taken into account, with the aim of exploiting every kJ of energy in the production process. Following the above-mentioned Principle of Energy Efficiency, whose other name is Design for Energy Efficiency, as a fundamental requirement, minimizes the use of energy. The possible ways to improve energy efficiency in the chemical industry [31].

It is necessary to design the chemical processes /products in such a way that it utilizes less energy to form desired product, this can accompanied by keeping the chemical processes at ambient temperature and pressure in the presence of suitable catalyst.

Example :

Formation of ammonia from Haber's process [32].
$$N_2 + 3H_2 \rightarrow 2NH_3$$
Temperature = 673-723 Kelvin, pressure = 200 atm, catalyst = Iron

3.7 Use Of Renewable Feedstock'S :

The seventh principle of green chemistry advocates Use of Renewable Feedstocks wherever it is technically and economically acceptable. For example, it is more convenient to use renewable raw materials than a variety of plastic materials, and then to waste away the waste materials. Because of this, the making of biodegradable plastic materials is a current trend. Biodegradable packaging has a future in the food industry. Numerous factors, including politics and changes in legislation, as well as global demand for food and energy resources, certainly affect the development of biodegradable packaging [33].

In the case of bioplastics, the use of renewable raw materials in production positively affects energy consumption and CO_2 emissions. Coca-Cola, a world-widescale company for the time being, manufactures bottles made of 30% polyethylene (PE) blends, while American company NatureWorks uses bottles made from lactic acid polymers (PLA) made from lactic acid, obtained by fermentation of dextrose obtained from starch, Most commonly corn. About 1 kg of PLA requires about 2.5 kg of corn [34].

For sustainable development, it is better to avoid exploitation of non-renewable natural resources like petroleum, coal and natural gas etc.

But use of renewable resources for its sustainable development did not create much problem because it is restored by natural processes and biogeochemical cycle.

Example :

Formation of furfural from bagasse and waste biomass of wheat and rice plant etc [35]

3.8 Reduce Chemical Derivatives :

During a chemical processes, waste product are formed or generated if additional chemical reagent are used to block or protect any groups, so avoid such type of blocking, protecting groups or even any modifications, if possible.

Reduced usage of derivatives and protecting groups in the synthesis of target molecules is one of the main concepts of green chemistry. Derivatization demands the consumption of additional energy and reagents, as well as the formation of additional waste during the synthesis. It also involves the application of protective or deprotecting substances, as well as any short-term changes to the physical and chemical process. The selection of the protective group is a critical aspect in the effective implementation of a synthetic process. The choice of the protective group has a significant impact on the overall efficiency and length of the synthetic process. Selectivity in the reaction will be induced by derivatizing the desired reactive site to make it more receptive to the reacting species. Using derivatives as little as possible in chemical synthesis can be achieved by avoiding the use of protecting groups which will result in an increase of atom economy on the reaction.

A prominent example is the manufacturing of penicillin-based antibiotics (Fig.2) or the substitution of traditional chemical enzymatic techniques in which 6-aminopenicillic acid is produced by interacting with the catalyzed immobilized enzyme penicillin amide. This resulted in the substitution of many chemical processes by an enzymatic reaction, which no longer required a low temperature (-60°C), organic solvents, and completely improper conditions, which increased and complicated production in the case of chemical synthesis [36].

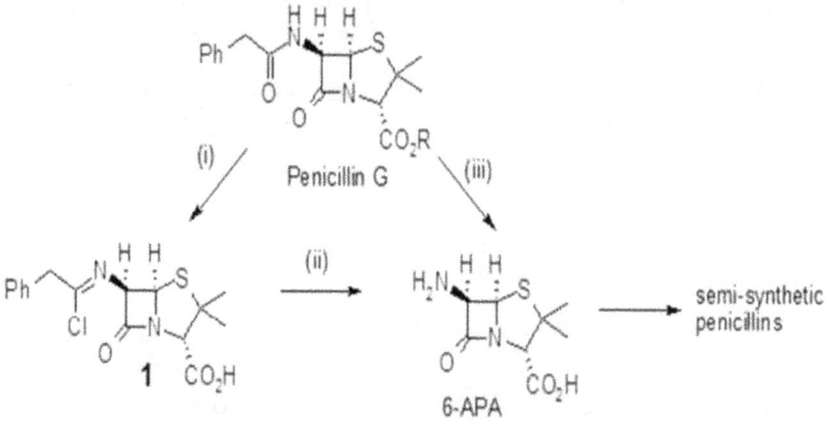

Fig.2: Synthesis of 6-aminopenicilic acid catalyzed by immobilized penicillin G amide.

In this manner another newer technique involving greener route to produce ethanal commercially can be prepared by oxidation of ethene, in the presence of an ionic catalyst in an aqueous medium. This is also greener method and gives 90% of yield.

Likewise, Tetrachloroethene was used as a solvent for dry cleaning purposes. It is a suspected carcinogen and groundwater contaminant. It is replaced by greener solvent like supercritical CO_2.

The synthetic methods should avoid using or generating substances toxic to humans and/or the environment. Hence less hazardous chemical synthesis is an important principle.

Photochemical reaction occurs when light energy gets absorbed by a substances' molecule. It is a green route as no by product will be formed. Vitamin D3 synthesis is assisted by a photochemical reaction.

We were bleach the paper, by using chlorine gas because it have excellent oxidising characteristics. Now H_2O_2 with a proper catalyst is being utilised for bleaching since it does not pollute groundwater.

Halogenated solvents contaminate groundwater. Whereas liquified CO_2 leaves a lower amount of residue. It is also a non-toxic and attractive solvent for temperature-sensitive materials.

Hydrogen peroxide can easily breakdown into water and oxygen. It is a good oxidizing agent and a strong bleaching agent. Use of H_2O_2 gives better results and makes use of a lesser amount of water.

When compared to conventional solvents, liquified CO_2 leaves a lower amount of residue. It is also a non-toxic and attractive solvent for temperature-sensitive materials

thus these all are excellent example of Green Chemistry making a genuine difference.

Example :

Use of enzymes to avoid protecting groups and cleanup process is the industrial synthesis of semi synthetic antibiotics such as ampicillin and amoxicillin [37].

3.9 Catalyst :

In order to protect the environment, the catalysis principle promotes the use of biodegradable catalysts, which imply less energy use, avoiding the use of organochlorine compounds and reducing the use of water or less waste water.

Like all catalysts, enzymes function in a way that lowers the activation energy of an individual reaction, and thus accelerates, up to several million times. In doing so, the enzyme remains unchanged throughout the duration of the reaction to which it affects, and this allows it to become completely unchanged when the reaction comes to an end. Also, enzymes do not affect the relative energy between the reactants and the products, nor to the related reactions.

Catalyst is the chemical substance which is used in small quantities, enhance the rate of reaction by decreasing activation energy and regenerate itself at the end of reaction [38]. But the stoichiometric reagent are used in large quantities and do not generate at the end of reaction [39].

Example:

[Reaction scheme: Acetophenone + NaBH₄ + 4H₂O → 1-phenylethanol + H₃BO₃ + NaOH]

Atom Economy = 81%

[Reaction scheme: Acetophenone + H₂O —Pd-on-C→ 1-phenylethanol]

3.10. Design For Degradation :

The principle of creating degradable chemicals and products or design for degradation demands the creation of enzymatic processes whereby the 6-aminopenicillic acid is obtained by reacting with the catalyzed immobilized enzyme penicillin amide. This resulted in several chemical steps being replaced by an enzymatic reaction, and no longer required a low temperature (-60°C), organic solvents, and completely unsuitable conditions that increased and complicated production in the case of chemical synthesis [36].

The chemical processes and products should be design in a way that the desired products and waste product formed by the process are biodegradable in natural environment. The desired products are break down into harmless small substances by physical, chemical and biological means and do not persist in the natural environment.

The product should not be bio accumulative in nature and do not show biomagnifications

Example :

Biodegradable and bioactive thermoplastic aliphatic polyester polylactic acid (PLA) [40]

3.11. Real Time Analysis For Pollution Prevention :

Traditional analytical chemistry implies large amounts of sample for analysis, abundant use of solvents and energy. With the development of new methods and precision mobile instruments, it is possible that the analyzes work with a small sample size at the sampling site and with much less solvent.

The principle of Real-Time Analysis for Pollution Prevention requires further development of analytical methodology to enable real-time monitoring of the chemical production process with the aim of preventing the formation of dangerous substances, ie it is necessary to constantly monitor the production process at each stage Would prevent the occurrence of errors that could lead to the emergence of dangerous substances, harmful to the environment and human health.

It is important to know the event's or the products formation during a chemical processes at different temperature, pressure, and time to control the formation of desired products and to avoid formation of any hazardous substances or waste substances as byproduct. [41]

Example :

$$\text{C}_6\text{H}_5\text{-Cl} \xrightarrow[\text{Diethyl ether}]{\text{Mg}} \text{C}_6\text{H}_5\text{-MgCl}$$

$$\xrightarrow{\text{H}_2\text{C=O}} \text{C}_6\text{H}_5\text{-CH}_2\text{OMgCl}$$

$$\xrightarrow{\text{H}_3\text{O}^+} \text{C}_6\text{H}_5\text{-CH}_2\text{OH}$$

3.12 Inherently Benign Chemistry For Accident Prevention :

The Twelfth Principle of Green Chemistry is the principle of Inherently Safer Chemistry for Accident Prevention. The basic requirement is to reduce the use of substances in chemical processes that can cause adverse effects (explosion, fire and harmful vapor). An example is today the increasing use of supercritical CO_2 that replaces organic solvents and which, unlike organic solvents, is not toxic or explosive and is environmentally acceptable.

Safety can be defined as a control of known hazards by achieving an acceptable level of risk and is achieved at several levels of the lowest use of Personal Protective Equipment. Then it follows the level of Administrative and Work Practice Controls) and implies establishing effective procedures, rotating work tasks, adjusting work schedules so that workers are not over-exposed to the impact of dangerous chemicals, etc. The next higher level of security control is the expert Engineering Controls, which implies the implementation of physical process change To reduce contact with hazardous chemicals, isolate the process, use wet methods to reduce dust formation, ventilation, digestion, etc. The highest level of safety control is achieved by eliminating or replacing the procedure with safer alternatives **(Fig. 3)**.

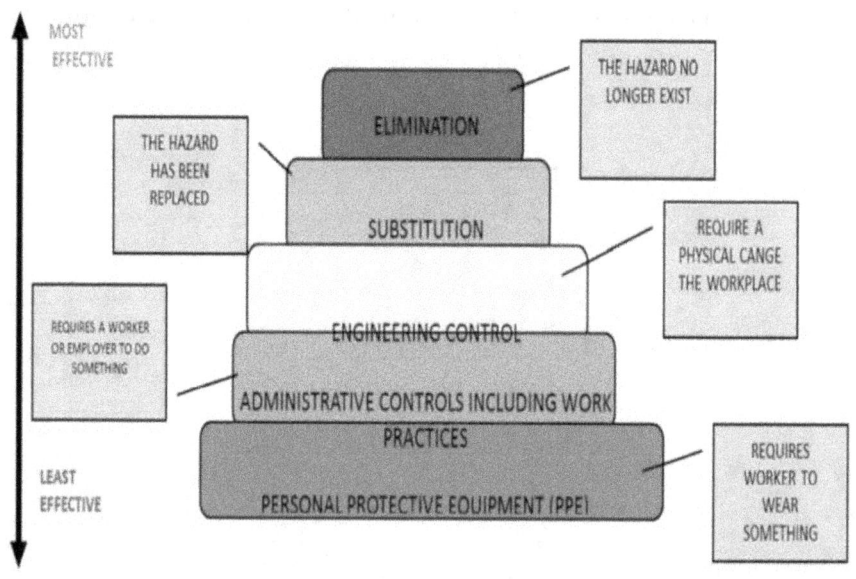

Fig. 3. Hierarchy of security control

Design chemical processes and products and their physical states like solid, liquid and gaseous form to minimize or eliminate the potential of chemical accident's including explosion, fire, and smoke produce due to chemical and release into the natural environment. Hazardous Substances are Corrosive, Flammable,

Explosive, Reactive, Toxic etc.

To prevent accidents and injuries the following right steps should be taken before handling any hazardous substances, Read labels and SDSs to learn about hazardous and required safety precautions. Check for adequate ventilation.Remove items from the work area that could ignite or react with the hazardous materials. Know the location of fire extinguisher, emergency alarms, eyewash stations and first-aid kits [42].

Disadvantages of Green Chemistry :

This goal is also the biggest handicap-lack of green chemistry that is reflected in time, costs and lack of information. More specifically, switching from an old, conventional product or process to a new "green" product or process requires a lot of time, designor redesign of a new product and process is often difficult and quite expensive, and there is also a lack of unity on what is considered safe. With the high cost of implementation and the lack of information, the lack of green chemistry is also the fact that there is no known alternative to used chemical raw materials or alternative technologies for green processes. In addition, there is also a lack of human resources and skills.

The risks of switching to green products and processes are not divided within the supply chain, and there is a lack of resources for further research. Ionic liquids are considered to be the future of green chemistry. Although there is no doubt that those are useful in chemical synthesis, the question is increasingly raised whether they meet expectations. When applying twelve principles that describe green chemicals, ionic liquids do not look particularly green. There is an opinion that at the presentstage of science progress it is unrealistic to expect that in the next ten years a wide application of ionic liquids will be seen.

Although, as is well known, ionic liquids are slightly volatile due to the low vapor pressure, yet it is only one of the many things that make a substance really green. For example, ionbased, imidazole-based and fluoro-anion-based liquids are likely to be poisonous but can not reach the environment by evaporation. The problem is that most ionic liquids are watersoluble and can easily reach the biosphere through that pathway [43].

5. Conclusions

Establishing a balance in the use of natural resources, economic growth and environmental conservation is possible through the introduction of a green chemistry process whose task is to design such chemical processes and products that are harmless to human health and the environment. The application of the concept of green chemistry that introduces chemical safety implies adequate legal support through the legal regulation of certain procedures and activities that are unavoidable for the implementation of such a concept.

The concept of green chemistry is based on twelve principles that speak of reducing or eliminating hazardous or harmful substances from the synthesis, production and application of chemical products and thus the use of substances that are hazardous to human health and the environment is reduced or eliminated. When designing a green chemistry process, it is impossible to meet the requirements of all twelve principles of the process at the same time, but it attempts to apply as many principles as possible during certain stages of synthesis. The goals of green chemistry in environmental protection and economic gain are achieved through several dominant directions. Some of them are: biocatalysis, catalysis, use of alternative renewable raw materials (biomass), alternative reaction media (water, ionic liquids, supercritical fluids), alternative reaction conditions (microwave activation) as well as new photocatalytic reactions.

Catalysis as the foundation of green chemistry with new catalytic reactions and types of new catalysts offers a number of benefits in terms of process utilization, selectivity, energy reduction and the use of alternative reaction media. The huge potential of microorganisms and enzymes in the transformation of synthetic substances with selectivity gives biocatalyst a dominant position in the "green" program. Photocatalytic reactions that represent new methods of cleaning contaminated air and water also contribute to green chemistry creating conditions for achieving sustainability.

References:
[1]. P. T. Anastas and J. C. Warner, in Green Chemistry: Theory and Practice, Oxford University Press, New York, 1998 Search PubMed; I. Horvath and P. T. Anastas, Chem. Rev., 2007, 107, 2167 Search PubMed.
[2]. P. T. Anastas and T. C. Williamson, in Green Chemistry: Designing Chemistry for the Environment, American Chemical Series Books, Washington, DC, 1996, pp. 1–20 Search PubMed.
[3]. T. J. Collins, in Green Chemistry, Macmillan Encyclopedia of Chemistry, Simon and SchusterMacmillan, New York, 1997, vol. 2, pp. 691–697 Search PubMed.
[4]. P. T. Anastas, Green Chem., 2003, 5, 29 Search PubMed.
[5]. W. McDonough, M. Braungart, P. T. Anastas and J. B. Zimmerman, Environ. Sci. Technol., 2003, 37, 434A CAS.
[6]. Office of Pollution Prevention and Toxics, The Presidential Green Chemistry Challenge Awards Program, Summary of 1996 Award Entries and Recipients, US Environmental Protection Agency, Washington, DC, EPA744K96001, 1996 Search PubMed.
[7]. Forum, Green Chem., 1999, 1, G11 Search PubMed.
[8]. J. Clark, Green Chem., 1999, 1, G1 RSC.
[9]. Office of Pollution Prevention and Toxics, The Presidential Green Chemistry Challenge, Award Recipients, 1996–2009, US Environmental Protection Agency, Washington, DC, EPA 744K09002, 2009 Search PubMed.
[10]. S2669, Green Chemistry Research and Development Act of 2008, 2008.
[11] Ritter, S. K. (2001): Green Chemistry. Chem. Eng. News, 79 (29), 27-34.
[12] Vojvodić, V. (2009): Environmental Protection: Green Manufacturing in the Pharmaceutical Industry and Cost Reduction, Kem Ind 58 (1): 32-33, In Croatian.
[13] Riđanović, L., Ćatović, F., Riđanović, S. (2013): The Green Chemistry-Ecological Revolution in the Classroom. 8thResearch/Expert Conference with International Participations "QUALITY 2013", Neum, B&H, June 06 – 08, 447-452., InBosnian.

[14] Jukić, M., Djaković, S., Filipović-Kovačević, Ž., Kovač, V. and Vorkapić-Furač, J. (2005): Dominant trends of green chemistry. Kem Ind 54 (5): 255-272, In Croatian.
[315]
[16] Environmental effect of war-Lenntech, www.lenntech.com
[17] Fundamental concept of Environmental chemistry, G.S. Sodhi
[18] Pesticide chemistry and toxicology-Bentham e books
[19] Mijin, D., Stanković, M. I., Petrović, S. (2003): Ibuprofen: Gain and Properties, Hem. Ind. 57 (5) 199-214, In Serbian.
[20] Anastas, P. T., Warner, J. C. (1998): Green Chemistry Theory and Practice. New York: Oxford University Press, 10-55.
[21] Anastas, P. T., Kirchhoff, M. M., Williamson, T. C. (2001): Catalysis as a foundational pillar of green chemistry. Appl Catal A: General, 221: 3-13.
[22] Fisher science education, www.fisheredu.com
[23] Atom economy –yield Green industry www.greens-industry.org.uk
[24] Riđanović, L., Ćatović, F., Riđanović, S. (2013): The Green Chemistry-Ecological Revolution in the Classroom. 8thResearch/Expert Conference with International Participations "QUALITY 2013", Neum, B&H, June 06 – 08, 447-452., InBosnian.
[25] Environmental Chemistry by A.K.DE
[26] Fisher science education, www.fisheredu.com
[27] Wayne Hill, H. and Brady, D. G. (1976): Properties, environmental stability, and molding characteristics of polyphenylene sulfide, Polymer Engineering & Science, Vol 16, Iss 12,pp 831–835
[28] 2, 4-D-Beyond pesticide, www.beyondpesticides.org
[29] Kärkkäinen, J. (2007): Preparation and characterization of some ionic liquids and their use in the dimerization reaction of 2-methylpropene. Dissertation, University of Oulu.
[30] Handbook of green chemistry Volume.IV, green solvents, supercritical solvents, By Paul T. Anastas.
[31] Hoffert, M. I., Caldeira, K., Benford, G., David R. Criswell, D. R., Christopher Green, C., Herzog, H., Jain, A. K., Kheshgi, H. S., Lackner, K. S., Lewis, J. S., Lightfoot, H. D., Manheimer, W., Mankins, J. C., Mauel, M. E., Perkins, L. J., Schlesinger

M. E., Volk, T., Wigley, T. (2002): Advanced Technology Paths to Global Climate Stability: Energy for a Greenhouse Planet, Science, Vol. 298, Issue 5595, pp. 981-987, DOI: 10.1126/science.1072357

[32] The Haber process for manufacture of Ammonia, www.chemguide.co.uk
[33] Ivanković, A., Zeljko, K., Talić, S., Martinović Bevanda, A. and Lasić, M.(2017): Biodegradable packaging in the food industry, Archiv für Lebensmittelhygiene 68, Heft 1.
[34] Rujnić-Sokele, M. (2007): Truths and mistakes about bioplastics. Polymers: Journal of Rubber and Plastics, Rubber and Plastics Corporation, Zagreb, 28_3: pp178-181. In Croatian.
[35] Green synthesis from biomass by, Paulo M. Donated/Springer Open
[36] Findrik Blažević, Z. (2013): Bioreactivity Technique I, Internal Script. Zagreb: University of Zagreb, Faculty of Chemical Engineering and Technology, In Croatian
[37] American chemical society/Green chemistry principle #8
[38] Handbook of green chemistry Volume-I, Green catalysis, Homogeneous catalysis by, Paul T. Anastas
[39] Introduction: Green Chemistry and catalysis by Wiley –VC
[40] Production process for polylactic acid (PLA) Industrial Plant: Hitachi, www.hitachi.com
[41] March Advanced organic chemistry
[42] Green chemistry principle # 12 (ACS), minimize the potential for accident, ehsdailyadvisor.blr.com
[43] Bharadwaj, M. and Neelam (2015): The Advantages and Disadvantages of Green Technology, Journal of Basic and Applied Engineering Research, p-ISSN: 2350-0077; e-ISSN: 2350-0255; Volume 2, Issue 22; October-December, 2015, pp. 1957-1960.

U.G, P.G. & Research Centre,
Department of Chemistry,
Shivaji, Art's, Comm. & Science College Kannad.Dist.
Aurangabad.431103, (M.S.) India.
email : **sakharedhondiram@yahoo.com**

19. Green Chemistry Principles and Environmental Sustainability

[1]Dr. Varsha Saxena* and [2]Dr. Sama Jain

Abstract

Green chemistry principles when comprehensively deployed in industries and educational institutes can bring about climate protection and sustainable development around the world.

Importance must be given to framing integrated strategies for GCP implementation in these areas. Redesigning and remanufacturing from medical waste, electronic waste, and industrial waste can improve the resource utilization. Management of water and energy consumption for crop production can also prove energy efficiency and cost effective parameters.

The design phase of a new chemical is most appropriate stage to induct the principles of green chemistry. This may start from introducing changes in few steps of product formation to entirely changing the process of production/synthesis. Implementing green chemistry principles in educational curriculum and establishment of interdepartmental collaboration can enormously benefit the environmental system.

This study focuses on implementation of green audit and green chemistry principles in various industries and educational institutes and its possible positive effect on environment sustainability.

Keywords : Green Chemistry, Green Audit, Sustainable Development, Resource Utilization

1. Introduction

Twentieth century witnessed the growth of chemistry in solving many problems of mankind . Discovery of catalyst alone led to manufacturing of many polymers which were used in everyday life . Chloflorocarbons gained popularity as refrigerants. Around the same time, discovery of new drugs led to control of many infectious diseases. At that time, researchers did not realize its long term impact on environment. With the passage of time, harmful effects of chemicals like DDT, BPA , Freons etc became the topic of concern. Dramatic reduction in bird population, development of drug resistant diseases, holes in ozone layer, transformation of by-products into various other toxic products was not anticipated by scientists.

Environmental chemistry comprises of all the chemical reactions taking place in environment including the natural cycle of biochemical and chemical transformation which helps in maintaining ecological balance. This natural balance of chemical transformation cycle has been disrupted by human activities. Exponential increase in human population has led to many combinations of chemicals for everyday use . In the name of development , many chemical products are being manufactured (xenobiotic substances) and by-products are released in environment. Some chemicals like pesticides and fertilizers are necessary to increase crop production and hence are released in environment deliberately. But some compounds are accidently discharged in the form of chemical waste from manufacturing units or chemical laboratories. All these chemicals may combine in any form to produce more toxic chemicals which in future may pose serious health hazards .

To protect environment and implement sustainable development in chemical technology, academia , industrial management and government policies ,a special program was launched by US environmental Protection Agency in 1991. A working party on green chemistry was created in 1996 which acted under the framework of IUPAC. The Royal Society of Chemistry came up with first book on principles of green chemistry.

Green chemistry principles provide the framework to tweak or reinvent the production process and reutilize the source of chemicals thereby making a paradigm shift from use of hazardous chemicals to reusable and safe chemicals.

New approach to synthesis, and application of chemicals is described in such a manner so as to decrease harmful effects on health and environment [1-7]

2. Drivers of Green Chemistry

Three basic drivers for application of green chemistry principles are economic, health and research.

2.1 Economic Drivers : Global adaptation and acceptance of green principles need consumer awareness and demand for green products.

Green regulations and restructuring of market across supply chain can lead to better economy.

2.2 Health Drivers : Discovery of new drugs or pesticides can involve computer based technology. This will be energy and atom efficient.

2.3 Research Drivers : Use of catalysts and universal solvents wherever possible can reduce waste. Redesigning of reaction path so as to reduce threshold energy required for particular reactions can emply green principles.

2.4 Application of Green Chemistry Principles

Application of green principles in all these fields will eventually lead to sustainable development

2.5 Industries

The twelve principles of green chemistry which can be applied in industries include

i) Prevention : The concept of E factor or environment prevention factor was introduced by Roger Sheldon (8) which quantifies the amount of waste generated per kilogram.

ii) Atom economy or atom efficiency involves the concept of having as many number of atoms in product as possible from the reactants.

iii) Less Hazardous Chemical Synthesis : Cycloaddition and rearrangement reactions have been redesigned using these principles.(9,10)

iv) Designing Safer Chemicals : Transformation of molecules in biosphere has a major impact on environment. Design of new molecules which can cater to safer environment can be achieved through these principles.

v) Safer Solvents and Auxiliaries : Toxic and corrosive nature of solvents have contributed to pollution. Use of water as widespread solvent can be encouraged.

vi) Design for Energy Efficiency : Unutilised Energy can be considered as waste. Design of chemical routes which may reduce threshold energy can be encouraged.

vii) Use of Renewable Feedstock : Use of biomass can largely reduce dependence on petroleum feedstock.

viii) Reduce derivatives : derivatisation based on intermolecular conversions should be encouraged. (11)

ix) Catalysis : Use of catalysts for synthetic chemistry has been proposed as a way to improve atom economy.

x) Design for Degradation : Biodegradability of many products chemical products is the need of hour.

xi) Real time analysis for pollution prevention- Monitoring and limiting the release of waste in environment is one of the main goals.

xii) Inherently Safer Chemistry for Accident Prevention : Accident prone chemicals should be replaced with less hazardous ones.

2.6 Educational Institutes

Material efficiency, energy efficiency, toxicity and innovative design metrics are few parameters which can greatly reduce pollutants from chemistry laboratories.

Material efficiency assumes complete transformation of reactants to products. It is calculated by dividing molecular weight of products by total weight of all reactants summed together . But it does not takes into account the waste generated by solvents and by products. It was first calculated by E factor . E factor is calculated by dividing total mass of waste by that of product.

Energy efficiency can be attained by using recyclable materials or raw material with high biodegradable content. Reactions occurring at high temperature use more fuel. By using microwave technology ,energy consumption can be reduced significantly.

Understanding the release of toxic materials and innovative design metrics can help in redesigning of chemical reactions. Redesigning of molecules at base level is the key to production of non toxic waste.

Educational institutes must take steps to inspire students to adapt to green chemistry principles by conducting regular lectures, by introducing them to study material pertaining to green principles, by making them aware of environmental hazards of not disposing chemicals properly and by introducing them to various metrics.

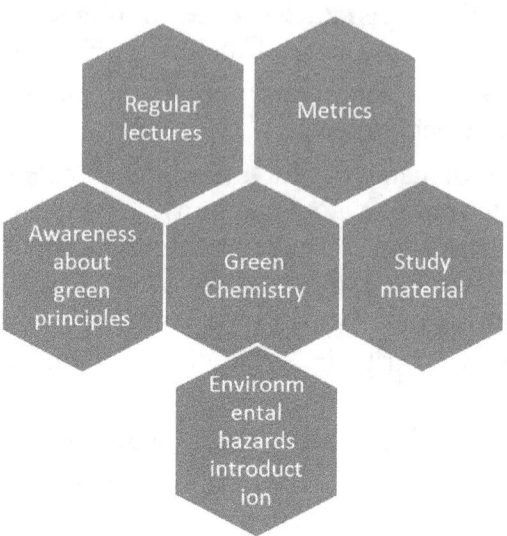

Rain water harvesting units, solar panels, and regular green auditing by universities can be of immense help in environmental sustainability.

3. Conclusion

The aim of green principles is to attain sustainability at molecular level. Driven by these goals, it has been applied in various fields of aerospace, cosmetics, house hold products, agriculture. Enthusiastic response of scientists, industrialists and educational institutes has led to and will further lead to development of new strategies towards achieving these goals. Improved diaphragms valves, magnetic drivers, double seal are few precautions which can prevent industrial accidental leakage. Spreading awareness by regular lectures can help students understand the positive impact of using green principles in educational institutes.

Refrences
1. Anastas. P.T, Warner J.C, Green chemistry Theory and Practice, OxfordUniversity, Press, New York, 1998.
2. Anastas P.T, Hovarsth I.T, Innovations and Green Chemistry, Chemistry review, 2007; 107.
3. Ravichandaran S., International Journal, 2010; 2(4): 2191.
4. Trost B.M, Atom economy-A challenge for organic synthesis :

Hompgeneous catalysis leads the way, 1995; 34: 259.
5. Sheldon R.A, Green solvents for sustainable organic synthesis: State of art, 2005; 7: 267.
6. Bharati V.B, Resonance, 2008; 1041.
7. Ahluwalia V.K and Kidwai M., New Trends in Green Chemistry, Anamaya Publisher, New Delhi, 2004.
8. R. A. Sheldon, *Green Chem.*, 2007, **9**, 1273
9. S. Kobayashi and K. A. Jorgensen, in *Cycloaddition Reactions in Organic Synthesis*, Wiley-VCH Verlag GmbH, Weinheim, 2002 Search PubMed ; N. Dennis, in *Organic Reaction Mechanisms, Addition Reactions: Cycloaddition*, John Wiley & Sons Ltd., West Sussex, 2008, ch. 12, p. 349 Search PubMed ; U. Chiacchio, A. Padwa and G. Romeo, *Curr. Org. Chem.*, 2009, **13**, 422 Search PubMed .
10. M. B. Smith and J. March, in *March's Advanced Organic Chemistry: Reactions, Mechanisms, and Structure*, John Wiley & Sons, Inc., New York, 5th edn, 2001, ch. 18, pp. 1377–1505 Search PubMed ; K. Banert and H. Hahn, in *Organic Reaction Mechanisms, Molecular Rearrangement: Part 1*, John Wiley & Sons Ltd, West Sussex, 2008, ch. 13, p. 451 Search PubMed ; A. Brandi and F. Pisaneschi, in *Organic Reaction Mechanisms, Molecular Rearrangement: Part 2*, John Wiley & Sons Ltd, West Sussex, 2008, ch. 14, p. 493 Search PubMed ; L. R. Overman, *Tetrahedron*, 2009, **65**, 6432 Search PubMed .
11. L. D. Taylor and J. C. Warner, *US Pat.*, 5 177 262, 1993 Search PubMed

[1]*Assistant Professor,
Department of Chemistry,
Sri Sathya Sai College for Women, Bhopal
[2]Professor,
Department of Chemistry,
Poornima Institute of Engineering and Technology, Jaipur
email : sinhavarsha@yahoo.com

20. Doctrines of Environmental Law in India

Dr. Pawan Kumar Srivastava

Abstract

Indian environmental law has seen considerable development in the last over three decades. Most of the principles under which environmental law works in India today were assembled over the last over three decades. A predominant share of essence of the existing law relating to the environment has developed through careful judicial thinking in the Supreme Court and the High Courts. In the process of adjudication on the environmental matters, the Supreme Court has actually come up with the new pattern of "judge-driven implementation" of environmental administration in India. The court has assumed a critical part in deciphering those laws and has effectively disconnected explicit ecological law standards upon the understanding of Indian resolutions and the Constitution, joined with a liberal view towards guaranteeing social equity and the assurance of common freedoms. So, when one analyses the Indian environmental law's development path, one will surely have to keep in mind the concept of judicial law making. In this article we have discussed some remarkable principles and doctrines propounded by the Indian judiciary.

Keywords : Doctrine, Liability, Precautionary, Sustainable Development, Indian judiciary

Introduction

India's modern environmental regulatory framework is founded on certain universal principles that have emanated from a creative reading of the Constitution of India, international treaties, and judicial precedents. The principles and doctrines have played a significant role in the development of environmental laws, the assignment of responsibility for environmental restoration to polluters, and the providing of guidance to courts and enforcement agencies for the handling of complex issues concerning pollution and the exploitation of natural resources.

Remarkable Principles and Doctrines

There are some remarkable principles and doctrines propounded by the Indian judiciary given as under:

1. Doctrine of Absolute Liability
The Bhopal Case : *Union Carbide Corporation* **versus** *Union of India*[1]

For this situation, the court held that, where an endeavor is busy with an intrinsically perilous or a risky action and mischief results to anyone by temperance of a setback in theactivity of such hazardous or normally dangerous development coming to fruition, forexample, in escape of noxious gas, the venture is stringently and totally committed toreimburse all of the people who are impacted by the mishap and such danger isn't dependentupon any exclusions. Likewise, Supreme Court made another pattern of Absolute Liabilitywith no exception.

One of the principle issues which the Bhopal Gas misfortune raises is the issue of supreme risk. This issue was extravagantly talked about on account of M.C Mehta versus Union of India. The standard of outright risk expresses that when an undertaking is occupied with unsafe or intrinsically perilous industry and assuming any mischief brings about record of such movement, the endeavor is totally obligated to make up for such damage and that it ought to be no response to the venture to say that it had taken all sensible consideration and that the damage happened with no carelessness on its part. In such industries, the principle of safe design would be that one does not guard merely against the most predictable, routine type of accidents. Rather one tries to anticipate the worst that could happen, even if it is highly unlikely, and not only guard against it, but prepare to contain it and make sure that there is no way for that even to take place.

This is the principle of absolute liability and liability can be fixed even if there is no negligence on part of the accused. In the case of absolute liability, even the defences available under strict liability would not apply. Thus, even if the accident is some freak incident, liability would still be fixed. In such a case, it would be no good defence to argue that the direct or the proximate cause of the accident or the causa causan of the accident was not the carrying of

---

[1] AIR 1990 SC 273

such hazardous activity, but it actually is an Act of God or that it is due to some third-party intervention. Even if the Company had taken extreme precautions to ensure that such events do not take place, responsibility would still be fixed on them. This principle of absolute liability in India evolved primarily because of the awakening that the Bhopal Gas Disaster and the Oleum Gas Leak case gave.

The Bhopal Gas Tragedy is also in a way responsible for the passing of the Public Liability Insurance Act, 1991 which provides for compulsory insurance of any unit or factory undertaking a hazardous activity.

Apart from all of this, the tragedy has recently been much discussed in the light of the Nuclear Liability Bill. This bill has a lot of controversial provisions which aim at capping the total liability in case of a nuclear accident. The bill also prohibits the victims from suing the suppliers directly and allows them to recover only from the operators. The bill also lays a cap on the amount that an operator can recover from the suppliers.

In the light of the events that followed Bhopal, clearly there is a necessity for a fitting instrument of pay and it is critical that any kind of cap on hazard should be disposed of as it would be unlawful.

2. Polluter Pays Principles

"If anyone intentionally spoils the water of another ... let him not only pay damages, but purify the stream or cistern which contains the water..."[2] – Plato

Polluter Pays Principle has become a very popular concept lately. 'In the event that you make a wreck, it's your obligation to tidy it up '- this is the essential premise of this trademark. It ought to be referenced that in climate law, the 'polluter pays rule' doesn't insinuate "issue." Instead, it upholds a healing philosophy which is worried about repairing regular damage. It's a standard in global ecological law where the dirtying party pays for the mischief or harm done to the indigenous habitat.

"The Polluter Pays" guideline has been held to be a sound rule by

---

[2] Karpagam, M., and Jaikumar, Geetha. Green Management: Theory & Applications. India, Ane Books Pvt Ltd, 2010.

this Court Indian Council for Enviro-Legal Action versus Union of India J.T. 1996 (2) 196. The Court noticed, "We are of the assessment that any standard developed for this 'sake ought to be basic functional and fit to the conditions getting in this country". The Court concluded that "When the activity proceeded is perilous or typically unsafe, the individual proceeding with such activity is capable to make extraordinary the setback caused to some other individual by his activity paying little mind to the truth whether he took reasonable thought while carrying on his development. The standard is introduced upon the genuine thought of the development proceeded". Subsequently, the contaminating businesses are "totally responsible to make up for the mischief brought about by them to locals in the influenced territory, to the dirt and to the underground water and thus, they will undoubtedly take all important means to eliminate ooze and different toxins lying in the influenced territories".

The "Polluter Pays" rule as unravelled by this Court suggests that the preeminent obligation regarding naughtiness to the environment loosens up not solely to compensate the overcomers of pollution yet also the cost of restoring the regular defilement. Remediation of the hurt environment is significant for the communication of "Sensible Development" and as such polluter is in danger to pay the cost for the individual casualties similarly as the cost of pivoting the hurt environment.

Vellore Citizen's Welfare Forum versus Union of India,[3] The Supreme Court has reported that the polluter pays rule is a principal segment of the sensible new development.

3. Precautionary Principle

The Supreme Court of India, in Vellore Citizens Forum Case, fostered the accompanying ideas for the preparatory standard:

Ecological measures should expect, forestall and assault the reasons for natural debasement.

Absence of logical assurance ought not be utilized as a justification deferring measures

---

[3] AIR 1996 SCC 212

Onus of verification is on the entertainer to show that his activity is amiable.

The preparatory standard has been acknowledged as a component of the rule that everyone must follow. Article 21 of the Constitution of India ensures insurance of life and individual freedom. Articles 47, 48A and 51A(g) of the Constitution are as under :

"Article 47. Obligation of the State to raise the degree of sustenance and the way of life and to improve general wellbeing. The State will respect the raising of the degree of nourishment and the way of life of its kin and the improvement of general wellbeing as among its essential obligations and specifically, The State will attempt to achieve restriction of the utilization aside from therapeutic reasons for inebriating drinks and of medications which are damaging to wellbeing. 48A. (g) Protection and improvement of climate and shielding of backwoods and natural life. The State will try to secure and improve the climate and to protect the woodlands and untamed life of the country.

51A(g) To ensure and improve the regular habitat including woods, takes, waterways and natural life, and to have sympathy for living animals."

4. Public Trust Doctrine

M.C.Mehta versus Kamal Nath and Others[4]

The public trust convention, as talked about by court in this judgment is a piece of the rule that everyone must follow.

The Public Trust Doctrine essentially lays on the rule that specific assets like air, water, ocean and the backwoods have a particularly extraordinary significance to individuals overall that it would be entirely ridiculous to make them a subject of private possession.

The discussions on the Doctrine of Public Trust and various case laws makes it evident that the state is not the owner of the natural resources in the country but a trustee who holds fiduciary relationship with the people. By accepting this task, the government is expected to be loyal to the interests of its citizens and to discharge its duty with the interest of the citizens at heart and involve them in

---

[4] *(1997)1 SCC 388*

decision-making process concerning the management of natural resources in the country.

The Public Trust Doctrine may provide the means for increasing the effectiveness of environmental impact assessment laws. Subsequently, under this regulation, the State has an obligation as a trustee under Art 48A to ensure and improve the climate and shield the backwoods and untamed life of the country. While applying Art 21 (right to life), the state is obliged to take account of Art 48A, a Directive Principle of State Policy. The state's trusteeship duties have been expanded to include a right to a healthy environment.

It is interesting to note that in the Kamal Nath case the Supreme Court held that even if there is a separate and a specific law to deal with the issue before the Court, it may still apply public trust doctrine. If there is no suitable legislation to preserve the natural resources, the public authorities should take advantage of this doctrine in addition to the fact that there was a branch of municipal law.

Also, the Supreme Court in M.I. builders, however, stated that public trust doctrine has grown from Article 21 of the constitution. By attaching this doctrine to the fundamental right to life, the Supreme Court appears to be willing to diversify the application of this doctrine. It seems likely that the court would give precedence to right to life when the public trust doctrine, as a part of right to a safe and healthy environment, is challenged by any other fundamental rights.

Moreover, by ordering the Mahapalika to restore the park to its original beauty, the Supreme Court redefined the duties of a trustee to its beneficiaries the users of the park. In effect, it aligned the local authorities' duty as a trustee with the concept of intra-generational and inter-generational equity. Further the case came before the court as a judicial review and not as challenge against the decision of the government from a beneficiary. As this doctrine acts as a check upon administrative action by providing a mechanism for judicial or resource allocation decisions. In this manner, public trust tenet could fill in as an extra instrument for environmental assurance especially where authoritative attentiveness has been manhandled.

5. Doctrine of Sustainable Development

The well recognized principle of sustainable development for the protection and improvement of environment has been unanimously accepted by the world countries as a strategy that caters to the needs of the present without depriving the future generations of their right to available natural resources. It has been rightly said that sustainable development is meant to secure a balance between developmental activities for the benefits of the people and environmental protection and therefore, "it is a guarantee to the present and bequeath to the future generations." The principle of sustainable development seeks to harmonise the conflict between development which may be industrial, economic or social, and right to healthy environment. In other words, the balance between environmental protection and developmental activities could only be maintained by strictly adhering to the principle of sustainable development.

Environmental studies have shown that the environment related problems of developed countries are mainly due to industrial and technological development whereas undeveloped countries have environmental problems because of poverty, over-population and illiteracy. Undoubtedly, encouragement and boost to developmental activities is in the socio-economic interest of a nation but this should not be at the cost of environmental degradation, because this will not only affect the present generation but have its adverse impact on the future generations. Therefore, sustainable development is the need of time so that development and environmental protection, both proceed maintaining a balance.

'Development' has been recognized as a human right under Rio-Declaration of 1992. But all the nations (parties) participating in this summit unanimously agreed that economic or industrial development should be carried out in a manner that it does not adversely affect the environment because environmental pollution is a potential danger to human life and in that case, what is the use of such development? It is for this reason that the principle of sustainable development was evolved in this world summit for maintaining a balance between development and environment, and it was realised that both should go hand in hand.

Aftermath of Climate Change

The World commission on Environment and Development (WCED) in its report prominently known as the 'Brundtland Report' named after the Chairman of the Commission Ms. GH Brundtland features the idea of maintainable turn of events. According to Brundtland Report, Sustainable advancement implies" improvement that addresses the issues of the present without bargaining the capacity of things to come ages to address their own issues"[5]. There is a need for the courts to strike a balance between development and environment.

India being a growing economy has seen rampant industrialisation and development in recent past, which resulted in adverse impact on the environment. Witnessing such degradation, the Supreme Court of India in a bid to protect the environment, played a significant role in shaping and adopting the doctrine of Sustainable Development. This crusade for safeguarding the environment was led by Justice Kuldip Singh, who famously came to be known as the 'Green Judge'.

The doctrine of Sustainable Development was carried out by the Supreme Court on account of Vellore Citizen Welfare Forum versus Association of India. The Petitioners therein had filed a petition in public interest under Article 32 of the Constitution of India against the pollution caused by discharge of untreated effluent by the tanneries and other industries in the river Palar in the State of Tamil Nadu. In the moment case, the Supreme Court held that the preparatory standard and polluter pays guideline are a piece of the natural law of India. The court in like manner held that: "Remediation of the hurt environment is fundamental for the association of 'Sensible Development' and as such polluter is dependable to pay the cost for the individual casualties similarly as the cost of pivoting the hurt science."

Thereafter in a number of judgments, the Apex Court explained and implemented the doctrine of Sustainable Development. The Hon'ble Supreme Court of India in Narmada BachaoAndolan versus Union of India saw that "Maintainable Development implies what type or degree of advancement can occur, which can be supported commonly or nature with or without relief". In T.N.

---

[5] S.Shanthakumar, ENVIRONMENTAL LAW AN INTRODUCTION, pp. 122, 123, Chennai: Surya Publication,(2001).

GodavaramanThirumulpad versus Union of India, the Hon'ble Supreme Court said "as an issue of introduction, we may communicate that adherence to the norm of Sustainable Development is by and by a holy essential. What sum damage to the environment and environment should be chosen current real factors of each case"? In Indian Council of Enviro-Legal Action versus Union of India, the Apex Court held: "while financial advancement ought not be permitted to happen at the expense of biology or by causing far and wide climate obliteration and infringement; simultaneously, the need to safeguard nature and climate ought not hamper monetary and different turns of events". Consequently, significance has been offered both to advancement and climate and the journey is to keep a fine harmony among climate and monetary turn of events.

The Supreme Court of India emphasised on the need to set up specialised environment courts for the effective and expeditious disposal of cases involving environmental issues, since the right to healthy environment has been construed as a part of right to life under Article 21 of the Constitution.

Conclusion

Therefore, after the analysis of aboveprinciples and doctrines, we find that,The Indian environmental justice system owes a lot to the proactive higher judiciary, which contributed significantly to the growth and evolution of sound and strong environmental principles and provided guidance on their adoption.In this way, the judiciary tries to fill in the gaps where there is laciness of the legislation. These new innovations and developments in India by the judicial activism open the numerous approaches to help the country.However, what has largely been lacking is the specific legislative intent when it comes to incorporating the principles of environmental jurisprudence in the applicable laws, administrative decisions, and effective enforcement, without which these principles remain theoretical.

**Assistant Professor,
Major S. D. Singh Law College, Farrukhabad**

www.ingramcontent.com/pod-product-compliance
Lightning Source LLC
Chambersburg PA
CBHW050251010526
44107CB00003B/282